TIGLATH-PILESER III,
FOUNDER OF THE ASSYRIAN EMPIRE

ARCHAEOLOGY AND BIBLICAL STUDIES

Brian B. Schmidt, General Editor

Editorial Board:
Andrea Berlin
Aaron Brody
Annie Caubet
Billie Jean Collins
Yuval Gadot
André Lemaire
Herbert Niehr
Christoph Uehlinger

Number 31

TIGLATH-PILESER III, FOUNDER OF THE ASSYRIAN EMPIRE

Josette Elayi

 PRESS

Atlanta

Copyright © 2022 by Josette Elayi

All rights reserved. No part of this work may be reproduced or transmitted in any form or by any means, electronic or mechanical, including photocopying and recording, or by means of any information storage or retrieval system, except as may be expressly permitted by the 1976 Copyright Act or in writing from the publisher. Requests for permission should be addressed in writing to the Rights and Permissions Office, SBL Press, 825 Houston Mill Road, Atlanta, GA 30329 USA.

Library of Congress Control Number: 2022940356

Contents

Abbreviations ix
Chronology of Tiglath-pileser III's Reign xv

Introduction 1

1. The Kingdom of Assyria in 745 BCE.......................................11
   1.1. Previous Attempts to Build the Empire   11
   1.2. The Crises of 826–746   15
   1.3. The Weakness of Assyria in 745   18

2. Was Tiglath-pileser III a Usurper?...25
   2.1. His Name and Family   25
   2.2. His Physical Portrait   29
   2.3. His Personality   31
   2.4. Royal Propaganda   41

3. Tiglath-pileser III's Ascent to the Throne 43
   3.1. The Revolt of Nimrud   43
   3.2. The Circumstances Surrounding Tiglath-pileser III's
        Ascent to the Throne   46

4. The Neutralization of High Dignitaries..................................49
   4.1. The Powerful High Dignitaries   49
   4.2. Restoring the Royal Power   57
   4.3. The Reforms for Neutralizing the High Dignitaries 58

5. The Strategy of Conquest 61
   5.1. Tiglath-pileser III's Objectives   61
   5.2. A Careful Preparation of Strategy   64
   5.3. The Place of the West in Tiglath-pileser III's Strategy 68

CONTENTS

6. The First Phase of the Campaigns (745–744) 71
   - 6.1. The Campaign against Babylonia and the Aramean Tribes — 71
   - 6.2. The Campaign in the Central Zagros and Media — 79
   - 6.3. The Creation of New Provinces — 85
   - 6.4. A New Deportation Policy — 92

7. The Second Phase of the Campaigns (743–738) 97
   - 7.1. The Campaigns against the Coalition of Syria and Urartu — 97
   - 7.2. The Fall of Arpad and Its Consequences — 103
   - 7.3. The Campaign against Ulluba — 105
   - 7.4. The Second Campaign to the West — 107
   - 7.5. Treaties and Loyalty Oaths — 114

8. The Third Phase of the Campaigns (737–735) 117
   - 8.1. A Second Campaign against Media — 117
   - 8.2. The Campaign to the Urartian Border — 121
   - 8.3. The Campaign into the Heart of Urartu — 122

9. The Fourth Phase of the Campaigns (734–732) 129
   - 9.1. The Campaign against the Phoenician Cities — 130
   - 9.2. The Campaign against the Philistine Cities — 135
   - 9.3. The Campaign against Israel and Judah — 138
   - 9.4. The Campaign against Damascus — 146
   - 9.5. The Campaign against the Arabs — 149

10. The Fifth Phase of the Campaigns (731–727) 153
    - 10.1. The Campaign against the Aramean and Chaldean Tribes — 153
    - 10.2. The Conquest of Babylon — 161

11. The King Is Dead! Long Live the King! 165
    - 11.1. The Mysterious End of Tiglath-pileser's Reign — 165
    - 11.2. Anticipating the Succession — 166

12. Building Activities 173
    - 12.1. Tiglath-pileser's Limited Interest in Building Activities — 173
    - 12.2. The Building of the Palace in Nimrud — 174
    - 12.3. Tiglath-pileser's Other Building Activities — 178

13. Conclusion: Assessment of Tiglath-pileser III's Reign 183

Selected Bibliography..189
Index of Ancient Sources..199
Index of Modern Authors..201
Index of Personal Names..207

Abbreviations

AB	Anchor Bible
ABD	Freedman, David Noel, ed. *Anchor Bible Dictionary*. 6 vols. New York: Doubleday, 1992.
ABS	Archaeology and Biblical Studies
ADPV	Abhandlungen des Deutschen Palästina-Vereins
AfO	*Archiv für Orientforschung*
AHL	*Ancient History of Lebanon*
AHw	Soden, Wolfram von. *Akkadisches Handwörterbuch*. 3 vols. Wiesbaden, 1965–1981.
AJA	*American Journal of Archaeology*
AMI	*Archäologische Mitteilungen aus Iran*
ANES	*Ancient Near Eastern Studies*
ANESSup	Ancient Near Eastern Studies Supplement
AnOr	Analecta Orientalia
AnSt	*Anatolian Studies*
AOAT	Alter Orient und Altes Testament
AoF	*Altorientalische Forschungen*
ARAB	Luckenbill, Daniel David. *Ancient Records of Assyria and Babylonia*. 2 vols. Chicago: University of Chicago Press, 1926–1927. Repr., New York: Greenwood, 1068.
BaF	Baghdader Forschungen
BASOR	*Bulletin of the American Schools of Oriental Research*
Bib	*Biblica*
BO	*Bibliotheca Orientalis*
BM	Tablets in the British Museum
CAD	*The Assyrian Dictionary of the Oriental Institute of the University of Chicago*. Chicago: The Oriental Institute of the University of Chicago, 1956–2006.
CAH	Cambridge Ancient History
CBQ	*Catholic Biblical Quarterly*

CHANE	Culture and History of the Ancient Near East
CRAI	*Comptes rendus de l'Académie des Inscriptions et Belles-Lettres*
CRIR	Culture and Religion in International Relations
CT	Cuneiform Texts from Babylonian Tablets in the British Museum
CTN	Cuneiform Texts from Nimrud
CTU	Salvini, Mirjo. *Corpus dei testi urartei*. Vols. 1–4. Rome: CNR, 2008–2012; Vol. 5. Paris: CNR, 2018.
DFI	*Délégation Archéologique Française en Iran*
ErIs	*Eretz-Israel*
HANE/S	History of the Ancient Near East/Studies
HchI	King, F. W. *Handbuch der Chaldischen Inschriften*. AfO 8. Graz: self-published, 1955.
HIMA	*Revue Internationale d'Histoire Militaire Ancienne*
HSAO	*Heidelberg Studien zum Alten Orient*
HW	History of Warfare
IEJ	*Israel Exploration Journal*
JA	*Journal Asiatique*
JAOS	*Journal of the American Oriental Society*
JCS	*Journal of Cuneiform Studies*
JESHO	*Journal for the Study of the Economic and Social History of the Orient*
JNES	*Journal of Near Eastern Studies*
JSS	*Journal of Semitic Studies*
KAI	Donner, Herbert, and Wolfgang Röllig. *Kanaanäische und Aramäische Inschriften*, Vols. 1–3. 2nd ed. Wiesbaden: Harrassowitz, 1966–1969.
KASKAL	*KASKAL: Rivista di storia, ambiente e culture del vicino oriente antico*
MVÄG	Mitteilungen der Vorderasiatische Ägyptischen Gesellschaft
NABU	*Nouvelles Assyriologiques Brèves et Utilitaires*
ND	Nimrud
NEA	*Near Eastern Archaeology*
NEAEHL	Stern, Ephraim, ed. *The New Encyclopedia of Archaeological Excavations in the Holy Land*. 5 vols. Jerusalem: Israel Exploration Society, 1993–2008.
NMC	Near and Middle Eastern Civilizations
OBO	Orbis Biblicus et Orientalis
OIP	Oriental Institute Publications

OLA	Orientalia Lovaniensia Analecta
OLZ	*Orientalistische Literaturzeitung*
OPSNKF	Occasional Publications of the Samuel Noah Kramer Fund
OrAnt	*Oriens Antiquus*
PEQ	*Palestine Exploration Quarterly*
PNA	Baker, Heather D., and Karen Radner ed. *The Prosopography of the Neo-Assyrian Empire*. 3 vols. Helsinki: The Neo-Assyrian Text Corpus Project, 1998–2011.
PRU	Nougayrol, Jean, and Charles Virolleaud. *Le palais royal d'Ugarit*. Vols. 2–6. Paris, 1955–1970.
PUF	Presses Universitaires de France
Qad	*Qadmoniot*
RA	*Revue d'Assyriologie et d'Archéologie orientale*
RAI	Rencontres Assyriologiques Internationales
RGTC	Répertoire Géographique des Textes Cunéiformes
RIMA 2	Grayson, Albert Kirk, ed. *Assyrian Rulers of the Early First Millennium BC I (1114–859 BC)*. RIMA 2. Toronto: University of Toronto Press, 1991.
RIMA 3	Grayson, Albert Kirk, ed. *Assyrian Rulers of the Early First Millennium BC II (858–745 BC)*. RIMA 3. Toronto: University of Toronto Press, 2002.
RINAP 1	Tadmor, Hayim, and Shigeo Yamada. *The Royal Inscriptions of Tiglath-pileser III (744–727 BC) and Shalmaneser V (726–722 BC), Kings of Assyria*. Winona Lake, IN: Eisenbrauns, 2011.
RlA	*Reallexicon der Assyriologie*
SAA 2	Parpola, Simo, and Kazuko Watanabe. *Neo-Assyrian Treaties and Loyalty Oaths*. SAA 2. Helsinki: Helsinki University Press, 1998.
SAA 5	Lanfranchi, Giovanni Battista, and Simo Parpola. *The Correspondence of Sargon II. Part 2*. SAA 5. Helsinki: Helsinki University Press, 1990.
SAA 6	Kwasman, Theodore, and Simo Parpola. *Tiglath-pileser III through Esarhaddon. Part 1 of Legal Transactions of the Royal Court of Nineveh*. SAA 6. Helsinki: Helsinki University Press, 1991.
SAA 11	Fales, Frederick Mario, and John Nicholas Postgate. *Imperial Administrative Records. Part 2*. SAA 11. Helsinki: Helsinki University Press, 1995.

SAA 12	Kataja, Laura, and Robert Whiting. *Grants, Decrees and Gifts of the Neo-Assyrian Period.* SAA 12. Helsinki: Helsinki University Press, 1995.
SAA 15	Fuchs, Andreas, and Simo Parpola. *Letters from Babylonia and the Eastern Provinces.* Part 3 of *The Neo-Babylonian Correspondence of Sargon II.* SAA 15. Helsinki: Helsinki University Press, 2001.
SAA 19	Luukko, Mikko. *The Correspondence of Tiglath-pileser III and Sargon II from Calah/Nimrud.* SAA 19. Helsinki: Helsinki University Press, 2012.
SAAB	*State Archives of Assyria Bulletin*
SAAS	*State Archives of Assyria Studies*
SAAS 2	Millard, Alan R. *The Eponyms of the Assyrian Empire (910–612 BC).* SAAS 2. Helsinki: Neo-Assyrian Text Corpus Project, 1994.
SANTAG	*SANTAG: Arbeiten und Untersuchungen zur Keilschriftkunde*
SEL	*Studi Epigrafici e Linguistici sul Vicino Oriente Antico*
Sir	*Studia Iranica*
TA	*Tel Aviv*
TAVO	*Tübinger Atlas des Vorderen Orients*
Trans	*Transeuphratène*
UKN	Melikišvili, G.A. *Urartskie Klinoobraznye Nadpisi.* Moscow: Izd-vo Akademii nauk SSSR, 1960.
WdO	*Die Welt des Orients*
WVDOG	*Wissenschaftliche Veröffentlichungen der deutschen Orient-Gesellschaft*
ZA	*Zeitschrift für Assyriologie*
ZAR	*Zeitschrift für altorientalische und biblische Rechtsgeschichte*
ZÄS	*Zeitschrift für Ägyptische Sprache*
ZDMG	*Zeitschrift der Deutschen Morgenländischen Gesellschaft*
ZDVP	*Zeitschrift des Deutschen Palästina-Vereins*

Key to Transliterated Words

Kibrāt	Akkadian words are indicated by italics.
DINGIR	Sumerian word signs are indicated by capital letters

Explanation of Symbols

[ ]   single brackets enclose restorations.
( )   parentheses enclose additions in the English translation.
...   a row of dots indicates gaps in the text or untranslatable words.

When personal names are not presented in transcription or transliteration, their spelling is simplified for convenience, for example, *sh* instead of š or šš and h instead of ḫ.

Chronology of Tiglath-pileser III's Reign

Dates (BCE)	Year of Reign	Campaigns and Activities
745	Accession year (first *palû*)	Accession to the throne on the thirteenth day of Ayyâru (May). Measure of the *andurâru*. Campaign against Babylonia and Aramean tribes. New policy of deportations.
744	Year 1 (second *palû*)	Campaign to Central Zagros. First Median campaign. Parsua and Bît-Hamban annexed. Submission of Iranzu, king of Mannea.
743	Year 2 (third *palû*)	Campaign against the coalition of Mati'-ilu of Arpad and Sarduri II of Urartu. Defeat in the kingdom of Kummuhu. Arpad besieged.
742	Year 3 (fourth *palû*)	Arpad besieged.
741	Year 4 (fifth *palû*)	Arpad besieged.
740	Year 5 (sixth *palû*)	Fall and annexation of Arpad. Allegiance of several western rulers.
739	Year 6 (seventh *palû*)	Campaign against Ulluba. The fortress was seized. Foundation of Ashur-iqisha.
738	Year 7 (eighth *palû*)	Revolt of Tutammû of Unqi. Capture of Kullania. Annexation of Unqi, Hatarikka, and Simirra. Tribute sent by all the western rulers.
737	Year 8 (ninth *palû*)	Second campaign against Media. Creation of the provinces of Parsua and Bît-Hamban.
736	Year 9 (tenth *palû*)	Campaign to the foot of Mount Nal on the Urartian border. Capture of some Urartian fortresses.
735	Year 10 (eleventh *palû*)	Campaign into the heart of Urartu after the failure of diplomatic negotiations. Sarduri was enclosed in his capital Turushpa, which was not captured.

734	Year 11 (twelfth *palû*)	Campaign against the Phoenician cities. Annexation of Kashpûna. Submission of Mattanba'al II of Arwad. Tribute of Hiram of Tyre. Capture of Gezer. Campaign against the Philistine cities. Submission of Hanunu of Gaza.
733	Year 12 (thirteenth *palû*)	Submission of Mitinti of Ashkelon. Loyalty of Ashdod. Syro-Ephraimite war. Tiglath-pileser's aid in Ahaz's defense of Judah. Devastation of Israel. Siege of Damascus. Defeat of Samsi, queen of the Arabs.
732	Year 13 (fourteenth *palû*)	Siege and fall of Damascus. Conquest of Galilee and of a part of Israel. Allegiance of Ahaz of Judah. Submission of the Arab tribes.
731	Year 14 (fifteenth *palû*)	Campaign against Aramean and Chaldean tribes of central and southern Babylonia. Attack of the tribes of Bît-Shilâni, Bît-Sha'alli, and Bît-Amukkâni. Siege of Shapîya.
730	Year 15 (sixteenth *palû*)	Preparation of the campaign against Babylonia.
729	Year 16 (seventeenth *palû*)	Defeat of Mukîn-zêri, king of Babylon. The king "took the hands of Bêl," meaning he ascended the Babylonian throne under the name of Pulû.
728	Year 17 (eighteenth *palû*)	Tiglath-pileser participated in the *akîtu*-festival. Campaign against the city Ḫi[…
727	Year 18 (nineteenth *palû*)	Campaign against the city [… Death of Tiglath-pileser III in the month of Tebêtu (January). Shalmaneser V ascended the throne.

Introduction

Tiglath-pileser III reigned over Assyria for eighteen years, from 745 to 727 BCE. He is considered by most modern historians as the true founder of the Assyrian Empire. He was the first Assyrian king to be mentioned in the Bible, although a contemporary Assyrian inscription mentions King Shalmaneser III as the one who led his army into battle in 853 against a coalition of Levantine states, including Israel's king Ahab.[1] Tiglath-pileser is mentioned in 2 Kings and 1 and 2 Chronicles under both his Assyrian name and his Babylonian name. Pulû (*pwl*) appears in 2 Kgs 15:19, and Tiglath-pileser (*tglt pl'sr*) appears in 2 Kgs 15:29, 16:7, 10. There is an intrusive *n* in 1 Chr 5:6 and 2 Chr 28:20 (*tglt pln'sr*).[2] Pulû and Tiglath-pileser were viewed as references to two different kings in 1 Chr 5:26. The biblical references, although inconsistent, are not surprising. Both Israel and Judah were impacted geopolitically by Assyrian expansionist policies in the eighth century BCE. While Ahaz, the king of Judah who had voluntarily allied himself with the Assyrians, was allowed to keep his throne, much of Israel's former territory was transformed into the Assyrian provinces of Dor, Megiddo, and Gilead, with Israel becoming a puppet kingdom of Assyria.[3] The contemporary Aramaic and Phoenician inscriptions of Sam'al (Zincirli) also mention Tiglath-pileser. Again, this is not surprising. Sam'al's King Panamuwa II was Tiglath-pileser's vassal ruler who paid Assyria tribute, while Panamuwa's son Bar-Rakib was ceremonially installed on Sam'al's throne by

---

1. RIMA 3:23, A.0.102.2, ii.91.
2. Alan R. Millard, "Assyrian Royal Names in Biblical Hebrew," *JSS* 21 (1976): 7, 10. The intrusive *n* may be treated as an inner-Hebrew variation.
3. Susan Ackerman, "Assyria and the Bible," in *Assyrian Reliefs from the Palace of Ashurnasirpal II: A Cultural Biography*, ed. Ada Cohen and Steven E. Kangas (Hanover: Hood Museum of Art, 2010), 129–31. See below, chapter 6, n. 119.

the king of Assyria.[4] The inscriptions of Sarduri II, king of Urartu, relate not only his victory against Ashur-nârârî V but also his confrontation with Tiglath-pileser in 743, including an interpretation of the outcome that is quite different from that of the royal Assyrian inscriptions.[5] Babylonia was more directly concerned with Assyrian expansionism. Therefore, the Babylonian Chronicles briefly mention several previous Assyrian kings, such as Ashur-bêl-kala, Adad-nârârî III, Tukultî-Ninurta II, Ashurnasirpal II, and Shalmaneser III.[6] Yet as many as twenty-six lines of Chronicle 1 are devoted to the reign of Tiglath-pileser. The Babylonian King List A also refers to two years of Pulû's reign over Babylon.[7] The Ptolemaic Canon mentions five years of reign by Poros or Pulû.[8] Tiglath-pileser is absent from classical sources, which mention only Ninus (a mythic figure), Sardanapalus, Semiramis, and Sennacherib. Berossus, the Babylonian priest who published the *Babyloniaca* during the reign of the Seleucid king Antiochus I, cites a Chaldean king named Phulos or Pulû.[9] Berossus refers to him only as king of Babylon, not as king of Assyria.

Unlike the reign of his predecessor Ashur-nârârî V, about which there is virtually no information, the Assyrian inscriptions related to the history of Tiglath-pileser's reign are numerous and even overabundant. Most of them are housed in the museum collections such as those in the Iraq Museum in Baghdad, the British Museum in London, and the Vorderasiatisches Museum in Berlin. Still others are scattered across Europe and the United States in various museums, such as the Louvre Museum in Paris, the Hamburg Museum, the Kunsthistorisches Museum in Vienna, the Archäologisches Institut der Universität Zürich, Yale Babylonian

---

4. *KAI* 224, 215.15; 233, 216.2; 234, 217.2; Trevor Bryce, *The World of the Neo-Hittite Kingdoms* (Oxford: Oxford University Press, 2012), 169–75.

5. UKN 155–156; Mirjo Salvini, "Assyrie-Urartu: guerres sans conquêtes," in *Guerre et conquête dans le Proche-Orient ancien*, ed. Leila Nehmé (Paris: Maisonneuve, 1999), 55–59.

6. Albert Kirk Grayson, *Assyrian and Babylonian Chronicles* (Winona Lake, IN: Eisenbrauns, 2000), 70–72, Chronicle 1; 183, Chronicle 24.

7. Albert Kirk Grayson, "Konigslisten und Chroniken (B. Akkadisch)," *RlA* 6 (1980): 90–96, §3.3; RINAP 1:15, A2.

8. Grayson, "Konigslisten und Chroniken," 201, §3.8; RINAP 1:16, A3.

9. Stanley Meyer Burstein, *The Babyloniaca of Berossus* (Malibu: Undena, 1978), 23, D1; Robert Rollinger, "Assyria in Classical Sources," in *A Companion to Assyria*, ed. Eckart Frahm (Malden, MA: Wiley Blackwell, 2017), 571–82.

Museum in New Haven, the Detroit Institute of the Arts, the Istanbul Archaeological Museum, the Israel Museum, the Aleppo Museum, and the Raqqa Museum, and there are others held in private collections. Several inscriptions are still unpublished. Tiglath-pileser's inscriptions can be divided into two categories: royal and nonroyal. The so-called Kalhu Annals were written near the end of his reign on sculpted slabs that decorated the rooms and corridors in his palace at Nimrud (Kalhu).[10] Series A of the Kalhu Annals was etched on seven lines, between the upper and lower registers of the slabs, and Series B in twelve lines. Series C was written across the sculpted figures of the slabs. Since many slabs were destroyed or removed from their original positions in antiquity, the text that has survived represents barely one third, if not less, of the full textual corpus. The annals are complemented by other annalistic-style texts, such as those inscribed on a stone stela originating from western Iran, a rock inscription from Mila Mergi in Iraqi Kurdistan (the earliest annalistic account), and a statue from Nimrud. There are also summary inscriptions preserved on pavement slabs and clay tablets and miscellaneous fragmentary texts that could be regarded as display inscriptions. In 1851, Austen Henry Layard was the first to publish Tiglath-pileser III's inscriptions.[11] Following the publications by Henry Rawlinson, Edwin Norris, George Smith, and Eberhard Schrader, Paul Rost published a book in 1893, which for many decades served as the standard for the study of this king.[12] The first modern, comprehensive edition is that of Hayim Tadmor published in 1994; it was followed by the revised and expanded edition of Tadmor and Shigeo Yamada in 2011.[13] All of these royal inscriptions generally provide detailed accounts of Tiglath-pileser's military campaigns presented in chronological order and of his building

---

10. Hayim Tadmor, *The Inscriptions of Tiglath-pileser III King of Assyria* (Jerusalem: Israel Academy of Sciences and Humanities, 1994); RINAP 1:4–11.

11. Austen Henry Layard, *Inscriptions in the Cuneiform Character from Assyrian Monuments* (London: Harrison & Son, 1851).

12. RINAP 1:3; Paul Rost, *Die Keilschrifttexte Tiglat-Pilesers III* (Leipzig: Pfeiffer, 1893); *ARAB* 1.761–826 (translation in English).

13. Tadmor, *Inscriptions of Tiglath-pileser III*; Hayim Tadmor and Shigeo Yamada, *The Royal Inscriptions of Tiglath-pileser III (744–727 BC) and Shalmaneser V (726–722 BC), Kings of Assyria*, RINAP 1 (Winona Lake, IN: Eisenbrauns, 2011); Simonetta Ponchia, review of *The Inscriptions of Tiglath-pileser III King of Assyria*, by Hayim Tadmor, *ZA* 106 (2016): 112–13.

operations. Allusions can also be found to Tiglath-pileser's reign in the royal inscriptions of his successors.[14]

Two problems are associated with Tiglath-pileser's royal inscriptions: dating and propaganda. The annals are reconstructed from four or five different versions.[15] The largest gaps extend over several years: the fourth and fifth *palûs* (742–741), the seventh *palû* (739), the tenth *palû* (736), the twelfth *palû* (734), and the fourteenth *palû* (732) are totally missing. Numerous smaller gaps occur in the account covering certain years. However, most of the gaps can be supplemented by combining the different sources, and the chronology of the reign can be established on the basis of information preserved in the Assyrian Eponym List.[16] The summary inscriptions generally follow a geographical arrangement, without exact year distinctions. Propaganda is the second problem that the historian has to address when analyzing the different sources in order to identify distorted information.[17] Such information has to be extracted from its ideological and literary frame. This is very difficult, especially when an event is attested in one source only.

The nonroyal inscriptions are much less distorted by propaganda, but they are often undated. The stela from Tell Abta on the Wadi Tharthar, engraved by the palace herald Bêl-Harrân-bêlu-usur, mentions Tiglath-pileser's name.[18] Some chronographic texts, such as the Eponym List, the Assyrian King Lists, the Babylonian King List, and two Babylonian Chronicles, are useful for dating events.[19] There are also administrative documents, land grants, an inscribed duck weight, and royal correspondence sent to the king by state officials, spies, and other correspondents. These items were discovered in Nimrud, in the so-called North-West Palace, the Governor's Palace, and the Burnt Pal-

---

14. *PNA* 3.2:1330 (with bibliography).

15. Tadmor, *Inscriptions of Tiglath-pileser III*, 27–39.

16. SAAS 2:43–46 and 59; Heather D. Baker, "Tiglatpileser III," *RlA* 14 (2014): 21–23.

17. Frederick Mario Fales, "Tiglath-pileser III tra annalistica reale ed epistolografia quotidiana," in *Narrare gli eventi*, ed. Franca Pecchioli Daddi and Maria Cristina Guidotti (Rome: Herder, 2005), 163–92.

18. RIMA 3:241–42, A.0.105.2.

19. SAAS 2:43–46 and 59; Grayson, "Konigslisten und Chroniken," 101–15, §3.9; 90–96, §3.3; Grayson, *Assyrian and Babylonian Chronicles*, 70–72, Chronicle 1; 183, Chronicle 24.

ace.[20] A few letters written after Tiglath-pileser's death allude to events from his reign.[21]

Nonwritten documentation dating from Tiglath-pileser's reign is also historically important. Information is provided by the reliefs from his palace in Nimrud, the so-called Central Palace, which included a "cedar palace" and "a bīt-ḫilāni, a replica of a palace of the land of Hatti."[22] The reliefs are partly representations of the Assyrian king's conquests, focusing on spectacular actions and occasionally accompanied by an epigraph, similar to our modern-day comics.[23] The Central Palace was discovered in November 1845 and was then excavated in 1845–1847 and again in 1849–1851 by Layard. Sir Stratford Canning paid for the first excavations at Nimrud. Hormuzd Rassam, who had been Layard's assistant in his excavations, worked at Nimrud in 1853–1854 and made some finds in the center of the mound: "In the ... Center Palace, I discovered heaps upon heaps of all kinds of sculptures."[24] The Central Palace was then excavated by William Kennett Loftus in 1854 and again in 1878–1879 by Rassam. Excavations were carried out in this palace in 1975–1976 by a Polish expedition conducted by Kazimierz Michalowski.

Several modern scholarly works, large and small, mention Tiglath-pileser III. Every general history of Assyria or Mesopotamia includes short studies, the last one being the useful book written by Eckart Frahm.[25] The first one was Abraham S. Anspacher's *Tiglath Pileser III*, published

---

20. SAA 12:15–16, 13–16; 82, 75; SAA 6:4–6, 1–5; SAA 19:4–151, 1–151; John Nicholas Postgate, *The Governor's Palace Archive* (London: British School of Archaeology in Iraq, 1973); Stephanie Dalley and John Nicholas Postgate, *The Tablets from Fort Shalmaneser* (London: British School of Archaeology in Iraq, 1984); Henry William Frederick Saggs, *The Nimrud Letters* (London: British School of Archaeology in Iraq, 2001); John Oates and David Oates, *Nimrud: An Assyrian Imperial City Revealed* (London: British School of Archaeology in Iraq, 2001), 88.

21. *PNA* 3,2:1331 (with bibliography).

22. RINAP 1:67, 25.1′; 123, 47.17′; Julian E. Reade, "The Palace of Tiglath-pileser III," *Iraq* 30 (1968): 69–73.

23. Richard D. Barnett and Margarete Falkner, *The Sculptures of Aššur-naṣir-apli II (883–859 B.C.), Tiglath-pileser III (745–727 B.C.), Esarhaddon (681–669 B.C.) from the Central and South-West Palaces at Nimrud* (London: British Museum, 1962), 34–46; John Nicholas Postgate and Julian E. Reade, "Kalḫu," *RlA* 5 (1976–1980): 304–15 (with bibliography).

24. Barnett and Falkner, *Sculptures*, 4.

25. Eckart Frahm, *A Companion to Assyria* (Malden, MA: Wiley Blackwell, 2017).

in New York in 1912; this succinct account, based on Rost's first publication of Tiglath-pileser's inscriptions, gives an overview of some of his military campaigns. Most of the works, for example those of Michael Astour, Stephanie Dalley, Stefan Zawadski, Jacob Kaplan, and Sajjad Alibaigi,[26] were related to a specific historical feature of Tiglath-pileser's reign, such as his ascent to the throne, the Assyrian army, and military expeditions. Several other works, such as those of Albrecht Alt, Ernst Vogt, Mordechai Cogan, Nadav Na'aman, Gershon Galil, and Luis Robert Siddall,[27] focused on expeditions to Israel and Judah. Works by Richard D. Barnett and Julian E. Reade focused on Tiglath-pileser's palace in Nimrud.[28]

My specific aim in this book is to study, for the first time, the history of Tiglath-pileser's reign, which was fertile in events, in all its facets—political, military, economic, social, ideological, religious, technical, and artistic—knowing that some aspects are considerably more documented than others. However, just like the history of Sargon's reign, that of Tiglath-pileser is poorly documented with respect to his family background, his youth, and the period before he ascended the throne. Hence it is difficult to propose a comprehensive assessment of the psychological factors that shaped his character and how, in turn, those factors influenced his approach to politics.

---

26. Michael Astour, "The Arena of Tiglath-pileser III's Campaign against Sarduri II (743 B.C.)," *Assur* 2 (1979): 69–88; Stephanie Dalley, "Foreign Chariotry and Cavalry in the Armies of Tiglath-pileser III and Sargon II," *Iraq* 47 (1985): 31–48; Stefan Zawadski, "The Revolt of 746 BC and the Coming of Tiglath-pileser III to the Throne," *SAAB* 6 (1992): 21–33; Jacob Kaplan, "Recruitment of Foreign Soldiers into the Neo-Assyrian Army during the Reign of Tiglath-pileser III," in *Treasures on Camel's Humps, Historical and Literary Studies from the Ancient Near East Presented to Israel Eph'al*, ed. Mordechai Cogan and Dan'el Kahn (Jerusalem: Magnes Press, 2008), 135–52; Sajjad Alibaigi, "The Location of the Second Stele Commemorating Tiglath-pileser III's Campaign to the East in 737 BC," *SAAB* 23 (2017): 47–53.

27. Albrecht Alt, "Tiglatpileser III, erster Feldzug nach Palästina," in *Kleine Schriften zur Geschichte des Volkes Israel*, vol. 2 (Munich, 1953), 150–62; Ernst Vogt, "Die Texte Tiglat-pilesers III. über die Eroberung Palästinas," *Bib* 45 (1964): 348–54; Hayim Tadmor and Mordechai Cogan, "Ahaz and Tiglathpileser in the Book of Kings: Historiographic Considerations," *Bib* 60 (1979): 491–508; Nadav Na'aman, "Tiglath-pileser III's Campaigns against Tyre and Israel (734–732 B.C.E.)," *Tel Aviv* 22 (1995): 268–78; Na'aman, "Tiglath-pileser III's Annexations According to the Iran Stele (II B)," *NABU* (1998): 16, no. 14; Gershon Galil, "A New Look at the Inscriptions of Tiglath-pileser III," *Bib* 81 (2000): 511–20; Luis Robert Siddall, "Tiglath-pileser III's Aid to Ahaz," *ANES* 46 (2009): 93–106.

28. Barnett and Falkner, *Sculptures*; Reade, "Palace of Tiglath-pileser III," 1–42.

The history of Tiglath-pileser's reign belongs to a trilogy, along with that of Sargon II and that of Sennacherib, that is, grandfather, father, and son.[29] The present book provides an understanding of the course of Tiglath-pileser's reign in relation to his personal choices and the context of his time. Several issues are raised and answered whenever possible: Was Tiglath-pileser a usurper? In what circumstances did he ascend to the throne? What were his qualities and skills? What were his shortcomings? What did he attempt to achieve, and how did he go about fulfilling his objectives? Did he have a clear plan or program at the beginning of his reign? Can he be considered the true founder of the Assyrian Empire? How did he manage to build the empire? Did he think it was more important to expand or to embellish the empire? Was he more a conqueror or an administrator? Was he more a reformer or a conservative? Were his achievements more novelty or continuity? What can be said of his personal evolution during his reign? In what areas did he succeed or, conversely, fail?

Concerning my conception of history, my methodology consists in adapting to the specific topic of the book and to the available sources.[30] My approach is multidisciplinary: political, strategic, economic, geographic, and ethnographic, along with text studies and onomastic analyses when necessary. I always adhere closely to the documents available, because only then is it possible to move on to a historical synthesis, which I provide in a partial summary at the end of each chapter. The progression of the present book is built around decisive events and determining facts. I was forced to make choices from a mass of overabundant data that to me appeared fundamental and relevant for the topic. Some facts and minor features had to be omitted because of the limited framework of the book. Among the different scholarly explanations, I have selected those which, in my opinion, offer the most plausible interpretations. However, different interpretations are also mentioned and sometimes discussed. In a few cases, given the current state of research, I have been unable to choose between several interpretations.

In order to determine whether Tiglath-pileser was the true founder of the Assyrian Empire, chapter 1, "The Kingdom of Assyria in 745 BCE," first

---

29. Josette Elayi, *Sargon II, King of Assyria*, ABS 22 (Atlanta: SBL Press, 2017); Elayi, *Sennacherib, King of Assyria*, ABS 24 (Atlanta: SBL Press, 2018).

30. Josette Elayi, "Être historienne de la Phénicie ici et maintenant," *Trans* 31 (2006): 41–54.

must determine what constituted the state of Assyria and what condition it was in when he ascended the throne. To be able to answer this question, we need to compare the Assyria of 745 with that of 727. Chapter 2, "Was Tiglath-pileser III a Usurper?," investigates the question of Tiglath-pileser's legitimacy because his ascent to the throne is far from clear. This in itself poses several problems. This chapter encompasses the study of Tiglath-pileser's name, his family, his youth, his previous function, his physical portrait, and his personality, based on inscriptions, even if distorted by royal propaganda. Chapter 3, "Tiglath-pileser III's Ascent to the Throne," examines the difficult historical context of Tiglath-pileser's early regnal years and the first measures he adopted to solidify his position. Chapter 4, "The Neutralization of High Dignitaries," explains how high dignitaries such as Shamshî-ilu had become powerful and how Tiglath-pileser proceeded to restore royal power. Chapter 5, "The Strategy of Conquest," investigates the king's objectives, his careful preparation of military strategy, and the place of the West in his strategy. In chapters 6–10, the book follows a chronological order, mainly based on the various texts of the annals. Chapter 6, "The First Phase of the Campaigns (745–744)," analyzes Tiglath-pileser's priority campaigns, the creation of new provinces, and the new measure of deportation of populations. Chapter 7, "The Second Phase of the Campaigns (743–738)," analyzes the subsequent campaigns conducted against the coalition of Syria and Urartu, with the creation of new western provinces. Chapter 8, "The Third Phase of the Campaigns (737–735)," analyzes the campaigns against Media and Urartu and the creation of the new buffer-state concept. Chapter 9, "The Fourth Phase of the Campaigns (734–732)," covers the different campaigns toward the western states of Damascus, the Phoenician and Philistine cities, Israel, and Judah. Chapter 10, "The Fifth Phase of the Campaigns (731–727)," deals with the campaigns against Chaldean and Aramean tribes, concluding with the conquest of Babylonia. Chapter 11, "The King Is Dead! Long Live the King!," focuses on the mysterious death of Tiglath-pileser and the designation of a crown prince, Shalmaneser V. Chapter 12, "Building Activities," examines the building projects initiated by the king. Finally, "Conclusion: Assessment of Tiglath-pileser III's Reign," offers an assessment of Tiglath-pileser's reign, his contribution to the transformation of the kingdom of Assyria into the Assyrian Empire, and the positive and negative consequences of his decisions and actions.

At the end of the book, readers will find research aids: a selected bibliography for each chapter; an index of ancient texts used; an index of the personal names cited, followed by brief comments and dates of reign for situating them both in a diachronic and synchronic perspective; and an index of modern authors cited. Three maps locating the geographical references in the book are provided within the body of the book, together with a chronology of Tiglath-pileser's reign on pages xv–xvi.

1
THE KINGDOM OF ASSYRIA IN 745 BCE

1.1. Previous Attempts to Build the Empire

Some authors considered the kingdom of Sargon of Agade in the third millennium BCE as the first empire, but, if that was the case, it would have been the Empire of Akkad and not the Assyrian Empire.[1] Samsî-Addu (in Assyrian: Shamshî-Adad I; ca. 1807–1776) founded, not an empire, but a tripartite kingdom, with his son Ishme-Dagan as king of Ekallâtum, his son Yasmah-Addu as king of Mari, and himself as king of Assyria. Samsî-Addu was based in Shubat-Enlil, not in Assur,[2] and he developed the military power of Assyria by reorganizing the army and conducting an offensive policy. His sons failed to maintain the vast kingdom founded by their father. Under the reign of Ashur-uballit I (1365–1330), Assyria was liberated from Mitannian domination and again became a powerful independent kingdom.[3] After a period of difficulties, in 1243 Tukultî-Ninurta I ascended the throne of Assyria and conducted several campaigns, trying to terrorize his enemies. He defeated Kashtiliash IV, king of Babylon, and captured and devastated his city, deporting the Babylonian god Marduk to Assyria.[4] This megalomaniac king had a new capital built, Kâr-Tukultî-Ninurta, named after himself, in front of the city of Assur. However, his triumph was short-lived. Assyria was affected by the crisis of the twelfth

---

1. Mario Liverani, *Akkad, the First World Empire: Structure, Ideology, Traditions*, HANE/S 5 (Padova: S.a.r.g.o.n., 1993).
2. Pierre Villard, "Shamshi-Adad and Sons: the Rise and Fall of an Upper Mesopotamian Empire," in *Civilizations of the Ancient Near East*, ed. Jack M. Sasson (New York: Scribner, 1995), 873–83.
3. *PNA* 1.1:227–28.
4. Paul Garelli and André Lemaire, *Les empires mésopotamiens, Israël*, vol. 2 of *Le Proche-Orient Asiatique*, 3rd ed. (Paris: PUF, 1997), 203–4.

century, provoked by various migrations of populations, the major one being the invasion of the "peoples of the sea." The Aramean invasions followed this invasion up to Mesopotamia.[5]

Following the decline of the kingdom of Assyria in the eleventh and tenth centuries, especially after the reign of Tiglath-pileser I (1114–1076), the former Assyrian territory was occupied by Aramean tribes who settled throughout most of northern Mesopotamia and Syria. As a consequence of these invasions and a series of bad harvests, Assyria's territorial holdings were greatly reduced, and its administrative and economic system collapsed. However, during the ninth century, new rulers conducted aggressive military campaigns. Their intention was to recover land once considered the "land of (the god) Assur." This period of reconquest was the preimperial phase of the Assyrian Empire. It started with the kings Ashur-Dân II, Adad-nârârî II, and Tukultî-Ninurta II and reached its peak with the ambitious campaigns of the great conquerors Ashurnasirpal II, Shalmaneser III, and, after difficulties during the reign of Shamshî-Adad V, with Adad-nârârî III.[6] Ashur-Dân II explained his program, which was also that of his successors: "I brought back the exhausted [people] of Assyria [who] had abandoned [their cities (and) houses in the face of] want, hunger, (and) famine (and) [had gone up] to other lands. [I settled] them in cities (and) houses [which were suitable] (and) they dwelt in peace. I constructed [palaces in] the (various) districts of my land.... [I piled up] more grain than ever before...."[7] When Ashur-Dân II was fighting against his enemies, he used intimidation tactics in order to terrorize them by devastating, destroying, and burning their cities. He also adopted the nomads' tactics: continuous harassing of the enemies, capturing towns by surprise, and stocking the necessary supplies for further attacks close by rebellious towns. The

---

5. William A. Ward and Martha S. Joukowsky, *The Crisis Years: The Twelfth Century B.C.; From Beyond the Danube to the Tigris* (Dubuque: Kendall/Hunt 1992); Robert Drews, *The End of the Bronze Age: Changes in Warfare and the Catastrophe ca. 1200 BC* (Princeton: Princeton University Press, 1997); Seymour Gitin, Amihay Mazar, and Ephraim Stern, *Mediterranean Peoples in Transition, Thirteenth to Early Tenth Centuries BCE* (Jerusalem: Israel Exploration Society 1998); Horst Klenger, "The 'Crisis Years' and the New Political System in Early Iron Age Syria: Some Introductory Remarks," in *Essays on Syria in the Iron Age*, ed. Guy Bunnens (Leuven: Peeters, 2000), 21–30.

6. Garelli and Lemaire, *Les empires mésopotamiens, Israël*, 73–79; Shigeo Yamada, *The Construction of the Assyrian Empire* (Leiden: Brill, 2000), 68–76.

7. RIMA 2:134–35, A.0.98.1, 60–67.

Assyrian army became a kind of tax and booty collector, looking like a big caravan returning to Assyria. Adad-nârârî II pursued his father's policy and started the first phase of reconquest of high Mesopotamia (Hanibalgat) and the western fringe of the Zagros.[8] His son Tukultî-Ninurta II conducted the same policy, with the objective of consolidating the borders and enriching Assyria by bringing back enormous riches.[9]

The second phase of reconquest, when Assyria became the most powerful state in the Near East, started with King Ashurnasirpal II. He continued his father's policy, campaigning in the same areas, continuously repressing the revolts, and levying the tribute. He had special methods because he was bloodthirsty and sadistic. However, his objective was not only to satisfy his sadistic instinct but to institute a policy of calculated terror as a radical method of conquest.[10] It was efficient as most peoples submitted spontaneously. Ashurnasirpal's numerous military campaigns, at least fourteen, multiplied his conquests in all directions but not to Babylon. His conquest also had economic objectives, and he was a builder king too, using the riches seized in the campaigns to create a new capital at Nimrud and to launch other building projects. At the end of his reign, Assyria had become a powerful kingdom, able to control its borders.

Shalmaneser III continued his father's aggressive policy and the territorial expansion of Assyria. He could have founded the Assyrian Empire during his long, thirty-five-year reign because his predecessors had prepared for such transformation, but he did not. Assyria had become sufficiently rich by dint of accumulating booty, and its army was hardened after so many expeditions. The army had been reorganized, with increased numbers of cavalrymen, bowmen, slingers, and siege machines that were more sophisticated. From the beginning of his reign, Shalmaneser conducted many campaigns eastwards, extending his control up to the Zagros and northward against the kingdom of Urartu, which he crossed completely in 856 BCE. He was mainly fascinated by the West. He implemented

---

8. RIMA 2:142–62; *PNA* 1.1:30–31.

9. RIMA 2:163–88; *PNA* 3.2:1332–333.

10. RIMA 2:189–393; *PNA* 1.1:204–7; Irène J. Winter, "The Program of the Throne-Room of Assurnasirpal II," in *Essays on Near Eastern Art and Archaeology*, ed. Prudence O. Harper and Holly Pittman (New York: Metropolitan Museum of Art, 1983), 15–31; Barbara Nevling Porter, "Intimidation and Friendly Persuasion: Reevaluating the Propaganda of Ashurnasirpal II," *ErIs* 27 (2003): 180–91; Lionel Marti, "Le banquet d'Aššurnaṣirpal II," *JA* 299 (2011): 505–20.

the policy of terror applied by his father, but it was no longer as efficient: instead of pushing the peoples to submit, his policy urged them to unite in order to resist. The Assyrian king first attacked Ahuni, king of the Bît-Adini; it took Shalmaneser three years to defeat Ahuni and to turn his kingdom into an Assyrian province. Then Shalmaneser came up against a coalition of twelve kings of Hatti and of the coastal area, led by Irhuleni, king of Hamath, and Adad-idri, king of Damascus (Bar-Hadad II, the biblical Hadad-ezer).[11] The confrontation occurred in 853 at Qarqar on the Orontes, probably near the city of Hamath.[12] Although Shalmaneser claimed victory, it was, in fact, a failure for him because he could advance no further, and he brought no booty back to Assyria. The king again launched offensives against the coalition in 849, 848, and 845, but he failed each time, even though his army of 120,000 soldiers was the largest ever assembled. In 841 and 838, he conducted two unsuccessful campaigns against Hazael, the new king of Damascus. Shalmaneser crossed the Euphrates more than twenty-five times, but he failed in his conquest of the West.[13] His failure could be explained by a too rapid expansion over a territory that was too vast, by his inability to create stable political structures, and maybe too by the northern threat of Urartu. Not only was Shalmaneser unable to master all these difficulties, but he also failed to settle his succession.

A last attempt to make Assyria a major power was embarked upon by King Adad-nârârî III. Adad-nârârî's reign followed an immensely troublesome period during the last four years of Shalmaneser's reign and the first three years of Shalmaneser's successor, Shamshî-Adad V: twenty-seven Assyrian cities, with the exception of Nimrud, revolted.[14] After suppressing the revolt, Shamshî-Adad V undertook no campaign to reconquer north Syria; he also failed in the Zagros against the Bît-Hamban and Namri. But he conquered Babylon, capturing the Babylonian king Marduk-balâssu-iqbi and his successor Bâba-ah-iddina.[15] King Adad-nârârî III was probably still a minor when he succeeded his father in 810 and was therefore helped by his mother Sammuramat (Semiramis of Herodotus). He had

---

11. RIMA 3:45, A.0.102.8, 16′–19′.

12. Josette Elayi and Alain G. Elayi, *Arwad, cité phénicienne du nord* (Pendé: Gabalda, 2015), 87–88.

13. Yamada, *Construction of the Assyrian Empire*, 300–308.

14. SAAS 2:57.

15. RIMA 3:187–88, A.0.103.1, iii–iv; 190–91, A.0.103.2, iii–iv; Grayson, *Assyrian and Babylonian Chronicles*, 168–69, Chronicle 21, iii.6′–9′; iv.1–14.

1. THE KINGDOM OF ASSYRIA IN 745 BCE 15

to recuperate the western provinces and to manage the situation with the powerful high dignitaries. Adad-nârârî succeeded in restoring control over all the western territories and received the tribute of all the western kings. He suppressed several revolts in the north and in the west, encouraged by Urartu and Elam. He adopted a policy of appeasement toward Babylonia, assuming the title of "king of Assyria and Karduniash (Babylon)."[16] He protected the Babylonian cities against the attacks of Chaldean tribes, and he maintained good relations with the local clergy. In the remote provinces, Adad-nârârî relied on reliable governors whom he gratified with many privileges, which contributed to increasing their power. However, these ambitious and energetic kings failed to achieve both supremacy and lasting dominion over all these territories; they only succeeded in displaying a show of military might (fig. 1).

1.2. The Crises of 826–746

Revolts broke out in Assyria in 826 according to the Eponym List.[17] This crisis that followed from 826 to 746 was different from the one provoked previously by the Aramean invasions. It was a crisis of development, both social and institutional. Relentless territorial expansion had weakened Assyria, and the successive Assyrian kings were unable or unwilling to implement necessary reforms. Assyria found itself in a precarious situation.

The revolt of 826–820 was a nobility revolt, complicated by disagreements over the royal succession. Ashur-da"in-aplu, son of Shalmaneser III, contested the choice of Shamshî-Adad, the youngest son, as crown prince. In his revolt against his father, Ashur-da"in-aplu was supported by Daiân-Ashur, commander-in-chief of the army and eponym in 853 and 826.[18] Together, Ashur-da"in-aplu and Daiân-Ashur initiated a revolt of twenty-seven Assyrian cities, among which figured Nineveh, Imgur-Enlil, Assur, Shibaniba, Kahat, Huzirina, Zaban, Lubdu, Arrapha (Kirkuk), and Arbela (Erbil).[19] These cities were largely located in the ancient provinces, although they were supported by some of the newer provinces that had been created through conquests.

---

16. RIMA 3:239–44.
17. SAAS 2:57; Garelli and Lemaire, *Les empires mésopotamiens, Israël*, 87–105.
18. *PNA* 1.2:368; SAAS 2:56–57.
19. RIMA 3:183, A.0.103.1, i.45–50.

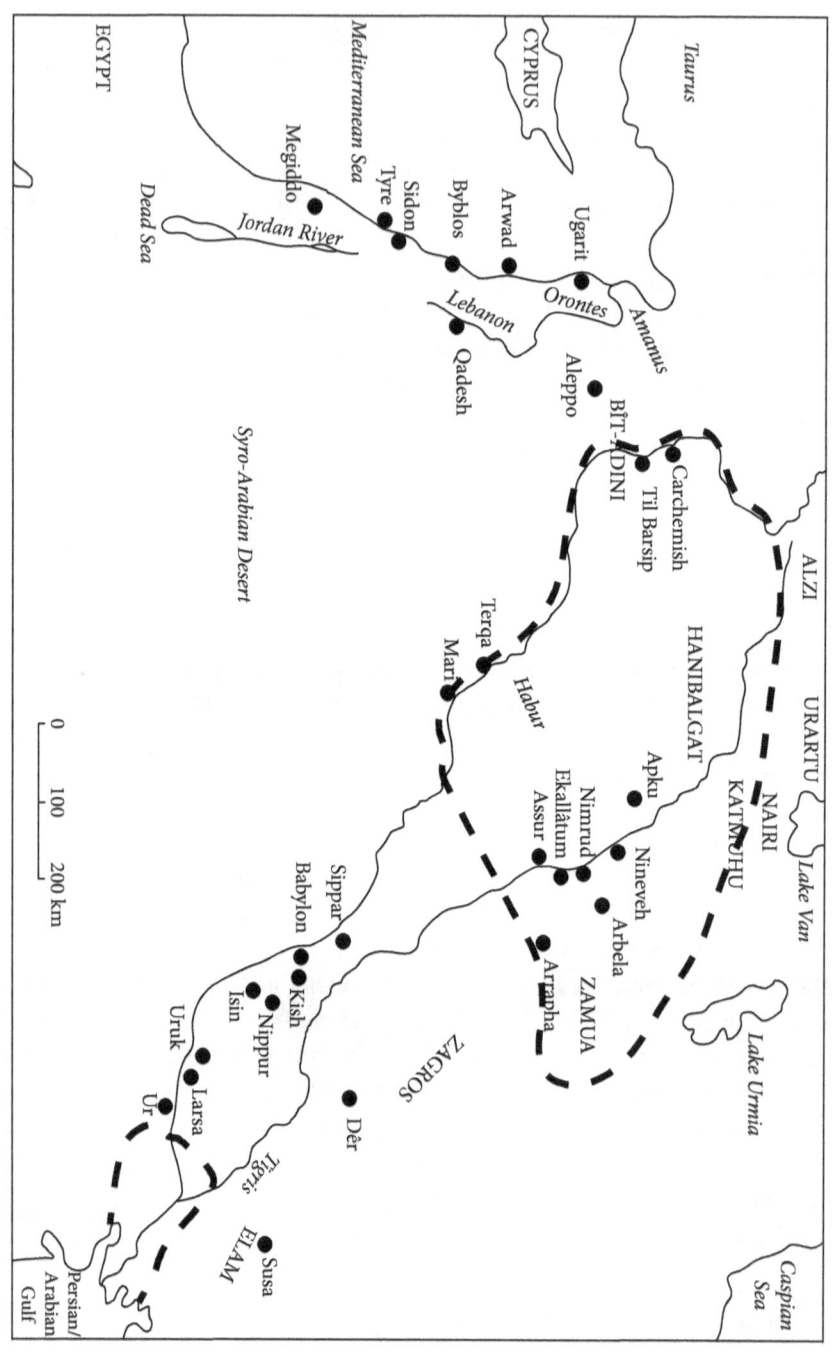

Fig. 1. The Assyrian kingdom, ca. 860 BCE

1. THE KINGDOM OF ASSYRIA IN 745 BCE   17

By the ninth century BCE, the governors of these provinces had become powerful, though how powerful varied depending on the size of the province.[20] The ancient provinces and the newer provinces were of different sizes. Territory in ancient Assyria was divided into small provinces, while the vast areas annexed at the beginning of the ninth century were divided into larger provinces. Since the governors lived on the income from their provinces, governors of the large new provinces had the greatest resources. For example, Daiân-Ashur, as commander-in-chief, was in charge of the vast province of Harrân, which encompassed all the territories inside the great loop of the Euphrates. He thus had substantial resources at his disposal. Governors like Daiân-Ashur were largely drawn from the class of high dignitaries, as can be seen by the fact that they rank as eponyms. For the most part, they were not landowning nobility, though they could occasionally acquire estates.[21] This system favored rivalry and intrigue, and the increasing power of high dignitaries obviously diminished the power of the king. This explains why the high dignitaries could eventually participate in the wars of succession, for example, after Shalmaneser III's death.

During this period of crisis, some other states grew substantially in power and rivaled the might of Assyria, benefiting from the latter's weakening status. Assyrian supremacy was no longer automatically accepted, especially by the small kingdoms of Syria and Anatolia. In the north Urartu and in the west Damascus both imposed their hegemony on several neighboring states. The kingdom of Urartu was similar to that of Assyria, and its army was probably as strong as the Assyrian army. Therefore, the treaties binding the neighboring states to Assyria, and guaranteeing their allegiance and submission to the tribute, were called into question, and allegiance sworn to Urartu instead provided an interesting alternative.[22] King Hazael of Damascus, free from Assyrian dominion, attempted to build a great kingdom of Aram.[23] He conducted several campaigns against Israel and

---

20. Albert Kirk Grayson, "Assyrian Officials and Power in the Ninth and Eight Centuries," *SAAB* 7 (1993): 19–52.

21. Paul Garelli, "L'État et la légitimité royale sous l'Empire assyrien," in *Power and Propaganda: A Symposium on Ancient Empires*, ed. Mogens Trolle Larsen (Copenhagen: Akademisk Forlag, 1979), 324–25.

22. Karen Radner, review of *The Inscriptions of Tiglath-Pileser III, King of Assyria*, by Hayim Tadmor, *JCS* 60 (2008): 137.

23. *PNA* 2.1:467–68.

Judah.[24] He annexed the territory of Galaad and left only a very small army to King Joachaz. King Joas of Judah gave all the treasures of his palace and of the temple of Jerusalem to Hazael. The Aramean kingdoms of Syria and the Phoenician cities also submitted. At the end of his reign, Hazael dominated the whole of Syria-Palestine and its thirty-two kings. However, it was more like a confederation of allies, not really structured or centralized.[25] After Hazael's death, his son Bar-Hadad II did not succeed in maintaining this confederation.[26] To the south of Assyria, there was a gradual disintegration of centralized authority in Babylonia. Nomadic and seminomadic Aramean tribes regularly clashed with the cities of Babylon, Sippar, and Nippur, which were important religious and economic centers. The king of Babylon was so disrupted by these attacks that he had to appeal to the king of Assyria for military support, at least before the period when Assyria was too weakened by its own military failures and internal instability.

In reality, this period is very difficult to analyze due to the small number of royal inscriptions. Is this lack of evidence due to a matter of chance in terms of archaeological discoveries, or is it indicative of a period of difficulties for Assyria? The Eponym Chronicle suggests that far-flung campaigns and victories against major rival states decreased in number. The mention "in the land" (*ina māti*) became more and more frequent in 810, 768, 764, 757, 756, 753, 752, 751, 750, and 747: this phrase means that there were no military campaigns and that the king remained in his capital city.[27] When the number of campaigns, that is, victorious campaigns, decreased so much, it can only be assumed that the Assyrian kings had no outstanding action to relate in the royal inscriptions to help sustain their propaganda.

1.3. The Weakness of Assyria in 745

The period from 782 to 745 is particularly obscure in Assyrian history. Very few royal inscriptions are preserved, but there are a number of

---

24. 2 Kgs 10:32–33.

25. Wayne T. Pitard, *Ancient Damascus: A Historical Study of the Syrian City-State* (Winona Lake, IN: Eisenbrauns, 1987), 145–89; André Lemaire, "Hazaël de Damas, roi d'Aram," in *Marchands, diplomates et empereurs, Études sur la civilisation mésopotamienne offertes à Paul Garelli* (Paris: Éditions Recherche sur les Civilisations, 1991), 91–108.

26. 1 Kgs 20; 2 Kgs 23:14–25; André Lemaire, "Joas de Samarie, Barhadad de Damas, Zakkur de Hamat: La Syrie-Palestine vers 800 av. J.-C.," *ErIs* 24 (1993): 148*–57*.

27. SAAS 2:56–57.

inscriptions by some high dignitaries who exercised considerable power in the kingdom at this time.

Shalmaneser IV succeeded his father Adad-nârârî III in 782.[28] The Eponym List mentioned six campaigns against Urartu (781–778, 776, 774), which are also known through the annals of Argishti I, king of Urartu.[29] Argishti had a policy of brutal expansion, similar to that of the Assyrian kings, burning, plundering, and deporting. Consequently, Urartu become a major power in the Near East at that time. Shalmaneser's commander-in-chief, Shamshî-ilu, fought six campaigns against Urartu and finally halted the Urartian army in the mountains, possibly in the region of Arrapha. Although Urartu was very powerful, Shamshî-ilu succeeded in keeping it at arms' length for several years. He commemorated his victory against Urartu on two lions, more than two meters high, at the palace of Til Barsip, "his lordly city." He did not mention the Assyrian king and took the title of "governor of the land of Hatti, of the land of the Guti and all the land of Namri."[30] In addition to the function of commander-in-chief, Shamshî-ilu was also in charge of Hatti, Guti, and Namri from the western part to the eastern part of Assyria. He was commander-in-chief for about fifty years under four different kings: Adad-nârârî III, Shalmaneser IV, Ashur-Dân III, and Ashur-nârârî V. Shamshî-ilu has also been equated by some scholars with Bar-Ga'yah of *KTK* in the Mati'-ilu (Mati'el) treaty.[31] According to this hypothesis, he would have been a local king of the region of Til Barsip who pursued an outstanding career. He would have come back to his region of origin both as an Assyrian high dignitary, commander-in-chief, and governor of the large province of Harrân and as local king for the neighboring rulers of north Syria. Although attractive, this hypothesis needs to be confirmed. A stela, dated from 773, was found

---

28. *PNA* 3.1:1076–77; RIMA 3:239–44.

29. SAAS 2:56–57; Friedrich Wilhelm Röllig, *Handbuch der chaldischen Inschriften* (Graz: Weidner, 1957), 94, no. 80, §8.

30. RIMA 3:232, A.0.104.2010, 8.

31. André Lemaire and Jean-Marie Durand, *Les inscriptions araméennes de Sfiré et l'Assyrie de Shamshi-ilu* (Geneva: Droz, 1984); Shigeo Ikeda, "Looking from Til Barsip on the Euphrates: Assyria and West in Ninth and Eighth Centuries," in *Priests and Officials in the Ancient Near East*, ed. Kazuko Watanabe (Heidelberg: Winter, 1999), 286–92; Edward Lipiński, *The Aramaeans, Their Ancient History, Culture, Religion*, OLA 100 (Leuven: Peeters, 2000), 217–31; Andreas Fuchs, "Der Turtān Šamši-ilu und die große Zeit des assyrischen Großen (830–746)," *WdO* 38 (2008): 93.

near Marash during the construction of the Pazarcik dam.[32] Curiously, the stela names Shalmaneser IV but celebrates the Syrian campaign of Shamshî-ilu and indicates that he (or the king) received the tribute of Hadiânu, king of Damascus, and his daughter with an extensive dowry. Anyway, this inscription confirms the importance of Shamshî-ilu.

Another high dignitary, the palace herald Bêl-Harrân-bêlu-usur, was also influential from the reign of Shalmaneser to that of Tiglath-pileser III.[33] The stela bearing his proper name "Dûr-Bêl-Harrân-bêlu-usur" found at Tell Abta commemorated the foundation of a city in the desert area that hosted a temple for the great gods. Bêl-Harrân-bêlu-usur established freedom from taxation for the inhabitants of the city. He was probably represented on the stela instead of the king.[34] The name of the king was quoted, but only after the herald's own name. Moreover, the name of Shalmaneser was erased and replaced by that of Tiglath-pileser III. Bêl-Harrân-bêlu-usur seems to have updated the stela when he resumed his office after the ascent of Tiglath-pileser to the throne. The king was apparently inactive during the reigns of Ashur-Dân III and Ashur-nârârî V.[35] However, the text of the Tell Abta stela bears witness to the fact that Bêl-Harrân-bêlu-usur enjoyed a high degree of independence from the king. In short, Shalmaneser IV's reign was characterized by a weakening of the royal power and an increase in the power held by some high dignitaries: these features were still more pronounced during the reign of his successors.

Shalmaneser's brother Ashur-Dân III succeeded him on the throne of Assyria in 772.[36] Although Ashur-Dân's reign lasted eighteen years, only one small fragment of a royal inscription related to him has been recovered from Assur. The text, inscribed on a clay cone, described restoration work on the main courtyard of the Assur temple.[37] However, additional information is provided by the King Lists, the Eponym List, and the Eponym

---

32. RIMA 2:239–40, A.0.105.1; SAAS 2:58; *PNA* 3.2:1226. Another unusual feature of this stela is the fact that the other side bears an inscription of Adad-nârârî III and Sammuramat establishing the border between Kummuhu and Gurgum (RIMA 2:205, A.0.104.3).

33. *PNA* 1.2:301; RIMA 3:243–44, A.0.105.3.

34. Ursula Magen, *Assyrische Königsdarstellungen-Aspekte der Herrschaft* (Mainz am Rhein: Philipp von Zabern, 1986), 50.

35. Grayson, "Assyrian Officials and Power in the Ninth and Eighth Centuries," 28–29.

36. *PNA* 1.1:179.

37. RIMA 2:245, A.0.106.

Chronicle.³⁸ Eight military expeditions toward the east and the west are mentioned: against Media, Gûzâna (Tell Halaf), and Hatarikka (Hazrik, biblical Hadrach, modern Tell Afis). We do not know whether these expeditions were conducted by the king or by Shamshî-ilu, but it is highly likely that the powerful Shamshî-ilu played an important role. He was eponym in 770, the year after the king. Assyria was then on the defensive in relation to the neighboring states and was destabilized by internal revolts in Assur, Arrapha, and Gûzâna from 763 to 759.³⁹ These revolts were possibly overcome in 758. Moreover, Assyria was devastated by plague on two occasions, in 765 and 759. The eclipse of the sun mentioned for year 763 was probably interpreted as an ill omen. Four years were taken up by military campaigns: 768, 764, 757, and 756.

The following reign, that of Ashur-nârârî V, is just as obscure as that of his predecessor and probably worse in terms of achievement.⁴⁰ Ashur-nârârî V was the son of Adad-nârârî III and the uncle of Ashur-Dân III. He ruled for ten years (754–745). The first year of his reign, he conducted a campaign against King Mati'-ilu of Arpad (Bît-Agusi).⁴¹ Instead of fighting and capturing the city, Ashur-nârârî V signed a treaty with Mati'-ilu in order to obtain his loyalty and avoid the penetration of Urartu into Syria. A lamb was killed in case Mati'-ilu did not respect the terms of the treaty: "If Mati'-ilu [should sin] against this treaty, so may, just as the head of this spring lamb is c[ut] off … the head of Mati'-ilu be cut off."⁴² As was usually the case, curses of all kinds formed the backbone of the treaty. The damaged text only preserves part of the treaty stipulations: the king of Arpad had to be loyal to the king of Assyria and join his forces and chariotry to the Assyrian army when it went to war. Mati'-ilu remained loyal to Ashur-nârârî V until the end of his reign and then participated in the anti-Assyrian revolt after Tiglath-pileser III took the throne.

According to the Eponym List, Ashur-nârârî V led a campaign in the east against Namri in 749 and 748.⁴³ An inscription of Sarduri II, king of Urartu, mentioned a victory achieved against the Assyrian king.⁴⁴ However,

---

38. Grayson, "Königslisten und Chroniken," 114; SAAS 2:39, 58.
39. SAAS 2:58.
40. *PNA* 1.1:208; Grayson, "Königslisten und Chronike," 86–135.
41. SAAS 2:59; *PNA* 2.2:745.
42. SAAS 2:xliii–xlvi, 8–13, no. 2.
43. SAAS 2:59.
44. UKN 156, DI:8; *PNA* 1.1:208.

it could have been Shamshî-ilu, and not Ashur-nârârî V, who conducted these campaigns. At the very least, Shamshî-ilu probably contributed to limiting the defeats of the Assyrian army. Ashur-nârârî V knew how important the high dignitaries were, and he gave them privileges as is shown by a fragmentary royal decree.[45] The text bears the remains of a description of a battle followed by the granting of territory, tax-free, to Marduk-sharra-usur by the king of Assyria, probably because the dignitary had distinguished himself in battle. We have no information about the beneficiary, but he might be identified with the eponym of 784, governor of Kurbail (an important city distinct from Arbail).[46] Except for these campaigns against Arpad (754) and Namri (749, 748), the king remained in his capital from 753 to 750 and in 747. In 746 a revolt broke out in Nimrud itself.

In short, in 745 the kingdom of Assyria was almost paralyzed, with a powerless king and powerful independent high dignitaries unable to restore the might of the kingdom. Enemies were not invading Assyria, but they were threatening all of its borders, and the internal political, economic, and social situation was disastrous. The size of the Assyrian territory had been considerably reduced. Central Assyria was still the so-called Assur-Nineveh-Arbela triangle (fig. 2).[47] Nimrud (Kalhu), which was the Assyrian capital city at that time, was roughly located in the center of this triangle. The relocation of the seat of royal power away from Assur to Nimrud was due to Ashurnasirpal II in 879, and it was maintained there by his successors.[48] To the south, the entire region north of Babylonia, south of Arrapha and Assur, was under the control of the Babylonians. This area included Gananate where the Assyrians campaigned for two years in 761 and 760 and which was possibly lost. To the east, the province of Zamua (Mazamua, Lullumî) was created in the first half of the ninth century by Ashurnasirpal II, who annexed various mountain valleys surrounding the Shehrizor basin.[49] While Zamua was still Assyrian in 745, the neighboring

---

45. RIMA 3:246–47, A.0.107.

46. SAAS 2:58; *PNA* 2.2:727.

47. Karen Radner, "The Assur-Nineveh-Arbela Triangle: Central Assyria in the Neo-Assyrian Period," in *Between the Cultures: The Central Tigris Region from the Third to the First Millennium*, ed. Peter A. Miglus and Simone Mühl (Heidelberg: Heidelberger Orient-Verlag, 2011), 321–29.

48. Karen Radner, "The Neo-Assyrian Empire," in *Imperien und Reiche in der Weltgeschichte*, ed. Michael Gehler and Robert Rollinger (Wiesbaden: Harrassowitz Verlag, 2014), 107.

49. SAA 11:XIV, 4, ii. 4.

1. THE KINGDOM OF ASSYRIA IN 745 BCE

areas of Namri and Media experienced unrest and necessitated military campaigns in 774 and 766 respectively. To the north, Urartu was so powerful that it controlled more and more regions in high Mesopotamia, up as far as Gûzâna in the Habur, which revolted and necessitated an expedition in 759–758. The territories west of the Euphrates had been lost even though there were three campaigns against Hatarikka. The king of Urartu tried to control north Syria, and the treaty concluded by Ashur-nârârî V with Mati'-ilu was intended to prevent him from achieving this. However, the kingdom of Assyria remained weak in 745, and the area of its extension was limited.[50]

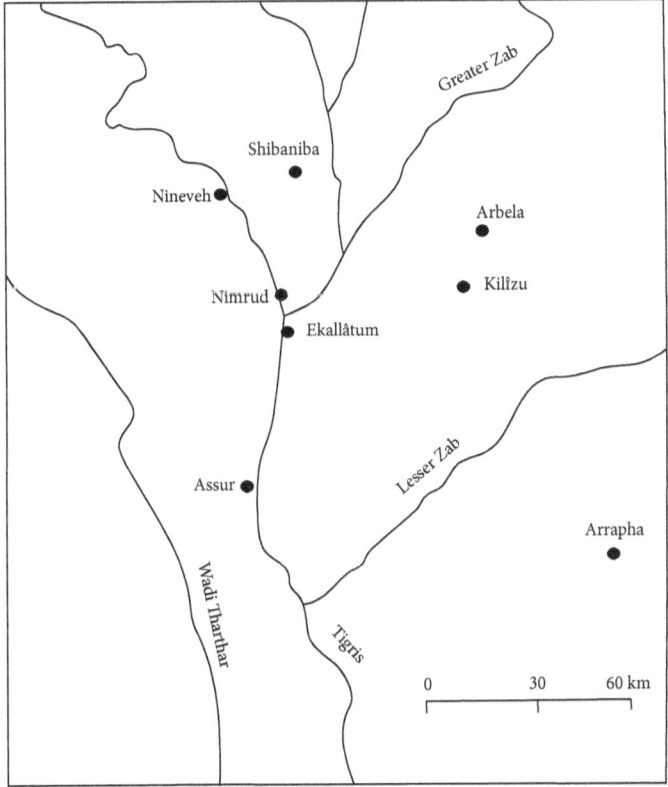

Fig. 2. Assur-Nineveh-Arbela triangle.

---

50. Mario Liverani, "The Fall of the Assyrian Empire: Ancient and Modern Interpretations," in *Empires: Perspectives from Archaeology and History*, ed. Susan E. Alcock (Cambridge: Cambridge University Press, 2001), 375, 15.1 (ca. 860 BCE). See also the map therein.

2
WAS TIGLATH-PILESER III A USURPER?

2.1. His Name and Family

The name of Tiglath-pileser III in Akkadian was *Tukultī-apil-Ešarra*, with some variants.[1] It meant "My support is the heir of Esharra."[2] Esharra referred to the Assur temple, and the heir of Esharra was Ninurta, considered to be the true founder of the Neo-Assyrian Empire. Ninurta was a war god, son of Enlil and the husband of the goddess Gula. He was worshiped in Nippur and obtained much success in Assyria where he was considered the son of the god Assur. Ninurta had a chapel in the Assur temple in the city of Assur, and King Ashurnasirpal II built a temple and a ziggurat for Ninurta in Nimrud.[3]

The name of Tiglath-pileser was translated *tglt pl'sr*, *tlgt pln'sr*, *tglt plsr*, or *tglt pln'sr* in Hebrew.[4] In Aramaic and Phoenician inscriptions from Sam'al, Bar-Rakib named his suzerain *tgltplsr* or *tgltplysr*.[5] In the Aramaic Ashur ostracon, written in Babylonia, there are two occurrences of the name: *plsr*, an abbreviated form, and *tklplsr*, maintaining the etymological *k* of *Tukultī*.[6] There were many variants in the Septuagint, such as θαγλαθφελλασαρ, θαλγαθφελλασαρ, θαλγαλφασαρ, θεγλαθφαλσαρ,

---

1. *PNA* 3.2:1329.
2. And not "My trust is (in) the son of Esharra" (i.e., in the god Assur), as stated by John A. Brinkman, *A Political History of Post-Kassite Babylonia 1158–722 B.C.*, AnOr 43 (Rome: Biblical Institute Press, 1968), 240, n. 1544.
3. Francis Joannès, *Dictionnaire de la civilisation mésopotamienne* (Paris: Robert Laffont, 2001), 577–78.
4. 2 Kgs 15:29, 16:7, 10; 1 Chr 5:6, 26; 2 Chr 28–20; 2 Kgs 16:7; Millard, "Assyrian Royal Names in Biblical Hebrew," 7–8.
5. *KAI* 224, 215.15; 233, 216.2; 234, 217.2.
6. *KAI* 283, 233.12 and 15.

θαγλαθφαλνασαρ, and θαγλαθφελλασαρ. Greek and Latin authors also used several forms, such as θαγλαθφαλλασαρ and Theglaphaassar.[7] If Tiglath-pileser was a throne name, it may have been a deliberate reference to Tiglath-pileser I, an illustrious forebear.[8]

The question as to whether Tiglath-pileser III was a usurper or not has long been debated. The opinion in favor of usurpation is mainly based on the silence of the sources over his origins and on the contradiction of the rare mentions of his patronymic, though the absence of patronymic in royal inscriptions was also a feature of Sargon II and Sennacherib.[9] There is only one official inscription of Tiglath-pileser III that mentions his parentage, duplicated on several bricks from Assur. The inscription is as follows: "Palace of Tiglath-pileser, king of Assyria, son of Adad-nārārī, king of Assyria: (this brick) belongs to the platform of the temple of (the god) Aššur."[10] This palace may have been the place where Tiglath-pileser lived when he was not in Nimrud or, more probably, when he visited the religious city of Assur. Anyway, the main problem is the mention of his patronymic. Since Adad-nârârî III was on the throne from 811 to 783, we should suppose that Tiglath-pileser was born at the end of Adad-nârârî's reign and that he was about forty or slightly older when he ascended the throne in 745. A land grant, dated from 762, curiously mentions King Adad-nârârî III (who was dead in 783) and a certain Tiglath-pileser who may have held an official position at that time.[11] Some scholars raise the

---

7. Brinkman, *Political History of Post-Kassite Babylonia*, 241, n. 1544 (with bibliography).

8. Donald John Wiseman, "Tiglath-pileser III," https://www.britannica.com/biography/Tiglath-pileser-III.

9. Elayi, *Sargon II*, 27. Authors in favor of usurpation: Hayim Tadmor, "History and Ideology in the Assyrian Royal Inscriptions," in *Assyrian Royal Inscriptions: New Horizons*, ed. Frederick Mario Fales (Rome: Instituto per l'Oriente, 1981), 26–27; Albert Kirk Grayson, "Assyria: Tiglath-pileser III to Sargon II (744–705 B.C.)," in *The Assyrian and Babylonian Empires and Other States of the Near East, from the Eighth to the Sixth Centuries BC*, ed. John Boardman et al., 2nd ed., CAH 3.2 (Cambridge: Cambridge University Press, 1991), 73–75; Grayson, "The Struggle for Power in Assyria," in *Priests and Officials in the Ancient Near East*, ed. Kazuko Watanabe (Heidelberg: Winter, 1999), 269: "Tiglath-pileser was almost certainly a usurper, or, at best a remote relation of the royal family."

10. RINAP 1:147–48, 58. It is unclear whether the bricks belonged to the palace or to the temple.

11. SAA 12:xxiv, 15, 13.r.3; RINAP 1:147.

possibility that Tiglath-pileser was governor of Nimrud prior to becoming king, although this remains unproven.[12] The Assyrian King Lists give a contradictory statement: "Tukultî-apil-Esharra (III) son of Ashur-nârârî (V) 18 years he ruled."[13] Some scholars consider "son" to be an error for "brother" because, in the King Lists, the scribes usually tended to describe all kings as their predecessor's sons; however, in these lists, Ashur-Dân III is referred to as the brother of Shalmaneser IV, making this interpretation unlikely.[14] If Tiglath-pileser was the son of Ashur-nârârî V, he was the grandson of Adad-nârârî III and not his son as is written on the bricks from Assur.[15] There is certainly an error, either in the royal inscriptions on the bricks or in the Assyrian King Lists.

Anyway, Tiglath-pileser was probably not the legitimate heir of Ashur-nârârî V, assuming that he was one of his sons, because he tried to legitimate himself by several means. He seems to have chosen Tiglath-pileser as a throne name to present himself as a legitimate king and a conqueror. He described himself as the one "who grew up to be king." He emphasized his claim to the throne by saying that he was the "precious scion of Baltil,"[16] the most ancient part of the city of Assur. In the Babylonian King List A, his son Shalmaneser V was said to belong to the "Dynasty of Baltil,"[17] the oldest legitimate dynasty. There could have been a link between the chronistic-scribal tradition of Baltil and the royal ideology of the "Dynasty of Baltil," which could explain why Tiglath-pileser was said

---

12. Emil O. Forrer, *Die Provinzeinteilung des assyrischen Reiches* (Leipzig: Hinrichs, 1920), 10; SAA 12:xxiv; PNA 3.2:1329; RINAP 1:147.

13. Ignace J. Gelb, "Two Assyrian King Lists," *JNES* 13 (1954): 223–24, iv.24–25.

14. Benno Landsberger, "Assyrische Königsliste und 'Dunkles Zeitalter,'" *JCS* 8 (1954): 42–43; Grayson, "Königslisten und Chroniken," 115. However, the error could not have been graphic: Keiko Yamada and Shigeo Yamada, "Shalmaneser V and His Era, Revisited," in *'Now It Happened in Those Days': Studies in Biblical, Assyrian, and Other Ancient Near Eastern Historiography Presented to Mordechai Cogan on His Seventy-Fifth Birthday*, ed. Amitai Baruchi-Unna et al. (Winona Lake: Eisenbrauns, 2017), 2:390 and n. 9; Gelb, "Two Assyrian King Lists," 229, iv.21–22.

15. Paul Garelli, "The Achievement of Tiglath-pileser III: Novelty or Continuity?," in *Ah, Assyria… Studies in Assyrian History and Ancient Near Eastern Historiography Presented to Hayim Tadmor*, ed. Mordechai Cogan and Israel Eph'al (Jerusalem: Magnes Press Hebrew University, 1991), 46; Tadmor, *Inscriptions of Tiglath-pileser III*, 212–13; Grayson, "Assyria: Tiglath-pileser III to Sargon II," 73.

16. RINAP 1:22, 1.1–3.

17. RINAP 1:15.

to be the son of Ashur-nârârî V in the Assyrian King Lists.[18] Since the city of Harrân gained extraordinary significance in the Sargonid period, it is also possible that Assyrian collateral branches had a special connection with Harrân starting with Tiglath-pileser. This dynasty was referred to in King List A as the "Dynasty of Ḫabi-GAL" (Ḫani-GAL-bat?), with the suggestion that Harrân could have been the capital.[19] Either Tiglath-pileser was a royal prince but not of the first order, or he came from a subsidiary line of the royal family, possibly from Harrân.[20] It is possible that he was one of the several sons of Adad-nârârî III and a brother of the previous king Ashur-nârârî V. Either way, Tiglath-pileser was illegitimate to succeed to him.

If Tiglath-pileser was a son of Adad-nârârî III, we do not know who his mother was. He had at least three brothers, all of whom had reigned: Shalmaneser IV, Ashur-Dân III, and Ashur-nârârî V. He had at least two sons who reigned: Shalmaneser V and Sargon II.[21] He possibly had a harem since the tradition of polygamy was practiced by Assyrian kings.[22] One of his wives is known by name: Iabâ, who was not Shalmaneser V's mother because she was also Shalmaneser's wife after Tiglath-pileser's death; the new king had apparently married his father's widow, an old strategy to further secure the succession. There is a mystery concerning the identity of Iabâ. In 1988–1990, a burial

---

18. Tadmor, "History and Ideology in the Assyrian Royal Inscriptions," 25–30; Tadmor, *Inscriptions of Tiglath-pileser III*, 40–41.

19. Natalie Naomi May, "Administrative and Other Reforms of Sargon II and Tiglath-pileser III," *SAAB* 21 (2015): 87–89 (with bibliography); Miguel Valerio, "Hani-Rabbat as the Semitic Name of Mitanni," *Journal of Language Relationship* 6 (2012): 173–83.

20. Yamada and Yamada, "Shalmaneser V and His Era, Revisited," 389–90 (with bibliography); May, "Administrative and Other Reforms of Sargon II and Tiglath-pileser III," 87–90; John A. Brinkman, *Prelude to Empire: Babylonian Society and Polities, 747–626 B.C.*, OPSNKF 7 (Philadelphia: Babylonian Section of the University Museum, 1984), 40, even doubted his royal parentage.

21. RIMA 2:239–47; RINAP 1:114–15, 46.28; *PNA* 3.1:1077; Felix Thomas, "Sargon II., der Sohn Tiglat-pilesers III.," in *Mesopotamica-Ugaritica-Biblica: Festschrift für Kurt Bergerhof*, ed. Manfred Dietrich and Oswald Loretz, AOAT 232 (Neukirchen-Vluyn: Neukirchener Verlag, 1993), 465–70.

22. Simo Parpola, "The Neo-Assyrian Royal Harem," in *Leggo! Studies Presented to Frederick Mario Fales on the Occasion of His Sixty-Fifth Birthday*, ed. Giovanni Battista Lanfranchi et al. (Wiesbaden: Harrassowitz, 2012), 620–26.

site with four tombs was discovered in Nimrud.[23] Tomb II contained gold bowls bearing the inscriptions of three queens, Iabâ, Banîtu, and Atalia, but only two skeletons. The inscriptions of Iabâ are as follows: "Belonging to queen Iabâ, wife of Tiglath-pileser, king of Assyria," and "Belonging to Iabâ, queen of Tiglath-pileser, king of Assyria"; the inscription of Banîtu is: "Belonging to Banîtu, queen of Shalmaneser, king of Assyria."[24] In order to explain the mention of three women when there are only two bodies, the following hypothesis has been proposed: Iabâ and Banîtu, Shalmaneser's wife, could have been one and the same person.[25] In fact, Iabâ seems to be a West Semitic name meaning "beautiful." The name would have been translated into Akkadian as Banîtu, which had the same meaning. The names Iabâ and Atalia, which might be Hebrew, would mean that the Assyrian kings married Judean or Israelite princesses at that time in order to seal alliances. After having analyzed what we know about his family, it is possible to answer the question as to whether Tiglath-pileser III was a usurper: he probably was a usurper because, even if he belonged to the reigning dynasty in some way, he was not the legitimate heir chosen by Ashur-nârârî V.

2.2. His Physical Portrait

There exist several representations of Tiglath-pileser III, mainly in the Central Palace of Nimrud, so we have some idea of his physical portrait.[26] We have to bear in mind that these representations were stereotyped and corresponded to the image that the king wanted to give of himself. Nevertheless, it is instructive to have this image. The king was represented in various attitudes and contexts, such as standing, seated on his throne, or carried in his chariot.[27] Most of the time he is depicted fighting, with or

---

23. Muayyad Said Damerji, "An Introduction to the Nimrud Tombs," in *New Light on Nimrud*, ed. John E. Curtis et al. (London: British Institute for the Study of Iraq, 2008), 81–82.

24. Farouk N. H. Al-Rawi, "Inscriptions from the Tombs of the Queens of Assyria," in Curtis et al., *New Light on Nimrud*, 136–38.

25. Stephanie Dalley, "Yabâ, Atalyā and the Foreign Policy of Late Assyrian Kings," *SAAB* 12 (1998): 83–98; Dalley, "The Identity of the Princesses in Tomb II and a New Analysis of Events in 701 BC," in Curtis et al., *New Light on Nimrud*, 171–75.

26. Barnett and Falkner, *Sculptures*, pls. I–CXIII.

27. Barnett and Falkner, *Sculptures*, pls. XXII, VIII, LXIX, LXXI, XCVIII.

without his chariot, or receiving his vizier, prisoners, or the submission of an enemy.[28] When he is fighting, he holds a bow or is shooting with it, sometimes preparing the next two arrows. He has a long sword in its scabbard, kept at the waist, the lower end extending behind him. He is also represented with a long spear or with a mace. Sometimes, his sword shows two lions' heads attached to it or two rings at his waist through which fringed bands are threaded, possibly attached to the sword or hanging over his shoulder.[29] When the king is receiving people, he raises his hand in salutation and holds a long staff, a fan, or a flower. He wears fine jewelry: triangular earrings hanging on a ring of a common type[30] and fourfold bracelets with a rosette in the middle but not arm-bangles like his successors; in a sculpture, he wears a necklace with the divine symbols of Sîn (crescent), Ishtar (star), Shamash (sun), Anu (horned cap), and Adad (trident).[31] Tiglath-pileser's costume consists of a long dress reaching down to the ankles, ornamented with motifs such as a rosette. Over this dress he wears a mantle that has a fringed border decorated with rosettes or disks alternating with squares. He has sandals on his feet. His headdress consists of a high, conical cap, flat at the top and surmounted by a small pointed tip decorated with bands of rosettes and a long (single or double) ribbon hanging down his back. The features of the king's face are carefully modeled: thick raised eyebrows, heavy lids with delineated iris, thin lips topped with a small mustache. He wears a long full beard and carefully curled hair. His tall headdress, making him taller, no doubt emphasized his status to the onlooker. With the same objective, his throne stands on a raised platform with rounded angles and long legs, which necessitate a footstool for the king's feet. He is also depicted as a brawny man, either to symbolize his physical strength or because this really was the case.

---

28. Fighting: Barnett and Falkner, *Sculptures*, pls. XV–XVI, LII, LXXIV. Receiving: Barnett and Falkner, *Sculptures*, pls. VIII, XVIII, LIX, LXXXIV–LXXXVII. On pl. LXXXIX, he is condemning an enemy.

29. As on some representations of Ashurnasirpal II: E. A. Wallis Budge, *Assyrian Sculptures in the British Museum, Reign of Ashur-nasir-pal* (London: Trustees of the British Museum, 1914), pls. XIII.1, XIX.1.2; Monica Rigo, "L'abbigliamento degli Assiri: Una nota sull' abito del re," in Lanfranchi et al., *Leggo!*, 719–24.

30. For example, a chief eunuch from the reign of Ashurnasirpal II bore the same earrings: SAA 19:3, fig. 13.

31. Barnett and Falkner, *Sculptures*, pls. LXXXIX, XCV–XCVI. See the divine symbols on a stela: SAA 19:70, fig. 19; RINAP 1:82, fig. 5.

When we compare the representations of Tiglath-pileser with those of Sargon II or Sennacherib, for example, they are more or less the conventional image of an Assyrian king. However, some slight differences can be noticed, such as the styling of the hair and the beard, the absence of arm-bangles, the presence of a necklace, the staff being held in the right hand instead of the left, and the two rings at the waist. There are also some differences in the choice of the scenes where the king is represented, for example, no hunting scenes as was the case for his successors. The Assyrians could notice these differences, but the key to identification was the location where each king was represented: Tiglath-pileser was mainly represented in his Central Palace of Nimrud.

2.3. His Personality

If Tiglath-pileser was a throne name, his personality explains why he took this king as a model by adopting the same name. As with Tiglath-pileser I,[32] the reign of Tiglath-pileser III marked a new rise of Assyria: his armies marched further afield than ever before, from Babylon in the southeast to Lebanon in the west. The extent of his conquests and political control were related yearly in the royal inscriptions. These military achievements were accompanied by economic and cultural advances in Assyria. The personality of Tiglath-pileser III can be deduced from his numerous inscriptions where he gave a self-presentation. However, as the royal inscriptions were dominated by propaganda and as the scribes used stereotyped formulae, they need to be examined with a critical eye. His self-presentation is mainly characterized by three points: his royal titles, the yearly dating system, and the image of an absolute empire builder-administrator.[33]

Most of the titles used in the annals are unknown because they are broken away. The two most frequent titles of Tiglath-pileser were "king of Sumer and Akkad" (*šar māt Šumeri [u] Akkadî*) and "king of the four quarters" (*šar kibrāt arba'i*). The first one can be found in the Iran stela and summary inscriptions, the second in the Mila Mergi inscription, Iran stela, and summary inscriptions. The first title was essentially Babylonian; it was previously used by Tukultî-Ninurta I and Shamshî-Adad V who attacked Babylon and temporarily extended the kingdom's influence over Babylonia. The

---

32. RIMA 2:5–84.
33. Shigeo Yamada, "Inscriptions of Tiglath-pileser III: Chronographic-Literary Styles and the King's Portrait," *Orient* 49 (2014): 42–48.

second title dated as far back as the third millennium and was later assumed by Tukultî-Ninurta I, Tiglath-pileser I, Adad-nârârî II, Ashurnasirpal II, and Shalmaneser III, that is, by all the kings who undertook numerous military campaigns in all directions.[34] The withdrawal of this title after Shalmaneser III's reign can be explained by the decline of the king's military activity. The renewal of military activity by Tiglath-pileser III explains why he reintroduced the title, already in the Mila Mergi inscription in 739. The king revived this prestigious title in order to proclaim that he had completed campaigns in all directions: to Babylonia in the south (745), to Namri in the east (744), to Urartu in the north (743), and to Syria in the west (742–740).

Some other traditional titles were taken up by Tiglath-pileser III, such as "prince" (*rubû*) and "vicar of Assur" (*iššiak Aššur*) in the Mila Mergi inscription and Iran stela, previously used by Shalmaneser III. "King of the world" (*šar kiššati*), used in the Iran stela, summary inscriptions, and short inscriptions, was taken up from Shamshî-Adad V, Adad-nârârî III, and Shalmaneser IV. The title "king of Assyria" (*šar māt Aššur*), used, for example, in the Iran stela, was taken up from most of the previous kings. "Prefect of Enlil" (*šakin Enlil*) was previously used by Ashur-Dân III. The standard titles such as "great king" (*šarru rabû*) and "strong king" (*šarru dannu*) were used by most of Tiglath-pileser's predecessors. According to the date of his royal inscriptions, the titles gradually become more and more numerous, reflecting the great pride Tiglath-pileser took in his achievements. For example, in the Iran stela, composed two years after the Mila Mergi inscription, that is, in 737, there was an accumulation of titles:

> the one appointed by the god Enlil, the prince, the priest of Aššur ... [king of the wo]rld, king of Assyria, king of Sumer [and Akkad, king of the] four [quar]ters (of the world), shepherd of (its) people, [the one who established the remis]sion (of debts) for Assyria, the one who pleases the heart of Ištar, [the one who enlarges] the boundary of Assyria, [the one who receives the tribute and gi]fts of the entire world.[35]

---

34. Marie-Joseph Seux, *Épithètes royales akkadiennes et sumériennes* (Paris: Letouzey & Ané, 1967), 302–8; Barbara Cifola, *Analysis of Variants in the Assyrian Royal Titulary from the Origins to Tiglath-pileser III* (Naples: Istituto universitario orientale, 1995); Vladimir Sazonov, "Some Notes on the King of The Four Corners," *NABU* 3 (2019): 102–5, no. 60; Jessie DeGrado, "King of the Four Quarters: Diversity as a Rhetorical Strategy of the Neo-Assyrian Empire," *Iraq* 81 (2019): 107–25.

35. RINAP 1:83, 35.i.25–30; Ludovico Portuese, "Concealed Paternalism of the Assyrian King: Which Audience?," *Mesopotamia* 52 (2017): 111–28.

2. WAS TIGLATH-PILESER III A USURPER? 33

In the summary inscriptions, redacted about seven years later, in ca. 731–730, there was a still longer set of traditional titles:

> great king, mighty king, king of the world, king of Assyria, king of Sumer <and> Akkad, king of the fo[ur] quarters (of the world), the one chosen by the glance of the god Enlil, the king who from the rising sun to the setting sun considered all of his enemies as (mere) ghosts and took control of (their) power, the one who exchanges the people of the upper land(s) with (those of) the lower land(s), the one who ousted their rulers (and) installed his governors (in their stead).[36]

The second point of Tiglath-pileser's self-presentation was the adoption of the *palû*-dating system. This yearly dating is first attested in the Mila Mergi inscription in 739 (seventh *palû*). It seems to have been used in all the annalistic inscriptions and in the summary inscriptions, but it is not always preserved in the damaged parts of the text. This system was first introduced in the royal inscriptions in the latter half of the ninth century under Shalmaneser III, who conducted military campaigns in almost every year of his reign. It also echoes the frequent campaigns of Tiglath-pileser I, who used the following expressions: "in my accession year" (*ina šurru šarrūtia*) and "at that time" (*ina ūmīšu*) for each campaign.[37] After Shalmaneser III, the *palû*-dating system was dropped because no Assyrian king was able to undertake numerous military expeditions, and the scribes managed to cover up the king's military inactivity. Tiglath-pileser III brought back the *palû*-dating system created by Shalmaneser III in order to emphasize his constant and unremitting military activities.[38] By using this system and the title "king of the four quarters," Tiglath-pileser wanted to be regarded as a great conqueror and ruler who restlessly campaigned far away in all directions in order to extend his rule over new territories. This presentation was strengthened by lists of the lands conquered and of the rulers who submitted to pay tax and tribute, already present in

---

36. RINAP 1:96, 39.1–3.
37. RIMA 2:14–28, A.0.87.1, i.62–vii.70.
38. Shigeo Yamada, "History and Ideology in the Inscriptions of Shalmaneser III: An Analysis of Stylistic Changes in the Assyrian Annals," in *Royal Assyrian Inscriptions: History, Historiography and Ideology; A Conference in Honour of Hayim Tadmor on the Occasion of His Eightieth Birthday, 20 November 2003*, ed. Israel Eph'al and Nadav Na'aman (Jerusalem: Israel Academy of Sciences and Humanities, 2009), vii–xxx.

the inscriptions of some of his predecessors. These lists are more frequent in the main later inscriptions such as the annals and summary inscriptions. What is new is the eloquent style adopted in presenting these lists: "I increased the territory of Assyria by taking hold of (foreign) lands (and) added countless people to its population. I constantly shepherd them in safe pastures."[39]

The third point of Tiglath-pileser's self-presentation was the image he wanted to convey, that of a great builder-administrator. Campaign narratives, as well as the literary style in which they were told, are found in the inscriptions of his predecessors. All of them wanted to present their heroic image and military accomplishment. What may be regarded as innovative in the inscriptions of Tiglath-pileser was the attention paid to administrative matters.[40] The long lists of lands and cities conquered are not only exhibited to underline that Tiglath-pileser was a great conqueror, but also to show that the conquered territory was incorporated anew under direct Assyrian administrative rule. Tiglath-pileser's inscriptions emphasized his administrative skills by describing the deportation of local inhabitants and the resettling of deportees, the nomination of eunuchs as provincial governors, and the imposition of corvée labor and taxes upon the people of the annexed areas.[41] These descriptions are formulated with a fixed phraseology, and the name of the provincial governors is very rarely given in order to show that the king himself had created a solid provincial system and had kept all the power in his own hands.[42]

This self-presentation was in accordance with the royal ideology: the Assyrian king, whoever he was, was portrayed as a king without rival anywhere else in the world. The god Assur chose the king to rule on earth and charged him to suppress chaos wherever it was and to establish order. The king accomplished this charge by conquering new territories and exploiting them.[43]

---

39. RINAP 1:86, 35.ii.15'-17'.
40. Cifola, *Analysis of Variants in the Assyrian Royal Titulary*, 138.
41. RINAP 1:26-29, 5-6.
42. RINAP 1:44, 13.18-20; Yamada, "Inscriptions of Tiglath-pileser III," 47-48.
43. Paul Garelli, "La conception de la royauté en Assyrie," in Fales, *Assyrian Royal Inscriptions*, 1-11; Garelli, "L'État et la légitimité royale sous l'Empire assyrien," 319-28; Simo Parpola, "Neo-Assyrian Concepts of Kingship and Their Heritage in Mediterranean Antiquity," in *Concepts of Kingship in Antiquity*, ed. Giovanni Battista Lanfranchi and Robert Rollinger (Padova: S.a.r.g.o.n., 2010), 15-24; Karen Radner,

2. WAS TIGLATH-PILESER III A USURPER? 35

Besides Tiglath-pileser's self-presentation and the Assyrian royal ideology, some characteristic features of his personality can be identified through the description of his actions. However, his inscriptions used many stereotyped formulae; they are neither developed nor did they contain any personal feelings like those of his successors. First, he believed that Ea, the sage of the gods, had endowed him "with the keen understanding (and) broad knowledge."[44] Tiglath-pileser was certain of being superior to previous kings, due to his intelligence and to his quality as a warrior. His weapons were more efficient than those of his ancestors; he went to places their chariots had never reached before; he was able to rehabilitate settlements on the periphery of Assyria abandoned by them; he built larger palaces than those of his ancestors.[45] In some of his inscriptions and figurative representations, the king displayed an excessive pride, but he presented his victories in an ambiguous form: "the deeds of (the god) Aššur my lord that I had done again and again to all the city rulers of the mountain regions."[46] Tiglath-pileser boasted of having extended the territory of Assyria and increased its population.[47]

Tiglath-pileser raised stelae and statues and engraved rock reliefs at different locations during his campaigns, often along the passageways. He mentioned eleven stelae in his inscriptions.[48] Some of them have been discovered: those of Luristan, Uramanat, and Mila Mergi.[49] During his campaign of 737 against the Medes, he placed his stelae in several places, such as the cities of Bît-Ishtar, Sibar (Sibur), Mount Ariarma, and Mount Silhazu.[50] He described in detail the stela he had made in the Zagros: "I dep[icted] on it (symbols of) the great gods, my lords, (and) I fashioned my royal image on it. I ins[cribed] on it the mighty deeds of (the god) Aššur, my lord, and [my] personal achievements (that) I accomplished again and again throughout (all of) the lands."[51] Then followed the curses

---

"Assyrian and Non-Assyrian Kingship in the First Millennium BC," in Lanfranchi and Rollinger, *Concepts of Kingship in Antiquity*, 35–44.
44. RINAP 1:123, 47.r.17′–19′.
45. RINAP 1:24, 3.1–4; 27–28, 5.11–12; 67, 25.1′–4′; 86, 35.ii.20′–21′.
46. RINAP 1:84, 35.i.15′–16′.
47. RINAP 1:86, 35.ii.15′–16′.
48. Daniele Morandi Bonacossi, "Stele e statue reali assire: Localizzazione, diffuzione e implicazioni ideologiche," *Mesopotamia* 23 (1988): 142.
49. Morandi Bonacossi, "Stele e statue reali assire," 153.
50. RINAP 1:86, 35.ii.27′–28′.
51. RINAP 1:87, 35.iii.31–36.

against a possible destroyer of the stela. Conversely, if a future ruler happened to read the inscription aloud, wash the stela with water, anoint it with oil, and make an offering, the gods depicted on the stela would hear his prayers.

Tiglath-pileser III was a warrior king who personally led numerous military campaigns. He described himself as a "powerful male," "valiant man," and "exalted lion-dragon," who could become ferocious and furious, able "to crush mighty mountains like potsherds."[52] He could jump across a river in a flood as if it was a simple ditch.[53] The conquest of a city was usually presented in three steps using a stereotyped formula: the king destroyed it, devastated it, and burnt it with fire.[54] Just like the other Assyrian kings, Tiglath-pileser was convinced that his gods approved his policies and that he was entitled to punish his enemies with unrestrained brutality. For example, he cut off their hands or impaled the foremost men alive while making the people of their land watch.[55] He pursued and killed the enemies mercilessly, filling the mountain gorges and the plains with their corpses, dying the rivers as red as dyed wool or flowers.[56] However, the descriptions of atrocities in Tiglath-pileser's inscriptions do not appear to express acts of sadism, as was the case for Ashurnasirpal II. To what degree such descriptions reflect reality remains an open question. It is difficult to distinguish the reality from the rhetoric of intimidation that the inscriptions expressed. Moreover, the intent of such rhetoric, called "deterrent propaganda," was an intimidation tactic, a kind of psychological warfare in the modern sense of the term.[57] In order to demoralize the inhabitants of the city he wanted to conquer, the king would display atrocities such as impaled live enemies. Tiglath-pileser was a master in the art of psychological warfare, and this influenced his successors, Sargon II and

---

52. RINAP 1:22, 1.5–7; 24, 3.5; 91, 37.14 and 25.
53. RINAP 1:89, 36.12'–13'.
54. RINAP 1:49, 15.10.
55. RINAP 1:31, 7.6–8; 59, 20.10'; 97, 39.8.
56. RINAP 1:34, 9.6'; 51, 16.9; 59, 20.3'–4'; 122, 47.48; 126, 48.10'.
57. Theodore J. Lewis, "You Have Heard What the Kings of Assyria Have Done: Disarmament Passages vis-à-vis Assyrian Rhetoric of Intimidation," in *Isaiah's Vision of Peace in Biblical and Modern International Relations: Swords into Plowshares*, ed. Raymond Cohen and Raymond Westbrook, CRIR (New York: Palgrave Macmillan, 2008), 88–89; Marc Van De Mieroop, "Metaphors of Massacre in Assyrian Royal Inscriptions," *KASKAL* 12 (2015): 299–309.

Sennacherib in particular.⁵⁸ He was a good strategist who knew how to analyze a situation and apply the appropriate solution to it. He was also realistic, pragmatic, and privileged his own self-interest over any desire for revenge. Tiglath-pileser displayed flexibility and adaptability; consequently he often tried to negotiate before fighting.

What kind of rapport did Tiglath-pileser have with his troops? Although we lack information to answer this question, we can imagine the nature of these relations from one significant passage. During his campaign against Kummuhu in 743, the king treated his troops with extreme hardness: "I marched [a distance of] seven leag[ues], day and night, and I did not give (them) water to drink, (and) did not pitch camp nor bivouac my soldiers (allowing them to recover from) their weariness."⁵⁹ However, these difficult conditions were probably accepted by the soldiers because Tiglath-pileser was enduring the same conditions as they were. The Assyrian king was a remarkable war lord as he succeeded to restore Assyria, making it a powerful empire. His soldiers were loyal to him because he was always victorious and distributed part of the booty to them or gave them the possibility to collect it. He probably knew how to lead his troops, reinforcing obedience and discipline.

Tiglath-pileser followed Assyrian tradition by extolling the role played by his gods. He had a special relationship with the god Assur, initiating campaigns at his command and attributing his victories to the "power and might" of this god.⁶⁰ As a result, the king set up the weapon of Assur in many of the conquered cities.⁶¹ However, in one of the summary inscriptions, Tiglath-pileser wrote that he was "the king who [marched about] at the command of the gods Aššur, Šamaš and Marduk."⁶² Marduk was probably quoted because this inscription was written after 629, when the Assyrian king became king of Babylon. As vicar of Assur and prefect of Enlil, Tiglath-pileser performed priestly services toward these two gods and others, offering them sacrifices.⁶³ Although we lack elements of information to be able to interpret Tiglath-pileser's religious beliefs, he undoubtedly appears as being pious. He was also conscious of the impor-

---

58. Elayi, *Sargon II*, 18–19; Elayi, *Sennacherib*, 21–23.
59. RINAP 1:85, 35.i.27′–30′.
60. RINAP 1:34, 9.5′–6′; 27, 5.11.
61. RINAP 1:55, 18.3.
62. RINAP 1:118, 47.3.
63. RINAP 1:97, 39.15–16; 118, 47.11–12.

tance of the gods when at war and before battles because they helped him to obtain victories and after when he thanked them for those victories. The king understood that religious rituals calmed fears, helped the soldiers in the most desperate situations, and convinced them that they were fighting for a just cause. For example, during the campaign of 744 in the Zagros Mountains, Tiglath-pileser offered horses, oxen, sheep and goats, and lapis lazuli to the great gods.[64] In 743, after having defeated Sarduri, king of Urartu, he offered his royal bed to the goddess Ishtar.[65] He offered sacrifices either to just one god or to several gods: to nine gods in the city of Hursagkalama and to six in the main cult centers of Babylonia (Sippar, Nippur, Babylon, Borsippa, Cutha, Kish, Dilbat, and Uruk).[66] In this last case, as the new king of Babylon, Tiglath-pileser's motives were probably more political than religious.

Tiglath-pileser prayed to the gods as did his predecessors and successors, but mention of his prayers is rare in his inscriptions, possibly because they are less developed and preserved than others. One of these prayers is, however, preserved on one of the two monumental basalt bulls discovered at Arslan Tash (ancient Hadattu). The name of the bull was "the one that attained victories for the king, that allowed him to achieve everything he desired, and that drove out evil and brought in good." The inscription reads: "I set them up in a place to be seen in the city Ḫadattu for (the preservation of) my life, the acceptance of my prayers, the prolongation of my reign, [the well-being of] my seed, the securing of the throne of my priestly office, (and in order) not to become ill, (and) for success at harvest time in [As]syria (and) [the well-being of] Assyria."[67] Even if this prayer was explicitly destined to be read by everybody, it possibly also expressed the king's personal feelings. The prayer concerned three groups: the king himself, his descendants, and all Assyrians. For himself, the king expressed customary wishes in such prayers: not to be killed in battle, not to be ill, to attain an old age, and to secure his throne; he wished to be heard by the gods and to continue his priestly office. He did not forget his descendants, briefly asking for their well-being. Finally, he cared about his subjects, requesting well-being and good harvests for them. He was not only interested in conquering new territories, but also in adding countless people to the population of Assyria. He

---

64. RINAP 1:32, 8.2–3.
65. RINAP 1:35, 9.16′.
66. RINAP 1:97, 39.15–16; 118, 47.11–12.
67. RINAP 1:142, 53.26–28. See also 90–91, 37.1–11.

considered them as inhabitants of Assyria, himself being "a shepherd who led them in safe pastures, and the light of all his people."[68] The king also fashioned images of the gods or of their symbols, sometimes together with his royal image or an image of him praying.[69]

Tiglath-pileser considered himself as a king of justice: his wars, approved by the gods, were just, and he behaved with justice. When a vassal betrayed him by neglecting the loyalty oath sworn by the great gods, he would become furious and punish him harshly, as he did, for instance, against Tutammû, king of Unqi.[70] Conversely, Tiglath-pileser was benevolent toward loyal vassals or enemies who submitted, such as Bâtânu of Bît-Kapsi.[71] In some cases, Tiglath-pileser forgave his enemies, even if they had revolted, and he maintained them on their throne. The king of Arwad Mattanba☒al II put on sackcloth and submitted, bringing to Tiglath-pileser rich offerings such as ivory and ebony, inlaid with precious stones and gold, fine oil, all types of aromatics, and Egyptian horses.[72] After having conducted a slaughter in a plain, possibly in the continental territory of Tyre, Tiglath-pileser said: "I accepted (their plea) [to forgi]ve their rebellion and I s[pared] their land."[73] Similarly, the Assyrian king conquered the rebellious city of Gaza and returned King Hanunu, who had first fled to Egypt, to the throne.[74] Maybe Tiglath-pileser was benevolent with these kings, but it was also a political calculation: in the case of Arwad, the Assyrian king was unable to capture the island since it was protected by a powerful war fleet, and in the case of Gaza, he preferred to keep the city autonomous as a buffer-state between Assyria and Egypt.

Tiglath-pileser was an excellent administrator, able to organize the vast newly conquered territories. Another traditional characteristic of Tiglath-pileser was that he was a builder-king, just like his predecessors, but not on such a large scale as Sargon II, for example, because Tiglath-pileser was more interested in military campaigns. His building activity

---

68. RINAP 1:27, 5.4; 83, 35.i.32–33; 86, 35.ii.15'; 22, 1.5.
69. RINAP 1:127, 48.16'–17'; 140, 53.21–22.
70. RINAP 1:39, 12.3'–11'.
71. RINAP 1:31, 7.10–11.
72. RINAP 1:126, 48.1'–10'; for my identification of the king in this somewhat damaged passage, see Josette Elayi, *The History of Phoenicia* (Atlanta: Lockwood, 2019), 148–49.
73. RINAP 1:126, 48.10'–14'; Tadmor, *Inscriptions of Tiglath-pileser III*, 176–77, 282.
74. RINAP 1:127, 48.14'–18'.

was initially linked to religion because he defined himself as "the one who restores sanctuaries."[75] In his first campaign against cities east of the Tigris, Tiglath-pileser built a new city named Kâr-Assur, where he founded a palace for his royal residence, set up the weapon of Assur, settled people from other conquered lands, and dug out the Patti-Enlil canal in order to provide abundant water.[76] This new city was governed by a eunuch. Then the king built a palace in Nimrud: the so-called Central Palace, which he described only briefly, in comparison with the numerous extensive accounts of his military campaigns.[77]

Tiglath-pileser was probably not a cultivated man like Ashurbanipal, for example, whose education is known. We lack sources on Tiglath-pileser's education, but it is clear that he was not educated as a prince destined to become king. He probably received the usual Assyrian education, that is, the education of a scribe: languages (Sumerian and Babylonian) and some elements of arithmetic. It is uncertain whether he followed the "second cycle" of studies, such as literature and the art of divination, in which his descendant Esarhaddon was talented.[78] In the royal inscriptions of Tiglath-pileser, there are some literary images such as "I overwhelmed the (tribe) Puqudu like a (cast) net," or "I ensnared Chaldea in its entirety as with a bird-snare," or "I en[veloped] him [like] a (dense) fog."[79] However, we do not know whether these images were inspired by the Assyrian king or imagined by the scribes. We do know that the libraries of Nimrud, the principal one being located in E-zida, the temple of the god Nabû, existed from the ninth century. In the North-West Palace, there was also a chancery office filled with letters and documents from the reigns of Tiglath-pileser, Shalmaneser V, and Sargon II.[80] The distinction between libraries and archives cannot always be maintained. Yet, Tiglath-pileser necessarily participated in the enrichment of both.

---

75. RINAP 1:114, 46.4.
76. RINAP 1:26–27, 5.1–4; 97, 39.6–7.
77. RINAP 1:123–25, 47.r.14–36.
78. Josette Elayi, "Assarhaddon et la conquête de l'Égypte," in *Dieux, rois et capitales dans le Proche-Orient ancien*, ed. M. Béranger, F. Nebiolo, and N. Ziegler, RAI 65 (Leuven: Peeters, forthcoming).
79. RINAP 1:118–19, 47.13 and 15; 62, 22.1–2.
80. Christopher Walker, "Archives of Nimrud," in Curtis et al., *New Light on Nimrud*, 256–59; Jeremy Black, "The Libraries of Kalhu," in Curtis et al., *New Light on Nimrud*, 261–65.

2.4. Royal Propaganda

Tiglath-pileser wanted to project an image of intelligence, ability, administrative skill, strength, energy, piety, justice, and benevolence. It has to be verified, however, through an analysis of his accession to the throne, his conquests, and the achievements of his reign, whether this image is not distorted by propaganda. The audiences to which the royal inscriptions and reliefs were destined also need to be investigated. In the end, the subject is difficult to analyze because there is very little information in the inscriptions; consequently the debate is not closed.

The first question is whether the inscriptions and reliefs were intended to be seen or not. In some cases, it is obvious that they were located so as to be visible. One of the two bulls installed in Arslan Tash bears the explicit mention that the king positioned them so that they would be seen in the city.[81] After having conquered Gaza, he wrote: "[I fashioned] (a statue bearing) image(s) of the gods, my lords, (and) my royal image out of gold, [erected (it) in the palace of the city Gaza."[82] After having defeated King Sarduri of Urartu, the Assyrian king fashioned his royal image and "erected (it) in front of [the city] of Ṭurušpâ."[83] In both of these cases, Tiglath-pileser's royal image was placed in sites that were visible. When he imagined that somebody could read his inscription, be it written with a good or a bad intention, one should suppose that the inscription was voluntary placed in a visible location.[84] However, some other inscriptions were situated in inaccessible places, meaning that nobody could reach and read them: for example, the Mila Mergi rock relief was located on a vertical rocky spur; the relief of Uramanat is sculpted on a vertical rock face 40 m above ground level. These few inaccessible inscriptions were probably targeting the gods. Still, since most of the stelae and rock reliefs related military campaigns, victories, and annexations of new territories, they were probably intended to be read by the subjects of the king because they celebrated his feats and, as such, conveyed the royal propaganda.[85]

---

81. RINAP 1:142, 53.26.
82. RINAP 1:106, 42.10–11; 127, 48.16–17; 132, 49.r.14.
83. RINAP 1:98, 39.23; 103, 41.24′; 129, 49.3′–4′.
84. RINAP 1:92, 37.45–54.
85. Morandi Bonacossi, "Stele e statue reali assire," 153. The attribution of the relief of Uramanat is uncertain: Tiglath-pileser III or Sargon II.

While any of the king's subjects who could read could have been influenced by this propaganda, in practice the average subject was not concerned by the inscriptions and reliefs located inside the royal palace as he would not have had access to the building. Hence, were the inscriptions intended for foreign emissaries who were allowed to enter the palace in order to meet the king? Probably not because the inscriptions would not have prevented the emissaries from initiating a revolt at some point in time. Were they intended for Assyrian high officials, priests, or scribes? These officials were already fully aware of the royal feats as many of them would have participated in them.[86] When, at the end of his reign, the aged king planned to exhibit the latest, longest, and decisively full version of his achievements in the annals combined with the summary inscriptions, the inscriptions were probably more intended to commemorate the king's glory for the next generations than to spread royal propaganda.[87] According to some scholars, the Assyrian reliefs, inscribed or not, were only targeting the gods because some of them were not visible and others were indeed explicitly addressed to the gods.[88] For example, the Luristan stela and the Mila Mergi inscription opened with an invocation of the ten major gods.[89] However, the inscriptions and reliefs of Tiglath-pileser cannot be explained merely as royal propaganda nor as homage to the gods. Both interpretations are possible, either jointly or alternately.

Anyway, the proud Assyrian king wanted to show his magnificence and his superiority in comparison with previous kings. By embellishing and sometimes distorting the accounts of his achievements, Tiglath-pileser intended to demonstrate that he was the best king who had ever existed and that all his subjects were right to remain loyal to him. This was undoubtedly some kind of royal propaganda that needs to be considered when reconstructing the history of Tiglath-pileser's reign.

---

86. Garelli, "La conception de la royauté en Assyrie," 8–11; Mario Liverani, *The Imperial Mission* (Winona Lake, IN: Eisenbrauns, 2017).

87. Yamada, "Inscriptions of Tiglath-pileser III," 42.

88. Luc Bachelot, "La fonction politique des reliefs néo-assyriens," in *Marchands, diplomates et empereurs: Études sur la civilisation mésopotamienne offertes à Paul Garelli*, ed. Dominique Charpin and Francis Joannès (Paris: Éditions Recherche sur les Civilisations, 1991), 115–21; Nicolas Gilmann, "Les bas-reliefs néo-assyriens: Une nouvelle tentative d'interprétation," *SAAB* 19 (2011–2012): 203–37.

89. RINAP 1:80–82, 35; 89–91, 37.

3
TIGLATH-PILESER III'S ASCENT TO THE THRONE

3.1. The Revolt of Nimrud

The "revolt of Nimrud" (*si-ḫu ina* URU *kal-ḫi*) is only known from the Assyrian Eponym List and Eponym Chronicle.[1] It occurred in 746, when Nergal-nâsir, governor of Nasibîna, was eponym.[2] Ashur-nârârî V, king of Assyria, was then in Nimrud, where he had decided to stay, without risking a campaign against his enemies, for a period lasting for five years of his ten-year reign. If the king did not campaign, it was probably because he had internal problems to face. As discussed above, this period was very disturbed and difficult for Assyria. For example, the Nimrud revolt of 746 was preceded by other revolts against Ashur-nârârî V's predecessor, Ashur-Dân III (772–755).[3]

Several hypotheses have been proposed to explain the revolt of 746. The first question is: Against whom was the revolt of 746 intended? As the previous revolts were directed against King Ashur-Dân, the revolt of 746 was logically intended against the powerless King Ashur-nârârî V.[4] The second question is: Who initiated this revolt? According to an old hypothesis proposed by Emil O. Forrer, Tiglath-pileser was governor of

---

1. Arthur Ungnad, "Eponymen," *RlA* 2 (1938): 430; SAAS 2:43, 59, 110.
2. *PNA* 2.2:950–51.
3. Albert Kirk Grayson, "Assyria: Ashur-dan II to Ashur-Nirari V (934–745 B.C.)," in Boardman et al., *Assyrian and Babylonian Empires and Other States of the Near East*, 269–79; Grayson, "Struggle for Power in Assyria," 266; *PNA* 1.2:301.
4. Radner, review of *Inscriptions of Tiglath-pileser III*, 137–40; Eckart Frahm, "Revolts in the Neo-Assyrian Period: A Preliminary Discourse Analysis," in *Revolt and Resistance in the Ancient Classical World and the Near East*, ed. John Collins and Joseph Gilbert Manning (Leiden: Brill, 2016), 76–89.

Nimrud and was the author of this revolt,[5] but as yet there is no evidence to support this view. Either Tiglath-pileser launched a coup d'etat, deposing his predecessor Ashur-nârârî V in order to become king in his place, or he was the instigator of the revolt, but Bêl-Dân, who was governor of Nimrud, supported and organized Tiglath-pileser's actions.[6] The arguments in favor of this last hypothesis are the fact that Bêl-Dân was again appointed eponym by Tiglath-pileser in 744 and 734, which would mean that he wanted to reward him for his help, and the account of the Eponym Chronicle would be sufficient to prove that Tiglath-pileser personally took part in the revolt because it elevated him to the throne. According to another hypothesis, Tiglath-pileser supported the revolt of the governors of Nimrud and Assur against Ashur-nârârî V because they were among the high officials remaining in power after 745.[7]

There is yet another hypothesis: Shamshî-ilu, the commander-in-chief, fomented the revolt, Ashur-nârârî V was forced to separate from him, and the revolt was crushed by Tiglath-pileser who was not responsible for it.[8] Under Ashur-Dân, the main high dignitaries (palace herald, chief cupbearer, and treasurer) had been excluded from eponymate; they were then reintroduced by Ashur-nârârî V. Except for Bêl-Dân, the high dignitaries were probably supporters of the first among them, the commander-in-chief Shamshî-ilu. The most important governors had also been excluded from the top rankings in the list of eponyms. This would have been a sufficient reason for all of them to revolt. As a matter of fact, the revolts of the mid-eighth century, in particular that of 746, were of a quite different nature from those of the ninth century.[9] At the head of the ninth-century revolts were the "small nobility" or royal sons, not the senior officials. Conversely, the revolts of the eighth century were led by high officials.

---

5. Forrer, *Die Provinzeinteilung des assyrischen Reiches*, 10; SAA 12:xxiv, 16, 15.

6. Baker, "Tiglath-pileser III," 21; *PNA* 1.1:208; Zawadzki, "Revolt of 746 B.C.," 53–54; Fuchs, "Der Turtān Šamšī-ilu," 94–96; Mario Fales, "The Eighth-Century Governors of Kalhu: A Reappraisal in Context," in *Stories of Long Ago: Festschrift Michael Roaf*, ed. Heather Baker, Kai Kaniuth, and Adelheid Otto (Münster: Ugarit-Verlag, 2012), 117–39.

7. Radner, review of *Inscriptions of Tiglath-pileser III*, 137–38.

8. Garelli, "Achievement of Tiglath-pileser III," 47–48.

9. Paul Garelli, "Les sujets du roi d'Assyrie," in *La voix de l'opposition en Mésopotamie*, ed. André Finet (Bruxelles: Institut des hautes études de Belgique, 1973), 190–91; Grayson, "Struggle for Power in Assyria," 267.

Their revolt would have been a refusal to recognize the supreme position of the royal family among the noble families of the officials.

All these hypotheses and analyses are interesting, but it is difficult to ascertain whether one of them is plausible and, if so, which one, due to the lack of documentation. We have to admit that we know nothing concerning the revolt of 746 and whether or not there was a relation between this revolt and the seizure of power by Tiglath-pileser in 745. If the revolt continued in 745, it would have been mentioned in the Eponym List, as was the case for the revolt of Arrapha in 761 and 760. In this case, two events would have been mentioned: the continuation of the revolt and Tiglath-pileser's accession to the throne, as was the case for the year 763 when the revolt in Assur and the sun eclipse are mentioned together.[10]

What do we know? According to the Assyrian King Lists, Ashur-nârârî V reigned for ten years, that is, from 754 to the beginning of the year 745, one and a half months before Tiglath-pileser's accession to the throne.[11] This means that Ashur-nârârî V was not deposed or killed during the revolt. We also know that Tiglath-pileser was not the legitimate heir. The high dignitaries were treated differently by him: there were those who were dismissed such as Shamshî-ilu, Marduk-Shallimanni, and Shamash-kenu-dugul, and those who were rewarded such as Bêl-Dân and Adad-belu-ka"in. Both actions were related to the revolt and/or with the seizure of power. In any case, Tiglath-pileser must have prepared his coup d'etat by assembling a support group and money. We could cautiously propose some possible scenarios: if the high dignitaries, who were normally supposed to protect the king, had revolted against him, Tiglath-pileser's coup d'etat was not initially directed against the king but against the high dignitaries, then only subsequently against the king whom he deposed in 745 in order to seize power. According to another scenario, Tiglath-pileser's coup d'etat was directed against the king in 745 and possibly his dignitaries who protected him. Even if there was no connection between the revolt and the coup d'etat, Tiglath-pileser would have taken advantage of an unstable situation in Nimrud. To say more in the present state of documentation would only be speculation.

---

10. SAAS 2:58.

11. Gelb, "Two Assyrian King Lists," 229; *PNA* 1.1:208; according to Andreas Fuchs, there would have been between the two kings a "formell Interregnum" ("Der Turtān Šamšī-ilu," 138–39).

3.2. The Circumstances Surrounding Tiglath-pileser III's Ascent to the Throne

The revolt of Nimrud in 746 seemed to be just another revolt in a weakened and declining kingdom, unable to overcome its difficulties. Nobody could have imagined that the situation would change so completely afterwards. According to the Babylonian Chronicles, Tiglath-pileser III ascended the throne of Assyria "the third year of Nabû-nâsir, king of Babylon,"[12] that is, in 745. In the Eponym List, after an entry in 746 for the revolt of Nimrud, when Nergal-nâṣir, governor of Nisibîna, was eponym, it is recorded that in 745, when Nabû-bêlu-usur, governor of Arrapha, was eponym, Tiglath-pileser "took the throne" (*ina kussî it-tu-šib*) on the thirteenth day of Ayyâru (the second month of the Assyrian calendar, May).[13] In his royal inscriptions, when he related the first campaign undertaken at the beginning of his reign in his first *pâlu* (745), Tiglath-pileser twice recorded that it was in the fifth or sixth month after he "sat on the throne of kingship."[14] It is possible that there were other mentions of Tiglath-pileser's accession to the throne, maybe more detailed, at the beginning of the annals, in the broken parts. On the one hand, we could ignore the fate of Ashur-nârârî V after 745, but the quasi-absence of references to his predecessor in all the corpus of his royal inscriptions seems to indicate an awkward succession. On the other hand, we do not know whether Tiglath-pileser became king in violent circumstances or whether he simply had to face a strong opposition. Whether he had himself conducted the revolt of 746 or whether he had merely taken advantage of it, Tiglath-pileser had nonetheless seized power by a coup d'etat in 745 since he was not the legitimate successor of Ashur-nârârî V.

The absence of military expeditions during the first five or six months of his reign, inconceivable for a warrior king, leads to the supposition that the new king emerged through internal difficulties. His son Sargon II also encountered massive opposition as soon as he ascended the throne. He needed more time than his father to secure his throne: his accession year, which lasted three months from Tebêtu (January) 722 to Nisannu

---

12. Grayson, *Assyrian and Babylonian Chronicles*, 70–72, Chronicle 1, i.1–2; 183, Chronicle 24, 19.
13. SAAS 2:43, 59.
14. RINAP 1:25, 4.2 (fifth month); 83, 35.i.36–37 (sixth month).

3. TIGLATH-PILESER III'S ASCENT TO THE THRONE 47

(April) 721, and his entire first year.[15] Since Tiglath-pileser was settled in Nimrud, where the revolt of 746 took place, he had to completely reestablish a secure situation in the city. He had first to carry out a purge among the high dignitaries, keeping the loyal ones and evicting the traitors. For example, Tiglath-pileser kept Bêl-Dân, the governor of Nimrud, making him eponym for the years 744 and 734, and Adad-bêlu-ka"in, governor of Assur, making him eponym for 738. Tiglath-pileser also reappointed Bêl-Harrân-bêlu-usur as a palace herald, just as other high officials and important military leaders were reinstated.[16] In his inscription from Tell Abta, Bêl-Harrân-bêlu-usur, already palace herald under Shalmaneser IV, replaced the name of Shalmaneser by that of Tiglath-pileser.[17] After a period of obscurity during the reigns of Ashur-Dân III and Ashur-nârârî V, Bêl-Harrân-bêlu-usur probably helped the new king to ascend the throne. It was only when Tiglath-pileser had secured the situation in Nimrud that he was ready to prepare his first military campaign: "I mustered the vast] troops of Assyria."[18]

Tiglath-pileser also used, probably at the beginning of his reign, a special measure in order to calm the Assyrians and gain their support.[19] This measure was the *andurâru* (*durâru* or *darâru*), an ancient measure consisting of a return to the previous financial situation so that all preceding debts were suppressed. This measure was still in use during the Neo-Assyrian period, usually enacted at the beginning of a reign, by Adad-nârârî III or Shalmaneser IV, Sargon II, Esarhaddon, and probably Ashurbanipal.[20] Such a measure would have been beneficial for people impoverished by a long period of crisis. The outstanding manner in which the Assyrian king had reestablished the situation and restored confidence and prosperity to

---

15. Elayi, *Sargon II*, 30–31.
16. Radner, review of *Inscriptions of Tiglath-Pileser III*, 137–38; Frahm, *Companion to Assyria*, 177.
17. Grayson, "Assyrian Officials and Power in the Ninth and Eighth Centuries," 28–29; RIMA 3:241–42, A.0.105.2; PNA 1.2:301.
18. RINAP 1:83, 35.i.38.
19. RINAP 1:83, 35.27–28.
20. CAD 1.2:116h; Julius Lewy, "The Biblical Institution of $D^eRÔR$ in the Light of Akkadian Documents," *ErIs* 5 (1958): 30*–31*; Dominique Charpin, "L'andurârum à Mari," *MARI* 6 (1990): 253–70; Brigitte Lion, "L'andurâru à l'époque médio-babylonienne, d'après les documents de Terqa, Nuzi et Arrapha," in *Nuzi at Seventy-Five*, ed. David I. Owen and Gernot Wilhelm (Bethesda: CDL, 1999), 313–28; Pierre Villard, "L'(an)durâru à l'époque néo-assyrienne," *RA* 101 (2007): 107–24 (with bibliography).

the Assyrians means that the measure of *andurâru* was efficient. Moreover, it is attested again in the correspondence that in 730 the king proposed the *andurâru* to the Babylonians, in the peace negotiations managed by his officials Shamash-bunaya and Nabû-nammir.[21]

---

21. SAA 19:xxiv, 104, 98.16.

4
THE NEUTRALIZATION OF HIGH DIGNITARIES

4.1. The Powerful High Dignitaries

One characteristic of the eighth century BCE in Assyria was the emergence of powerful high dignitaries. The power of these dignitaries was due to the fact that Assyria suffered serious problems and was on the decline, mainly since the reign of Adad-nârârî III. Several of these officials held office under successive kings, some of them until Tiglath-pileser's reign. Here I consider only the high dignitaries in relation to this last king: the most important ones by far were Shamshî-ilu and Bêl-Harrân-bêlu-usur. Bêl-Dân, Adad-bêlu-ka"in, Nabû-da"inanni, Nabû-êtiranni, Sîn-taklâk, Ninurta-bêlu-usur, and Ninurta-ilâya probably also had some importance as they had twice been eponyms or had born important titles.

Shamshî-ilu had a very long career as "commander-in-chief" (*turtānu*).[1] The first attestation of his name is found on the inscribed Antakya stela of Adad-nârârî III, dated from around 800, just after Arpad was reconquered, or from 796, in connection with a campaign to Mansuate.[2] Shamshî-ilu was also the commander-in-chief of Ashur-nârârî V, while Nabû-da"inanni was the new commander-in-chief named by Tiglath-pileser.[3] Shamshî-ilu was eponym for the years 780, 770, and 752, named respectively by Shalmaneser IV, Ashur-Dân III, and Ashur-nârârî

---

1. *PNA* 3.2:1226.
2. For the earlier date, see Grayson, "Assyrian Officials and Power in the Ninth and Eighth Centuries," 27; Grayson, "Struggle for Power in Assyria," 261 (ca. 800–752); SAAS 11:110–111. For the later date, see Ikeda, "Looking from Til Barsip on the Euphrates, 281–82, 292–93; Felix Blocher, "Assyrische Würdenträger und Gouverneure des 9. und 8. Jh.: Eine Neubewertung ihrer Rolle," *AoF* 28 (2001): 305–11; Fuchs, "Der Turtān Šamšī-ilu," 78–80, 83, 131–35, 138, 145 (ca. 787–746).
3. *PNA* 2.2:819; SAAS 2:59.

V.[4] Shamshî-ilu is known through several inscriptions, royal and personal. On the Antakya stela of Adad-nârârî III, Shamshî-ilu established, together with the king, the Orontes River as a boundary between the territories of King Zakkur of Hamath and King Attar-shumkî of Arpad.[5] The inscription guaranteed that the city of Nahlasi on the border, with its territories, was the property of Attar-shumkî and of his sons and of his grandsons after him. The inscription concluded with curses on anyone who would violate the border or damage the stela. Shamshî-ilu was also mentioned in an inscription of Shalmaneser IV, dated from 773, engraved on the reverse of the Pazarcik stela of Adad-nârârî III and Sammuramat (Semiramis).[6] Shamshî-ilu was the commander-in-chief who accompanied the Assyrian king to Damascus to receive the tribute of Hadiânu, king of Damascus. Shamshî-ilu's name, with the title of commander-in-chief, was also engraved on a golden bowl from Nimrud and on a stone bead from Assur, in a dedicatory inscription asking for (long) life for him.[7]

Other Shamshî-ilu inscriptions are personal inscriptions. Like the inscriptions of other powerful high dignitaries of the eighth century, these inscriptions commemorated Shamshî-ilu's deeds, just like an Assyrian king. They took the form of royal inscriptions, but without mentioning any royal name. These inscriptions were engraved on two colossal stone lions, more than two meters high, discovered at the northeastern gate of Til Barsip (modern Tell Ahmar). Til Barsip had been renamed Kâr-Shalmaneser by King Shalmaneser III in 856. Shamshî-ilu had no scruples in appropriating the royal residence. These inscriptions were dated from 874 according to Andreas Fuchs.[8] After a dedication to ten gods, Shamshî-ilu enumerated his titles: "commander-in-chief, chief herald, administrator of temples, chief of vast forces, and governor of the land of Hatti, of the land of the Guti and all the land of Nairi."[9] As administrator of the temples, Shamshî-ilu could probably raise funds for his own campaigns from the treasuries of local temples. The last title was not realistic because Hatti was in the west and Guti and Nairi were far to the east, but the title meant that he was the strong man

---

4. SAAS 2:38, 40, 42, 59, 120.
5. RIMA 3:203–4, A.0.104.2.
6. RIMA 3:239–40, A.0.105.1.
7. RIMA 3:236, A.0.104.2014; A.0.104.213; SAAS 11:110.
8. Fuchs, "Der Turtān Šamšī-ilu," 81.
9. RIMA 3:232, A.0.104.2010, 8–9; SAAS 11:110.

4. THE NEUTRALIZATION OF HIGH DIGNITARIES   51

of Assyria.[10] In his inscription, Shamshî-ilu mentioned victories against Musku (Mushki) and Urartu, which could have taken place during a campaign to the north under the reign of Shalmaneser IV. Shamshî-ilu's victory against Utû, Rubû, Hadalu (Hatallu?), and Labdudu concerned Aramean tribes to the south, on the banks of the Tigris, which are also mentioned later in Tiglath-pileser's inscriptions.[11] Shamshî-ilu then boasted of his victory over Argishti I, king of Urartu, who escaped like a thief, frightened by the battle.[12] This victory probably occurred during the reign of Shalmaneser IV when there were six campaigns against Urartu (781–778, 776, 774).[13] Shamshî-ilu then related that he erected two lions, giving each one a name. He called Kâr-Shalmaneser "my lordly city" (*āl bēlūti-ia*), as Nimrud was later called by Tiglath-pileser.[14] In describing how he defeated his enemy "like the *Anzu*-bird," Shamshî-ilu assumed a mythological role by gaining control over destinies and subduing cosmic chaos.[15] A fragment of a black stone stela, said to come from Dohuk, bears the description of the battle waged by Shamshî-ilu, "man fearless [in battle]" against the Urartian king, Argishti I.[16] It mentions Mushallim-Marduk, chief judge (*sartinnu*), and ends with a curse on anyone who would deface the stela. The style seems similar to that of the previous inscription.

Another inscription engraved on a broken stone tablet could be attributed to Shamshî-ilu because of the title "chief of the extensive army."[17] This inscription recorded the construction of a new fortified city on the border of Assur, naming it Sharru-iddina, which meant "The king has given to me." The name indicates that a royal favor was granted to an honored official,

---

10. The authority of the commander-in-chief over the governor at that time is clearly demonstrated by a letter sent to Mannu-kî-mât-Ashur, governor of Gûzâna and eponym in 793, in which Shamshî-ilu commanded the governor: "Be on the Tigris on the 5th!" See Johannes Friedrich, G. Rudolf Meyer, Arthur Ungnad, and Ernst F. Weidner, *Die Inschriften von Tell Halaf*, AfO 6 (Berlin: self-published, 1940), TH9; *PNA* 2.2:693.
11. RINAP 1:97, 39.5; 114, 46.5–6; 119, 47.14.
12. RIMA 3:233, A.0.104.2010, 15–18.
13. SAAS 2:58.
14. RIMA 3:233, A.0.104.2012, 19–24; RINAP 1:123, 47.r.17'.
15. RIMA 3:233, A.0.104.2010, 16; Stephanie Dalley, "Shamshi-ilu, Language and Power in the Western Assyrian Empire," in *Essays on Syria in the Iron Age*, ed. Guy Bunnens (Leuven: Peeters, 2000), 85–86.
16. RIMA 3:233–34, A.0.104.2011.
17. RIMA 3:235, A.0.104.2012; SAAS 11:111.

possibly Shamshî-ilu. If so, Shamshî-ilu probably wrote this inscription in order to establish his name for posterity: "May those who come after see this monumental inscription of mine. May they heed my name."[18]

Some scholars have equated Shamshî-ilu with Bar-Ga'yah, king of *KTK*, who is mentioned in a treaty concluded with Mati'-ilu, king of Arpad, in the Aramaic inscriptions of Sfire (close to Tell Halaf).[19] The first redaction of these inscriptions would then be linked to the campaign of Shamshî-ilu against Damascus and the establishment, by Adad-nârârî III and Shamshî-ilu, of the border of the kingdom of Arpad in about 796. Shamshî-ilu would be an Aramean, named Bar-Ga'yah, king of *KTK*, and at the same time the powerful Assyrian commander-in-chief. The identification of *KTK* with Til Barsip (Kâr-Shalmaneser), Shamshî-ilu's lordly city, remains uncertain. This double identity would find a parallel in the Tell el-Fekheriye inscription, dated from the second half of the ninth century[20]: Hadad-yis'i, "king" (*mlk*) of Gûzâna, was at the same time Adad-it'i, "governor" (*šaknu*) of Gûzâna, Sikanu, and Zaranu. According to Dalley, figures such as Shamshî-ilu were viceroys or kings who ruled with the full support of the Assyrian king: Shamshî-ilu was essentially a "king-in-the-west."[21] Dalley quotes the book of Isaiah, in which Assyria, personified, says: "Are not my officers all kings?"[22] For Alan R. Millard, these provincial kings might have belonged

---

18. RIMA 3:235, A.0.104.2012, 11'–14'.
19. André Dupont-Sommer, *Les inscriptions araméennes de Sfiré (Stèles I et II)* (Paris: Imprimerie nationale, 1958); *KAI* 238–74, 222–224; Edward Lipiński, "State Treaties between Katk and Arpad," in *Near Eastern Religious Texts Relating to the Old Testament*, ed. Walter Beyerlin (Philadelphia: Westminster, 1978), 256–66; Lemaire and Durand, *Les inscriptions*, 3–21 (with bibliography); Shigeo Ikeda, "Once Again *KTK* in the Sefire Inscriptions," *ErIs* 24 (1994): 105*–8*. According to John David Hawkins, "The Neo-Hittite States in Syria and Anatolia," in *The Prehistory of the Balkans, the Middle East and the Aegean World, Tenth to Eighth Centuries B.C.*, ed. John Boardman, I. E. S. Edwards, N. G. L. Hammond, and E. Sollberger, 2nd ed., CAH 3.1 (Cambridge: Cambridge University Press, 1982), 402, it is "a historical document of great importance and one of the great enigmas of the whole period."
20. Ali Abou-Assaf, Pierre Bordreuil, and Alan R. Millard, *La statue de Tell Fekheriye et son inscription bilingue assyro-araméenne* (Paris: Recherche sur les civilisations, 1982).
21. Dalley, "Shamshi-ilu, Language and Power in the Western Assyrian Empire," 84–85.
22. Isa 10:8; see also Abraham Malamat, "Amos 1:5 in the Light of the Til Barsip Inscriptions," *BASOR* 129 (1953): 25–26, who considered that "the sceptred one at Beth-Eden," in Amos 1:5 as a reference to Shamshî-ilu in Bît-Adini.

4. THE NEUTRALIZATION OF HIGH DIGNITARIES 53

to local princely houses that were loyal to Assyrian suzerainty.[23] Although the identification of Shamshî-ilu with Bar-Ga'yah is an interesting hypothesis, it is not accepted by all scholars.[24]

In short, during his long career of at least forty or fifty years, Shamshî-ilu was so powerful that Paul Garelli used the formula "the Assyria of Shamshî-ilu."[25] Shamshî-ilu did not succeed in reestablishing the might of Assyria, but he limited its decline and maintained its cohesion so that he could continue to function.

The second powerful high dignitary related to Tiglath-pileser was Bêl-Harrân-bêlu-usur. He was "palace herald" (*nāgir ekalli*), designated by the King Shalmaneser IV.[26] It has been suggested that Bêl-Harrân-bêlu-usur may have received a grant from King Adad-nârârî III and that his career started from 792, maybe earlier, but it seems unlikely.[27] The interpretation of the beginning of his career as a palace herald is based on the stela found at Tell Abta.[28] The inscription read "palace herald of Shalmaneser, king of Assyria" before the name of the king was changed to Tiglath-pileser. Bêl-Harrân-bêlu-usur was therefore designated palace herald during the reign of Shalmaneser IV, but after 778 because Bêl-lêshir was a palace herald in 778.[29] Bêl-Harrân-bêlu-usur's career was also interrupted under the reign of Ashur-nârârî V because Marduk-shallimanni was a palace herald in 751, and Bêl-Harrân-bêlu-usur again held this function in 741

---

23. Alan R. Millard, "Assyrians and Arameans," *Iraq* 45 (1983): 106. According to Wolfram Von Soden, "Das nordsyrische *KTK*/Kiski und der Turtan Šamši-ilu: Erwägungen zu einem neuen Buch," *SEL* 2 (1985): 136–38, Shamshî-ilu would be a younger son of Adad-nârârî III.

24. Edward Lipiński, review of *Les inscriptions araméennes de Sfiré et l'Assyrie de Shamshi-ilu*, by André Lemaire and Jean-Marie Durand, *OLZ* 81 (1986): 351–54; Frederick Mario Fales, review of *Les inscriptions araméennes de Sfiré et l'Assyrie de Shamshi-ilu*, by André Lemaire and Jean-Marie Durand, *RA* 80 (1986): 88–93; Grayson, "Assyrian Officials and Power in the Ninth and Eighth Centuries," 27; Ikeda, "Looking from Til Barsip on the Euphrates," 286–87; Lipiński, *Aramaeans*, 225 n. 32.

25. Garelli and Lemaire, *Les empires mésopotamiens, Israël*, 101–2; Grayson, "Struggle for Power in Assyria," 262–63.

26. *PNA* 1.2:301; *SAAS* 11:30–31.

27. John Nicholas Postgate, *Neo-Assyrian Royal Grants and Decrees* (Rome: Pontifical Biblical Institute, 1969), no. 1; Grayson, "Assyrian Officials and Power in the Ninth and Eighth Centuries," 28.

28. *RIMA* 3:242, A.0.105.3, 9.

29. *SAAS* 2:58.

under Tiglath-pileser.[30] Bêl-Harrân-bêlu-usur was eponym in 741, but it is uncertain whether he was the same as the governor of Gûzâna, who was eponym in 727.[31] Thus Bêl-Harrân-bêlu-usur's career started between 778 and 772, the date of Shalmaneser IV's death. There is no information about Bêl-Harrân-bêlu-usur's status during the reign of Ashur-Dân III, but his career was interrupted during the reign of Ashur-nârârî V and resumed under Tiglath-pileser. Dalley has suggested that it was not interrupted and that the changing of the royal name was a simple updating.[32] Other scholars have suggested that he was involved in the revolts against Ashur-Dân III in 772–755 and Ashur-nârârî V in 746.[33]

Bêl-Harrân-bêlu-usur was probably a eunuch, since he was represented by a standing beardless figure on the Tell Abta stela.[34] This stela was discovered at a site of the Wadi Tharthar in Irak. The inscription commemorated Bêl-Harrân-bêlu-usur's foundation of a new city in the desert at the command of the gods, including a temple for them, and divine symbols are represented above the inscription. Bêl-Harrân-bêlu-usur gave his name to the city: Dûr-Bêl-Harrân-bêlu-usur. Moreover, he made a personal monumental inscription, established offerings to the gods invoked on the stela, and exempted the new city from all kinds of taxation. These initiatives had normally been royal prerogatives. The name of the king was mentioned just once and only in a secondary position. All these features show the extent of Bêl-Harrân-bêlu-usur's independence from the king of Assyria. Bêl-Harrân-bêlu-usur was nevertheless loyal to Tiglath-pileser who depended heavily on him for support.

Other high officials probably also had some importance. Bêl-Dân, governor of Nimrud, was eponym and chief cupbearer in 750 and then

---

30. SAAS 2:58–59. Heather D. Baker, "Tiglatpileser III," *RlA* 14 (2014): 22, raised the possibility that it was Shalmaneser V and that Sargon II changed it into Tiglath-pileser because he wanted to obliterate the memory of his predecessor. This hypothesis does not seem very likely.

31. SAAS 2:59; Grayson, "Assyrian Officials and Power in the Ninth and Eighth Centuries," 28–29.

32. Dalley, "Shamshi-ilu, Language and Power in the Western Assyrian Empire," 84.

33. *PNA* 1.2:301; SAAS 11:31.

34. Eckhard Unger, *Die Stele des Bel-harran-beli-ussur ein Denkmal der Zeit Salmanassars IV* (Constantinople: Druck von A. Ihsan, 1917), 12; Julian E. Reade, "Neo-Assyrian Monuments in their Historical Context," in Fales, *Assyrian Royal Inscriptions*, 160; Magen, *Assyrische Königsdarstellungen-Aspekte der Herrschaft*, 50; *PNA* 1.2:301.

4. THE NEUTRALIZATION OF HIGH DIGNITARIES 55

eponym and governor of Nimrud in the year 744, two years after the revolt of 746, and again in 734.[35] Four letters addressed to him have been found in the Governor's Palace archive of Nimrud. Two of them came from Tiglath-pileser giving Bêl-Dân instructions. The other two were sent by Bêl-Dân's son Misharu-nâsir from Babylonia: one of them referred to the royal lineage of their family.[36] Adad-bêlu-ka"in, governor "of the land" (that is, the province of Assur), was eponym under Ashur-nârârî V in 748 and again under Tiglath-pileser in 738.[37] A stela in Assur was erected for Adad-bêlu-ka"in as governor of the Inner City, of Kâr-Tukultî-Ninurta, of Ekallate, of Itu'u, and of Ruqaha.[38] Nabû-da"inanni was the new commander-in-chief whom Tiglath-pileser chose to replace Shamshî-ilu. He was eponym in 742.[39] Nabû-êṭiranni was chief cup-bearer and eponym in 740; he was possibly killed in the defeat of the Assyrian army by the Urartians.[40] Sîn-taklâk was named treasurer and was eponym in 739.[41] Nabû-bêlu-usur, governor of Arrapha and eponym in year 745, may not have been the same Nabû-bêlu-usur who was governor of Simme and eponym in 732.[42] Ninurta-bêlu-usur is one of the best attested high officials during the reign of Tiglath-pileser. However, it is difficult to ascertain what he was doing and where: he was possibly governor of Kâr-Shalmaneser.[43] Ninurta-ilâya, governor of Nisibîna and eponym in 736, was possibly the governor of Kâr-Shalmaneser, but later, from the late 730s or early 720s.[44]

Some other high officials, who were provincial governors and eponyms, probably also played a role under Tiglath-pileser, such as Bêl-êmuranni, governor of Rasappa and eponym in 737; Ashur-shallimanni,

---

35. SAAS 2:59; Grayson, "Assyrian Officials and Power in the Ninth and Eighth Centuries," 33–34.
36. PNA 1.2:290; Postgate, *Governor's Palace Archive*, no. 201–202.
37. SAAS 2:59.
38. Walter Andrae, *Die Stelenreihen in Assur*, WVDOG 24 (Leipzig: Hinrichs, 1913), 47; PNA 1.1:23.
39. SAAS 2:59; SAAS 11:111; PNA 2.2:819.
40. SAAS 2:59; SAAS 11:45–46; PNA 2.2:830–31; SAA 19:xli (or more likely his predecessor chief cupbearer).
41. SAAS 2:59; SAAS 11:13, 15; PNA 3.1:1150.
42. SAAS 2:43, 59, 103; PNA 2.2:817.
43. SAA 19:xlv–xlvi.
44. SAA 19:xlvi–xlvii.

governor of Arrapha and eponym in 735;[45] Ashur-da"inanni, governor of Zamua and eponym in 733; Nergal-uballit, governor of Ahi-zuhina and eponym in 731; Bêl-lû-dâri, governor of Tillê and eponym in 730; Liphur-ilu, governor of Habruri and eponym in 729; and Dur-Ashur, governor of Tushhan and eponym in 728.[46] The high dignitaries played such an important role in the eighth century that John A. Brinkman designated this period as a "period of local autonomy" in Assyrian regions as well as in Babylonia.[47] The Assyrian kings were ruling through a few select officials who remained in office for long periods of time and who had exceptional power and wealth.[48] There were sometimes family ties between the officials and the royal family, for example, with Bêl-Dân, governor of Nimrud. According to Albert Kirk Grayson, this oligarchy of high dignitaries did not challenge the authority of one particular king, but it reflected "a refusal to recognize the supreme position of the royal family among the noble families from which the officials came. It was then an attack upon one of the foundations of the Assyrian monarchy, heredity."[49] It follows that some high dignitaries were at the head of the revolts of the eighth century, such as the revolt of 746, which would have been led by Shamshî-ilu. However, this hypothesis is somewhat in contradiction with the fact that the dignitaries were supposed to conduct military campaigns in the name of the king in order to protect the kingdom of Assyria. This was more necessary when, in particular, the king lacked the ability to rule effectively and had a weak character, as in the case of Adad-nârârî III and his three sons and successors, Shalmaneser IV, Ashur-Dân III, and Ashur-nârârî V. Those kings were unable to keep their officials at court in order to retain the power for themselves. Grayson's conclusion on these four kings is correct: "They could not exercise enough power to control the activities of a few strong officials so that the officials remained in office a long time, gradually eroding authority of the monarchy."[50]

---

45. SAA 19:xliii.
46. SAAS 2:59.
47. Brinkman, *Political History of Post-Kassite Babylonia*, 218–20.
48. Grayson, "Assyrian Officials and Power in the Ninth and Eighth Centuries," 19–52; Grayson, "Struggle for Power in Assyria," 261–68. See also Simonetta Ponchia, *L'Assiria e gli Stati Transeufratici* (Padova: S.a.r.g.o.n., 1991), 53–61.
49. Grayson, "Struggle for Power in Assyria," 267.
50. Grayson, "Struggle for Power in Assyria," 268.

4. THE NEUTRALIZATION OF HIGH DIGNITARIES 57

4.2. Restoring the Royal Power

Tiglath-pileser emerged out of the tumult of the mid-eighth century with the firm objective of reducing the influence of the powerful high dignitaries.[51] Even if they, or some of them, had contributed to maintaining the cohesion of Assyria under the four preceding kings, the decline of the kingdom was not halted, and it was urgent to restore the royal power. It was a preliminary condition before facing the dangerous situation prevailing at the borders of Assyria.

The first high dignitary to be neutralized was Shamshî-ilu. After 752 when he was commander-in-chief and eponym, Shamshî-ilu was no longer mentioned in the sources. He probably kept his charge of commander-in-chief until the end of the reign of Ashur-nârârî V and, possibly, in some way, participated in the revolt of Nimrud in 746. His age is unknown, but he was probably then an old man, maybe close to eighty,[52] so it could be that he died a natural death. However, it is more likely that he was eliminated by Tiglath-pileser, subject to *damnatio memoriae*, because his name and titles seem to have been deliberately erased from his lion inscriptions in Til Barsip.[53]

Ninurta-bêlu-usur, a eunuch of Shamshî-ilu, was another powerful high dignitary, governor of Kâr-Shalmaneser, who engraved his personal inscription in Akkadian, Aramaic, and Hieroglyphic Luwian on two pairs of basalt lions erected at the East and West Gates of Arslan Tash, not far from Til Barsip. He wrote: "At that time, I created, built, (and) completed the city Ḫadattu."[54] The inscription ended with a curse against any future ruler who would erase his name and inscribe his own. It was not dated, but it was possibly composed before Tiglath-pileser's reign. Then the new king came to Arslan Tash and erected a pair of inscribed monumental bulls, with an account of the construction, using the same formula as Ninurta-bêlu-usur: "I built (and) completed the city."[55] The king appears

---

51. Ikeda, "Looking from Til Barsip on the Euphrates," 269.
52. Ikeda, "Looking from Til Barsip on the Euphrates," 289.
53. François Thureau-Dangin, *Til-Barsip* (Paris: Geuthner, 1936), 44.
54. RINAP 1:163, 2001.6–7; Hannes Galter, "Der Himmel über Hadattu: Das religiöse Umfeld der Inschriften von Arslan Tash," in *Offizielle Religion, lokale Kulte und individuelle Religiosität*, ed. Manfred Hutter and Sylvia Hutter-Braunsar (Münster: Ugarit-Verlag, 2004), 173–88; Galter, "Die Torlöwen von Arslan Tash," in *Wiener Zeitschrift für die Kunde des Morgenlandes* 97 (2007): 196–200.
55. RINAP 1:140, 53.18–19.

to have entrusted the building to Ninurta-ilâya, possibly the governor of Nisibîna, eponym in 736.[56] Moreover, the driver of the royal chariot represented on the Western door seems to have been deliberately erased. This driver was probably the eunuch Ninurta-bêlu-usur since he was represented beardless.[57] I suggest that Tiglath-pileser wanted to suppress the influence of this high dignitary by the erasure of his representation and his building project and inscription in the city. Anyway, there is no further trace of Ninurta-bêlu-usur in the sources.

Another means for neutralizing powerful high dignitaries was to give them honors in order to make them loyal. The Assyrian king could not rule alone, and he was obliged to reward those who had helped him to ascend the throne. This was the case, for example, with the powerful Bêl-Harrân-bêlu-usur who was probably one of his main supports. Tiglath-pileser made him eponym and kept him as palace herald.[58] Bêl-Dân, governor of Nimrud and therefore probably also one of the main supports of the Assyrian king, was rewarded by being eponym in 744, immediately after Tiglath-pileser's accession to the throne, and in 734.[59] However, Natalie Naomi May has proposed an alternative explanation: Bêl-Dân's prominence might be due to him belonging to the royal family.[60]

4.3. The Reforms for Neutralizing the High Dignitaries

Tiglath-pileser also made reforms in order to neutralize those high dignitaries who were too influent. Since our sources from the time of this king are limited compared with the abundant sources from the time of Sargon II, several reforms have been wrongly attributed to Sargon II. However, in reality, most of these reforms can be traced to Tiglath-pileser's reign.

The "chief eunuch" (*rab ša rēši*) was raised to commander status during Tiglath-pileser's reign, probably in order to balance the might

---

56. SAAS 2:44, 59.
57. He was not Shamshî-ilu because he was not a eunuch and was settled at Til Barsip, as suggested by Lemaire and Durand, *Les inscriptions*, 108.
58. SAAS 2:59, 89; May, "Administrative and Other Reforms of Sargon II and Tiglath-pileser III," 108 and n. 152: Bêl-Harrân-bêlu-usur was not at the top of the list of eponyms but after the commander-in-chief.
59. SAAS 2:59.
60. May, "Administrative and Other Reforms of Sargon II and Tiglath-pileser III," 109.

4. THE NEUTRALIZATION OF HIGH DIGNITARIES 59

of the commander-in-chief after the bad experience of Shamshî-ilu.[61] Tiglath-pileser also promoted the "chief cupbearer" (*rab šāqê*) by creating a province for him on the border with Urartu.[62] Assyrian high dignitaries and military officers no longer had the right to commission inscriptions written in their own names.[63] Tiglath-pileser also suppressed the right of the eponyms to have their funerary stelae in the royal necropolis.[64] It has been said that Tiglath-pileser changed the order in the list of eponyms. The order in the list of eponyms varies, but the most common order we find is: king, commander-in-chief, palace herald, chief cupbearer, treasurer, then the main governors of the land, of Rasappa, and of Nisibina.[65] However, before the king in the list of eponyms, the first eponym was the governor of Nimrud in 744: it was not by chance that this was just after the suppression of the revolt of Nimrud.[66]

It was probably during the reign of Tiglath-pileser that the important posts were entrusted to a group of three persons: the titular, his assistant (*šaniu*), and a third man (*šalšu*).[67] This chain of command was, at the same time, intended to optimize the governance and to limit personal ambitions of the high dignitaries and military officers. Another measure is attributed to Tiglath-pileser: the stricter dependence of the governor on the king, which was expressed, for example, by the use of the title *bēl-pīḫāti* instead of *šaknu*.[68]

Tiglath-pileser liked to use eunuchs in his administration and as provincial governors and military commanders. The choice of eunuchs

---

61. SAAS 11:73, 152.
62. SAAS 11:163; it was older, according to Karen Radner, "Provinz. C. Assyrien," *RlA* 11 (2006–2008): 49.
63. For a possible exception, see B. Balcioğlu and Walter R. Mayer, "Eine neuassyrische Votivstele aus Turlu Höyük," *Orientalia* 75 (2006): 177–81; Frahm, *Companion to Assyria*, 177.
64. Garelli and Lemaire, *Les empires mésopotamiens, Israël*, 220; SAAS 2:11–12.
65. Garelli and Lemaire, *Les empires mésopotamiens, Israël*, 220; May, "Administrative and Other Reforms of Sargon II and Tiglath-pileser III," 80–82.
66. SAAS 2:59. In 745, the eponym was the governor of Arrapha; however, it was not decided by Tiglath-pileser who ascended the throne only on the 13th of Ayyâru of this year.
67. John Nicholas Postgate, "The Invisible Hierarchy: Assyrian Military and Civilian Administration in the Eighth and Seventh Centuries BC.," in *The Land of Assur and the Yoke of Assur: Studies on Assyria 1971–2005* (Oxford: Oxbow, 2007), 331–60.
68. However, the title of *bēl-pīḫāti* is already attested from the fourteenth century. See Garelli and Lemaire, *Les empires mésopotamiens, Israël*, 220.

ensured their loyalty to the king because of their physical inability to father children.[69] The eunuchs were anonymous, as is indicated by a standard phrase that was a typical feature of Tiglath-pileser's royal inscriptions: "I placed my eunuch(s) as governor(s) over them" (*šūt-rēšiya šaknu muhhišunu aškun*), which does not enable us to identify the governors in question.[70] Moreover, the number of high dignitaries who were provincial governors was relatively small during Tiglath-pileser's reign.[71]

Another means used to reduce the influence of the high dignitaries was to divide the large provinces, previously controlled by the dignitaries, into smaller provinces and to place them under the authority of loyal provincial governors.[72] Consequently, as Tiglath-pileser launched a massive policy of systematic annexation, creating new provinces, the limits of which are unknown, it is difficult to distinguish the new provinces from the ancient divided large provinces.[73] Anyway, the number of provinces doubled under Tiglath-pileser's reign.

However, the most efficient means to neutralize the ambitious and difficult-to-manage high dignitaries was to channel their energy into conquest wars, as French kings were to do later in history by sending their vassals to fight in the Crusades. Tiglath-pileser skillfully reduced the dissensions and ambitions of the high dignitaries by putting them in the service of his expansionist policy. The king did not want to weaken the high dignitaries since he maintained their privileges, but he channeled their ambitions for his own benefit and succeeded in totally restoring royal authority. This does not mean that struggles for power disappeared. The high dignitaries were only provisionally neutralized by the skillful policy of Tiglath-pileser, which was a combination of diplomacy and firmness.

---

69. Omar N'Shea, "Royal Eunuchs and Elite Masculinity in the Neo-Assyrian Empire," *NEA* 79 (2016): 214–21.

70. SAA 19:xvi–xvii; May, "Administrative and Other Reforms of Sargon II and Tiglath-pileser III," 83–84.

71. SAA 19:xvii–xviii.

72. Simo Parpola, "Assyria's Expansion in the Eighth and Seventh Centuries and Its Long-Term Repercussions in the West," in *Symbiosis, Symbolism, and the Power of the Past*, ed. William G. Dever and Seymour Gitin (Winona Lake, IN: Eisenbrauns, 2003), 99–111; Frahm, Companion to Assyria, 177.

73. Garelli and Lemaire, *Les empires mésopotamiens, Israël*, 220–21; Radner, "Provinz. C. Assyrien," 42–68.

5
The Strategy of Conquest

5.1. Tiglath-pileser III's Objectives

"World empires cannot be planned, but originate on the basis of certain objectives and are influenced by many internal and external, unpredictable factors."[1] In a difficult period of weakness and decline for Assyria, the first objective of Tiglath-pileser after he seized power was to restore its might. This was said explicitly in his annals for the first *palû*: "I restored Assyria" (*a-na eš-šu-te ak-šer-ma* KUR *aš-šur*).[2] Of course, this objective corresponded to Tiglath-pileser's strong personality and his personal ambition. He wanted to do better than his forefathers, which was quite easy because the last three kings were weak and powerless. Thus, the king boasted: "I appointed governors in places where the chariots of the kings, my ancestors, never crossed over."[3]

Tiglath-pileser's second objective, a political-ideological one, was to expand the borders of Assyria. This was linked with the first objective because, by conquering new territories, Tiglath-pileser would increase the wealth and might of Assyria. The king presented himself in his inscriptions as the extender of the borders, enlarging the territory of Assyria by adding countless people to its population.[4] As he states, he was commissioned by the god Assur "to widen (the borders of) Assyria" (*ana rupuš māt aššur*).[5] The duty of the Assyrian king to extend the borders of his land existed from an earlier period than that of the Neo-Assyrian Empire. It was clearly attested in the royal inscriptions of Adad-nārārî

---

1. Ariel M. Bagg, "Palestine under Assyrian Rule: A New Look at the Assyrian Imperial Policy in the West," *JAOS* 133 (2013): 119.
2. RINAP 1:29, 6.1.
3. RINAP 1:86, 35.ii.20'–22'.
4. RINAP 1:86, 35.ii.15'–16'.
5. RINAP 1:114, 46.3–4; 83, 35.i.29.

I (1307–1275), who presented himself as the "extender of borders and boundaries" (*murapiš miṣri u kuduri*) and assigned this title to three of his predecessors, the first one being Ashur-uballit I (1365–1330).[6] Tukultî-Ninurta I (1243–1207) also presented himself as the "extender of borders" (*murappiš miṣrī*).[7] Moreover, during a ceremony performed at the beginning of the Assyrian cultic year, the priest of the god Assur crowned the king, placed a scepter in his hands, and said: "with your scepter, extend your land!" (*mātka rappiš*).[8] This assertion is found much later in a similar coronation hymn of King Ashurbanipal: "spread your land wide [*mātka ruppiš*] at your feet!"[9] This recurrent motif, connected with the principle of perennial expansion and Assyrian royal ideology, was an image of the king as a hero and a claim of heroic priority.[10] Two universalist royal titles corresponded to the principle of territorial expansion: "king of the universe" (*šar kiššati*) and "king of the four quarters (of the world)" (*šar kibrat arba'i*).[11] Sargon of Agade introduced the former title, and all Mesopotamian rulers used the latter title from the third millennium on.

In this pattern of continuous expansion in all directions, what were the maximal borders claimed by the Assyrian king? They were theoretically the edges of the earth, which were marked in Mesopotamian geography by seas or lakes: the Upper Sea of the sunset (that is, the Mediterranean) and the Lower Sea of the sunrise (Lake Urmia or Lake Van). Reaching the Mediterranean Sea, which was previously a sporadic act, became common practice under the reign of Shalmaneser III.[12] The declaration of dominion

---

6. RIMA 1:131–32, A.0.76.1.15, 24, 27, 32.

7. RIMA 1:249, A.0.78.8.4'.

8. Karl Friedrich Müller, *Das assyrische Ritual*, MVÄG 41.3 (Leipzig: Hinrichs, 1937), 12.

9. SAA 3:26–27, 11.3, 17.

10. Roberto Gelio, "La délégation envoyée par Gygès, roi de Lydie: Un cas de propagande idéologique," in Fales, *Assyrian Royal Inscriptions*, 203–4 n. 3; Hayim Tadmor, "World Dominion: The Expanding Horizon of the Assyrian Empire," in *Landscapes, Territories, Frontiers and Horizons in the Ancient Near East*, ed. Lucio Milano, Stefano de Martino, Frederick Mario Fales, and Giovanni Battista Lanfranchi, RAI 44 (Padova: S.a.r.g.o.n., 1999), 55–56.

11. RINAP 1:116, 47.1; 138, 52.1; Marie-Joseph Seux, "Les titres royaux 'šar kiššati' et 'šar kibrāt arba'i,'" *RA* 59 (1965): 1–18; Sazonov, "Some Notes on the King of the Four Corners," no. 3, 102–5, 60 (with bibliography).

12. Josette Elayi, "Terminologie de la Mer Méditerranée dans les Annales assyriennes," *OrAnt* 23 (1984): 75–92.

5. THE STRATEGY OF CONQUEST

over the sea coast, at this stage, did not mean a permanent acquisition. Tiglath-pileser institutionalized this ideological claim: his objective was to become the permanent master of the whole earth as it was defined by the Assyrians, from the Upper to the Lower Seas.

The geographical extent of the Assyrian conquest was commemorated by monuments in the course of successful military campaigns, located further and further afield, as soon as the border of the empire moved.[13] The Assyrian king made a distinction between the "land of Assur" and the "yoke of Assur."[14] The former consisted of the historic Assyrian heartland, the Assur-Nineveh-Arbela triangle, plus the territories considered as originally part of it and reclaimed in yearly campaigns.[15] The territory under the "yoke of Assur" referred to lands more recently conquered, which continued to be ruled by vassal or client kings subject to loyalty oaths and treaties and tribute. Since Tiglath-pileser was commissioned by the god Assur to expand the borders of Assyria, he knew that he was under the god's protection during this ambitious undertaking. The Assyrian troops made extensive use of all possible religious means to guarantee supernatural support for their dangerous mission.[16]

The process of expanding the territory of Assyria did not have the sole objective of creating a vast territory; it also sought to increase the population and bring back riches. Tiglath-pileser's objective was that Assyria regain its prosperity and even enhance it, that it became a mighty and wealthy state, the major power in the Near East. As a matter of fact, the king was confronted with a dilemma: to be victorious and subsequently collect riches, Tiglath-pileser needed an efficient army, but to build an efficient army, he needed riches. Tiglath-pileser did not depend on booty alone, as horses were also imported from Egypt through trade. Moreover, foreigner advisors and experts were employed in the Assyrian army: for example, men of Israel already served as mercenaries at the beginning of the eighth century (2 Chr 25:6).

---

13. Morandi Bonacossi, "Stele e statue reali assire," 106–55; Heather D. Baker, "Tiglatpileser III," *RlA* 14 (2014): 23.

14. John Nicholas Postgate, *The Land of Assur and the Yoke of Assur: Studies on Assyria; 1971–2005* (Oxford: Oxbow, 2007).

15. Radner, "Assur-Nineveh-Arbela Triangle," 321–29.

16. Andreas Fuchs, "Assyria at War: Strategy and Conduct," in *Cuneiform Culture*, ed. Karen Radner and Eleanor Robson (Oxford: Oxford University Press, 2011), 386.

5.2. A Careful Preparation of Strategy

It would be interesting to know whether Tiglath-pileser proceeded in his conquests by leading campaigns at random in all directions or whether he had a precise strategy for planning his campaigns. It is difficult to answer this because of the poor state of preservation of his annals, which provided a detailed account of his campaigns. According to Garelli, Tiglath-pileser's first move was probably prompted by his coup d'Etat.[17] The annexation of new territories then developed gradually as rebellions prompted new campaigns: "it is not certain that he tried to change his predecessor's policy (Shalmaneser III) drastically along the lines of a preconceived plan. It is perhaps the success of the actions conducted in the traditional spirit of the past which accounted for the change in the political situation."[18] Tiglath-pileser probably did appropriate some strategic ideas developed by his predecessors such as in his Syrian campaign, which reminds us of that of Shalmaneser III. It is also possible that the successes of some campaigns or, conversely, the absence of significant results or of some unexpected consequences, induced the Assyrian king to modify his plans. For example, from 737 until 735, in the absence of significant results, Tiglath-pileser was forced to launch several campaigns against the Medes and Urartu.

Nevertheless, several elements in his inscriptions proved that Tiglath-pileser did not leave anything to chance and that he did build a precise strategy; yet he was flexible, adapting this strategy if unexpected events occurred. Theoretically, Tiglath-pileser adopted three strategic lines according to the situation: conquest resulting from a military campaign, submission obtained by the dissuasive presence of the Assyrian army without fighting, and allegiance expressed by the sending of tribute from states that, although not invaded, were threatened. The king aimed at three main targets, which were powerful states potentially dangerous for Assyria: Urartu, the kingdom of Damascus, and Babylonia. The military campaigns of Tiglath-pileser were methodically arranged in five main stages: the first (745–744) against Babylonia, the Aramean tribes, and Media; the second (743–738) against the Syrian-Urartian coalition; the third (737–735) against Media and Urartu; the fourth (734–732) against Damascus, Phoenicia, and Palestine; and the fifth (731–727) against Babylonia. Most of the

---

17. Garelli, "Achievement of Tiglath-pileser III," 47, 50.
18. Garelli, "Achievement of Tiglath-pileser III," 51.

5. THE STRATEGY OF CONQUEST

time, he did not settle the conflicts at one go in each area and was forced to return there, sometimes several times. For example, Tiglath-pileser conducted three campaigns against Babylonia in 745–744 and again, thirteen years later, in 731 and 729. He undertook two campaigns against Media, after an interval of seven years: in 744 and 737. It took several campaigns to crush the western revolts: during a first period from 743 to 740 and in 738, and during a second period from 734 to 732. It was thanks to these comings and goings that Tiglath-pileser succeeded in reaching his objectives in all these regions. As for the powerful kingdom of Urartu, Tiglath-pileser was obliged to make four attempts: a first campaign against King Sarduri, defeated at Arpad in 743; a second campaign in 739 on the border of Urartu; a third campaign in 736 on its border; and a fourth campaign in 735 when he reached the capital of Urartu. This progressive action over eight years reveals a strategy that was carefully prepared by Tiglath-pileser. After Assyria had been brought under firm control, he engaged in several theatres of war, concentrating in each campaign on just one foe alone because the Assyrian army had to fight in a single theater of war in order to be victorious. Before each campaign, the objective had to be chosen wisely.[19] It was also part of Tiglath-pileser's strategy to convince everybody of Assyria's invincibility by displaying the images of the hero king and his victories on the wall reliefs of the royal palace.[20]

Last but not least, a good military strategy depended on the capability of the army, which was reformed by Tiglath-pileser. The king used the army cautiously and successfully, giving the troops a lead in number, experience, and competence. He needed a professional and skilled army, large enough to secure control over vast territories and their large populations.[21] The difficulty in dealing with the question of his military reforms comes from the scarce evidence of Tiglath-pileser's sources compared with the abundant sources from the time of Sargon II. However, according

---

19. Fuchs, "Assyria at War," 388–89.
20. Fuchs, "Assyria at War," 386.
21. Israel Eph'al, "On Warfare and Military Control in the Ancient Near Eastern Empires: A Research Outline," in *History, Historiography and Interpretation: Studies in Biblical and Cuneiform Literatures*, ed. Hayim Tadmor and Moshe Weinfeld (Jerusalem: Magnes, 1983), 104; Kaplan, "Recruitment of Foreign Soldiers," 135–36; Tamás Dezsö, *The Assyrian Army, I: The Structure of the Neo-Assyrian Army as Reconstructed from the Assyrian Palace Reliefs and Cuneiform Sources*, 2 vols. (Budapest: Eötvös, 2012).

to May, "it can be firmly established that the reorganization of the army and the system of subjugation of the conquered territories was launched by Tiglath-pileser III and was only taken up by Sargon."[22] Tiglath-pileser reformed the army's logistics, strategy, and weaponry.[23] Much information can be found in the administrative documents from so-called Fort Shalmaneser in Nimrud, the central base of the chariot and equestrian units of the standing army in the time of Tiglath-pileser and Sargon.[24] These documents, known as "Horse Lists," contain information about the different units which made up the royal army.[25]

The army of conscripts, providing military service (*ilku*) only when the agricultural calendar permitted the absence of farm workers, was transformed into an army of professionals.[26] More than his predecessors, Tiglath-pileser seems to have used armed troops of specialized soldiers.[27] A document (ND 2619), dated by Jacob Kaplan from the reign of Tiglath-pileser instead of that of Sargon, provides information on the recruitment of foreign soldiers (from Chaldean tribes) into the Assyrian

---

22. May, "Administrative and Other Reforms of Sargon II and Tiglath-pileser III," 109.

23. Peter Dubovský, "Neo-Assyrian Warfare: Logistics and Weaponry during the Campaigns of Tiglath-pileser III," *Anodos* 4–5 (2004–2005): 61–67; Jamie Szudy, "Archery Equipment in the Neo-Assyrian Period," 2 vols. (PhD diss., University of Vienna, 2015), 1:18–59.

24. Dalley and Postgate, *Tablets from Fort Shalmaneser*.

25. Dalley, "Foreign Chariotry and Cavalry," 31–48.

26. Walther Manitius, "Das stehende Heer der Assyrerkönige und seine Organisation," *ZA* 24 (1910): 108; Andreas Fuchs, "War das Neuassyrischer Reich ein Militärstaat?," in *Krieg-Gesellschaft-Institutionen: Beiträge zu einer vergleichenden Kriegsgeschichte*, ed. Burkhard Meissner, Oliver Schmidt, and Michael Sommer (Berlin: Akademie, 2005), 35–60; John Nicholas Postgate, "The Invisible Hierarchy: Assyrian Military and Civilian Administration in the Eighth and Seventh Centuries BC," in Postgate, *Land of Assur and the Yoke of Assur*, 331–60; Robin Archer, "Chariotry to Cavalry: Developments in the Early First Millennium," in *New Perspectives on Ancient Warfare*, ed. Garrett G. Fagan and Matthew Trundle, HW 59 (Leiden: Brill, 2010), 57–80; Karen Radner, "The Assyrian Army," http://tinyurl.com/SBL1722b; John Marriott and Karen Radner, "Sustaining the Assyrian Army among Friends and Enemies in 714 BCE," *JCS* 67 (2015): 127–43.

27. May, "Administrative and Other Reforms of Sargon II and Tiglath-pileser III," 107, contra John Nicholas Postgate, *Taxation and Conscription in the Assyrian Empire*, Studia Pohl, Series Maior 3 (Rome: Biblical Institute Press, 1974), 218–26, who considered that recruits were mostly supplied by the provinces.

5. THE STRATEGY OF CONQUEST 67

military organization, particularly on their distribution among the provinces of the Neo-Assyrian Empire.[28] The distribution of these soldiers was possibly a deliberate policy in order to exploit their experience while decreasing the potential threat that they could have on the security of the empire. The formation of new multinational military units could solve the problem. However, the creation of a corps of Itueans (an Aramean tribe) was probably more ancient.[29] The archives of Nimrud mentioned several corps of Arameans in different parts of the empire. They were needed to complement the Assyrian troops, not sufficient to control the vast, newly conquered territories. Even if Tiglath-pileser did not create these corps of foreign specialized soldiers, he probably generalized this system.[30]

The various specialists of the Assyrian army were adapted to different tasks. Thus, sappers opened roads in difficult mountain areas while charioteers were used in plains and other specialists in naval operations. Couriers were used for reconnaissance operations and poliorcetic specialists for besieging fortified cities. Just as the Samarians were among the best at chariotry, so the Urartians were the best at cavalry operations by exploiting the special horses and rearing skills of the neighboring Manneans. All of them were employed in the Assyrian army. According to the Horse Lists, the unit of Samaria consisted of thirteen equestrian officers, "commanders of teams" (*rab urâte*), probably only charioteers.[31] The Nimrud Wine Lists suggest that there were horse experts at the court of Tiglath-pileser; they were Nubian emissaries sent by Pharaoh Piankhy (Piye), a charioteer-king, with whom Tiglath-pileser enjoyed good relations.[32] The soldiers' weapons and equipment also improved under this Assyrian king.[33] Tiglath-pileser was effective in terms of military intelligence and strategy in his quest for victory; he created a new intelligence system, using reports transmitted by staging posts.[34] He also used a rhetoric and

---

28. Barbara Parker, "Administrative Tablets from the North-West Palace, Nimrud," *Iraq* 23 (1961): 38; Kaplan, "Recruitment of Foreign Soldiers," 139–52.

29. Dezsö, *Assyrian Army*, 1:33–38; Natalie Naomi May, review of SAA 19, in *BiOr* 71 (2014): 479.

30. Garelli and Lemaire, *Les empires mésopotamiens, Israël*, 100; Dezsö, *Assyrian Army*, 1:33–51.

31. Dalley, "Foreign Chariotry and Cavalry," 32–33.

32. Dalley, "Foreign Chariotry and Cavalry," 43–45 (with bibliography).

33. Joannès, *Dictionnaire de la civilisation mésopotamienne*, 851.

34. Fuchs, "Assyria at War," 392–93; Peter Dubovský, "King's Direct Control: Neo-Assyrian Qepu Officials," in *Organization, Representation, and Symbols of Power in*

tactics of intimidation, a kind of psychological warfare, as followed by his successors Sargon II and Sennacherib.[35]

5.3. The Place of the West in Tiglath-pileser III's Strategy

The conquest of the western regions was an abiding goal of the Assyrian kings who were attracted by the western states. During two centuries, they marched sixty-seven times to the Levant.[36] Shalmaneser III was particularly fascinated by the West because he had been influenced by the western campaign of his father Ashurnasirpal II between 876 and 868. Access was easy, thereby revealing the wealth of this area.[37] Shalmaneser III crossed the Euphrates more than twenty-five times, but, as discussed above, he failed in the conquest of the West. The Assyrian kings were also attracted by the Mediterranean Sea, which for them represented the western limit of their land and which was reached several times by one-off expeditions. They intended to make the Assyrian Empire a maritime empire. The control or conquest of Egypt, which had dominated the Levantine region in the second millennium, was another of their dreams, but this dream could not be realized before they first had control of the West.

Were the Phoenician cities included in Tiglath-pileser's strategy for conquering the West? We tend to believe that the cities occupied a central place in Tiglath-pileser's western strategy because they were situated at an important crossroads, which favored trade and was a strategic location. As a matter of fact, the Phoenicians controlled the Homs gap, the main northern road toward the hinterland, and the southern Akko depression toward the Jordan valley. Moreover, in the eventuality of a conflict with Egypt for the control of the Near East, Assyria could need the Phoenician fleets. Nevertheless, Tiglath-pileser did not adopt this strategy, even if it might seem logical to us. He preferred to start by attacking the western states of the hinterland such as Arpad, Hamath, and

---

the *Assyrian Near East*, ed. Gernot Wilhelm, RAI 54 (Winona Lake, IN: Eisenbrauns, 2012), 449–60; Pierre Villard, "Quelques aspects du renseignement militaire dans l'empire néo-assyrien," *HIMA* 3 (2016): 87–97.

35. Lewis, "You Have Heard What the Kings of Assyria Have Done," 79–80; Ariel M. Bagg, "Where Is the Public? A New Look at the Brutality Scenes in Neo-Assyrian Royal Inscriptions and Art," in Cohen and Westbrook, *Swords into Plowshares*, 45–56.

36. Bagg, "Palestine under Assyrian Rule," 122.

37. Elayi, *History of Phoenicia*, 133–36.

5. THE STRATEGY OF CONQUEST

Damascus. He followed the principle of territorial contiguity, advancing further when the nearer territory was under control.[38] This strategy was the opposite of that of the preceding kings who mostly made one-off, short-lived raids. Tiglath-pileser's aim was to break down Assyria's isolation, to control the caravan trade routes and the access to the metal and wood resources of the Amanus and Taurus mountains. Tiglath-pileser's conquests of the coastal states of north Syria were only a side effect of his activities in the hinterland. Conversely, he was interested in the southern shore of the Mediterranean Sea because the Philistine cities gave access to Egypt. His interest in Egypt was mentioned in a broken context concerned with Egypt and Gaza: "[I considered] his [...]... as an Assyrian emporium" (*ú-ter-šu-ma...]-x-šu a-na bīt ka-a-ri māt aš-šur*).[39] Frahm suggested reading *alu-šú*, "his [ci]ty," that is, Gaza, King Hanunu's city.[40] Later, Sargon was also interested in an emporium at the Brook of Egypt.[41] However, before thinking of conquering Egypt one day, when the conditions would be right, Tiglath-pileser had to content himself with Assyrian-Egyptian trading activities. In the meantime, his deep interest in establishing "ports/quays" (*karrānu*) and "trading posts" (*bīt karrāni*) was to use them also as outposts at the borders.[42]

---

38. Bagg, "Palestine under Assyrian Rule," 120.
39. RINAP 1:127, 48.18′; 132, 49.r.16.
40. RINAP 1:132, 49.note r.16.
41. Elayi, *Sargon II*, 55–56.
42. K. Lawson Younger, "The Assyrian Economic Impact on the Southern Levant in the Light of Recent Study," *IEJ* 67 (2015): 183–84; Shigeo Yamada, "Neo-Assyrian Trading Posts on the East Mediterranean Coast and 'Ionians': An Aspect of Assyro-Greek Contact," *Orient*, Supplement 1 (2019): 224.

6
The First Phase of the Campaigns (745–744)

6.1. The Campaign against Babylonia and the Aramean Tribes

Five or six months after his accession to the throne, Tiglath-pileser "mustered the vast] troops of Assyria" (*ú-ši]-bu* ERIM.ḪI.A-*at* KUR *aš-šur*.KI [*gap-šá-a-ti*]).[1] He needed some time for this operation because part of the Assyrian army was possibly still in north Syria with the commander-in-chief Shamshî-ilu, and the king had to replace him with another commander-in-chief, Nabu-da"inanni.[2] According to the Eponym List, in "Tashrîtu [October 745], he marched to the (land) between the river(s)" (*t*]*ašrīti a-na bi-rit nāri it-ta-lak*).[3] *Birit nāri* means the inner part, that is, the territory between the Euphrates and the Tigris, in other words "Mesopotamia" (Μεσοποταμία) in its etymological sense. Tiglath-pileser, at the head of the Assyrian army, left Nimrud on the Tigris and went down southwards across Mesopotamia.

Tiglath-pileser's first campaign was directed against Babylonia and the Aramean tribes. The Assyrian intervention in Babylonia was different and more problematic than the approach adopted in other regions of the empire. It was different because the Assyrians respected the religious traditions of the Babylonians and had numerous cultural similarities with them. It was more problematic because Babylonia was a region of a heterogeneous people: native Babylonians, Aramean tribes, and later Chaldean tribes. Because of the presence of these tribes and semi-independent cities, Babylonia was an unstable region, and the power of its king was therefore limited; every tribe was more or less independent.

---

1. RINAP 1:83, 35.i.37–38.
2. SAAS 2:59.
3. SAAS 2:43; Tadmor, *Inscriptions of Tiglath-pileser III*, 232 and n. 4; RINAP 1:25, 4.2–3.

In which order did Tiglath-pileser conduct his campaigns? He attempted to confront Babylonia first but often interrupted his activities on that front to deal with the Aramean tribes, who were scattered across the region: partly settled in the alluvial plain between the lower reaches of the Tigris and Euphrates and partly circulating among the Babylonian cities.[4] The Babylonian Chronicles only mentioned Akkad: "In that same year (in 745), he (Tiglath-pileser) went down to Akkad, plundered Rabbilu and Hamranu, and abducted the gods of Shapazza."[5] The location of Hamranu on the Diyala River is practically certain because it was listed among the cities conquered by Sennacherib on the Elamo-Babylonian border. Rabbilu and Shapazza, mentioned in conjunction with Hamranu, are probably also located in the region of the Diyala.[6]

In the annals, Tiglath-pileser mentioned that he marched first against the Aramean tribes, quoting eighteen of them (tribes or cities of the tribes), but their locations are difficult to determine.[7] We can recognize Hamranu (spelt Hamarânu) and Rabbilu (spelled Rabi-ilu) from the Babylonian Chronicles. Ten new names of Aramean tribes are mentioned in another text of the annals related to the first campaign; only Adilê is repeated.[8] The question of the locations of all these tribes has been fully dealt with by Edward Lipiński.[9] No firm location has been determined for the tribes of Luhu'atu, Hatallu, Rubbû, Rapiqu, Kapiru, and Adilê.[10] Rapiqu is written either with the determinative LÚ, "people," or without it and could instead be a city on the Euphrates, north of Sippar.[11] Hîrânu, Nasiru, and Gulusu were probably tribes settled in the Sippar region.[12] The Li'ta'u and Gurumu tribes were possibly localized on the banks of the Uqnû River and Ubudu

---

4. Frederick Mario Fales, "Moving around Babylon: On the Aramean and Chaldean Presence in Southern Mesopotamia," in *Babylon, Wissenskultur in Orient und Okzident*, ed. Eva Cancik-Kirschbaum et al. (Berlin: de Gruyter, 2008), 91.
5. Grayson, *Assyrian and Babylonian Chronicles*, 71, Chronicle 1.3–5.
6. Grayson, *Assyrian and Babylonian Chronicles*, 255–56, 261–63.
7. RINAP 1:25, 4.3–7.
8. RINAP 1:27, 5.6–7.
9. Lipiński, *Aramaeans*, 437–89.
10. RINAP 1:25, 4.4–7; Lipiński, *Aramaeans*, 444–45, 451–52; Fales, "Moving around Babylon," 92.
11. RINAP 1:25, 4.4; 118, 47.6; Lipiński, *Aramaeans*, 445; Garelli and Lemaire, *Les empires mésopotamiens, Israël*, 53, 78, 327.
12. RINAP 1:25, 4.4–5; Lipiński, *Aramaeans*, 446–48.

6. THE FIRST PHASE OF THE CAMPAIGNS (745-744)   73

on the banks of the Tigris.[13] The Uqnû River corresponds to the modern River Kerkha.[14] The Nabâtu tribe raises a particular question concerning its identification: although it is generally distinguished from the Nabateans, Nabâtu could be a north Arabian tribe that is later associated with the tribe called *Nbyt/Nabayatu*.[15] Rummulitu and Gibrê were probably not Aramean but Arab tribes of desert nomads.[16] North Arabian tribes who lived in the same regions were often called "Arameans" in Assyrian inscriptions because they were generally confused with Aramean tribes. The Tanê tribe could be located in the area between Sippar and the Diyala and Lesser Zab.[17] Dunanu was a tribe and Pasitu a city of this tribe, located in the north or northwest of Nippur.[18] Nasikku is an unexpected name for a tribe, because *nasīku* often designated the head of an Aramean group in Assyro-Babylonian sources, but there may be no relation with this term.[19]

In the summary of the three campaigns against the Aramean tribes in 745, 731, and 729, which present the most complete list, thirty-five names are mentioned.[20] Twenty-six of these names have already been mentioned. The scribe of the summary inscription copied out the first list of eighteen names, following the same order, except for Li'ta'u.[21] Four other names were quoted in another summary inscription.[22] In fact, all the Aramean tribes (or cities of tribes) quoted in these lists were not conquered in the campaign of 745 but later.

In the inscriptions there are also isolated mentions of tribes such as Puqudu and Labdudu.[23] Puqudu was one of the most prominent Aramean

---

13. RINAP 1:25, 4.6-7; Lipiński, *Aramaeans*, 446, 467-68, 452-55.
14. Garelli and Lemaire, *Les empires mésopotamiens, Israël*, 327, map 2; Lipiński, *Aramaeans*, 413, fig. 16.
15. RINAP 1:25, 4.5; Lipiński, *Aramaeans*, 448-50; cf. Israel Eph'al, *The Ancient Arabs* (Jerusalem: Magnes, 1982), 221 (with references).
16. RINAP 1:25, 4.6-7; Lipiński, *Aramaeans*, 451-53: LÚ *Ru-um-mu-lu-tu* meant literally "desert people."
17. RINAP 1:27, 5.6; Lipiński, *Aramaeans*, 471-72.
18. RINAP 1:118, 47.7; 27, 5.6; Lipiński, *Aramaeans*, 458-59.
19. RINAP 1:27, 5.6; Lipiński, *Aramaeans*, 494-95. See Paul-Eugène Dion, *Les Araméens à l'âge du fer: Histoire politique et structures sociales* (Paris: Gabalda, 1997), 233-35.
20. RINAP 1:118, 47.5-9.
21. RINAP 1:25, 4.3-7.
22. RINAP 1:97, 39.4-5.
23. RINAP 1:97, 39.12; 114, 46.6-7 (Labdudu, Naqru); 27, 5.6. Another tribe,

tribes, sometimes simply called "Arameans"; it is mainly known from the governor's archive in Nippur, a first-hand source dated between ca. 755 and 732.[24] This tribe was active around Nippur, in Lahîru, east of the Tigris, between the Diyala and Dêr, and in the southern marshes along the Elamite border; in other words the tribe moved between the middle Euphrates to southern Mesopotamia. Labdudu was located in eastern Babylonia and was possibly a group of nomadic pastoralists.[25] It is not presented as a tribe but with the determinative KUR, "country." However, it was one of the tribes that Shamshî-ilu boasted of having overcome in the early eighth century, along with 'Utû', Rupû', and Hatallu.[26] Among the tribes (or cities of tribes) probably conquered by Tiglath-pileser after 745, several cannot be firmly located, such as Naqru, Nilqu, Radê, Ru'u'a, Qabi'u, Marusu, Hagarânu, and Dai[...]u.[27] Ubulu was possibly located east of the Tigris, Amatu on the banks of the Uqnû River, Hindiru on the Lower Uqnû, Hudadu in northern Babylonia between Sippar and the Tigris, and Naqru between Dûr-Kurigalzu and Sippar of Shamash.[28] Damunu and Karma'u belonged to north Arabian groups.[29] It is uncertain whether Amlatu was a tribe (determinative LÚ) or a city (determinative URU) or an Arabic name for assemblies of tribesmen.[30] The Itu'u tribe, which lived along the western bank of the Tigris north of Babylonia, had already been confronted by Tukultî-Ninurta II in the early ninth century and was said to have been overcome by Shamshî-ilu in the early eighth century.[31] The Itueans had presumably attained an ideal balance early on between their demographi-

---

Li'tamu, known only from a letter of Shamash-bunaya and Nabû-nammir, made allegiance to Tiglath-pileser: SAA 19:105, 98.r.9–13.

24. Steven W. Cole, *Nippur IV: The Early Neo-Babylonian Governor's Archive from Nippur*, OIP 114 (Chicago: The Oriental Institute of the University of Chicago, 1996), 1–6; Lipiński, *Aramaeans*, 429–37.

25. RINAP 1:114, 46.5; 119, 47.14; Lipiński, *Aramaeans*, 438–41.

26. RIMA 3:232, A.0.104.2010, 10–11.

27. RINAP 1:118, 47.6–8; Lipiński, *Aramaeans*, 459–60, 464–70.

28. RINAP 1:118, 47.7–8; 100, 40.5; 114, 46.8; Lipiński, *Aramaeans*, 455–57, 460, 469–70, 470–71. There were two cities named Sippar 7 km apart: Sippar of Shamash (Abu Habbah) and Sippar-Amnânum (Tell ed-Dêr). See Joannès, *Dictionnaire de la civilisation mésopotamienne*, 782–84.

29. RINAP 1:118, 47.7; Lipiński, *Aramaeans*, 461–62.

30. RINAP 1:118, 47.7; 68, 27.2; Lipiński, *Aramaeans*, 462–63.

31. RINAP 1:118, 47.5; Lipiński, *Aramaeans*, 437–38; RIMA 2:173, A.0.100.5, 49–50; RIMA 3:232, A.0.104.2010, 10.

6. THE FIRST PHASE OF THE CAMPAIGNS (745-744)   75

cal size, their specific territory, and their distinctive ethnicity. That is why Tiglath-pileser integrated them into the ranks of his administration as a trustworthy unit of military police.[32] The bowmen represented on some reliefs in the Assyrian palace could refer to this group.[33]

Some Babylonian cities were also conquered during the first campaign, such as Sippar of Shamash and Nippur.[34] However, the other cities conquered were possibly controlled by Arameans: "(those living in) the cities of Dūr-Kurigalzu (and) Adin[ni], the fortresses of Sarragitu, Labbanat, (and) Kār-bēl-mātāti."[35] Tiglath-pileser exerted authority "over all the Arameans who are on the banks of the Tigris (and) Surappu Rivers, as far as the Uqnû River, which is by the shore of the Lower Sea."[36] The king had undertaken to track the Arameans down from Dūr-Kurigalzu and Sippar to the Persian/Arabian Gulf since they were mainly settled on the banks of the Tigris, Euphrates, Surappu, and Uqnû Rivers.[37] The Lower Sea corresponds to the Persian/Arabian Gulf, which had a very different configuration in antiquity. It penetrated further into the mainland, probably up to the border of Bît-Yakîn.[38] As a result, Bît-Yakîn was not inland but on the coastline.

---

32. John Nicholas Postgate, "Itu'a," *RlA* 5 (1976–1980): 221–22.
33. Julian E. Reade, "The Neo-Assyrian Court and Army from the Sculptures," *Iraq* 34 (1972): 87–112; John Nicholas Postgate, "The Assyrian Army in Zamua," *Iraq* 62 (2000): 89–108.
34. RINAP 1:27, 5.5, 7–8; 96–97, 39.4–5.
35. RINAP 1:118, 47.8.
36. RINAP 1:97, 39.4–5.
37. RINAP 1:100, 40.9.
38. P. Kassler, "The Structural and Geomorphic Evolution of the Persian Gulf," in *The Persian Gulf: Holocene Carbonate Sedimentation and Diagenesis in a Shallow Epicontinental Sea*, ed. Bruce H. Purser (Berlin: Springer, 1973), 11–32; Hartmut Waetzoldt, "Zu den Strandverschiebungen am Persischen Golf und den Bezeichnungen der Hōrs," in *Strandverchiebungen und ihrer Bedeutung für Geowissenschaften und Archäologie*, ed. Jérôme Schäfer and W. Simon (Heidelberg: Vorstand der Vereinigung der Freunde der Studentenschaft der Universität, 1981), 159–84; Paul Sanlaville, "Considérations sur l'évolution de la basse Mésopotamie au cours des derniers millénaires," *Paléorient* 15 (1989): 5–27; Paul Sanlaville and Rémi Dalongeville, "L'évolution des espaces littoraux du golfe persique et du golfe d'Oman depuis la phase finale de la transgression post-glaciaire," *Paléorient* 31 (2005): 10–11 (map); Joannès, *Dictionnaire de la civilisation mésopotamienne*, 793 (map).

Who were the Arameans confronted by Tiglath-pileser? The origin of the Aramean tribal group in this area remains unclear.[39] They are attested from the eleventh century at least, and they occupied strategic areas in the so-called Jezirah, the Syrian steppe, and northern Mesopotamia. The first mention of the Arameans (Ahlamû) in Assyrian sources was the military expedition conducted by Tiglath-pileser I against them in 1111.[40] According to Babylonian sources, during the eleventh and tenth centuries, different tribal groups labeled "Arameans" or "Suteans," which designated West Semitic nomads, looted Sippar and other cities of the northern alluvial plain. The main Assyrian cities located on the Middle and Upper Tigris were threatened by Aramean plunderers. The Assyrians reacted strongly in the tenth and ninth centuries by forcing the tribal groups to migrate southwards and to occupy land from the Tigris riverbank to the Euphrates riverbank near Sippar and especially the southeastern plain between the Tigris and the border of Elam. Some residual connections probably continued between these southern Aramean tribes and the middle Euphrates area.

However, there are different hypotheses. For example, some scholars directly link the Aramean takeover of the southern reaches of the Tigris to the exactions of the eleventh century.[41] Some surveys on the southern Tigris-Euphrates alluvial plain have provided a detailed picture of its human occupation from the twelfth to the eighth centuries.[42] These

---

39. Brinkman, *Political History of Post-Kassite Babylonia*, 265–85; Brinkman, *Prelude to Empire*; Lipiński, *Aramaeans*, 409–89; Frederick Mario Fales, "Arameans and Chaldeans: Environment and Society," in *The Babylonian World*, ed. Gwendolyn Leick (New York: Routledge, 2007), 288–98; Mirko Novák, "Assyrians and Aramaeans: Modes of Cohabitation and Acculturation at Guzana (Tell Halaf)," in *Assyria to Iberia: Art and Culture in the Iron Age*, ed. Joan Aruz and Michael Seymour (New York: Metropolitan Museum of Art, 2016), 123–35.

40. *ARAB* 1.239; Françoise Briquel-Chatonnet, *Les Araméens et les premiers Arabes: Des royaumes araméens du IXe siècle à la chute du royaume nabatéen*, Encyclopédie de la Méditerranée 9 (Aix-en-Provence: Édisud, 2004), 9–17.

41. Brinkman, *Political History of Post-Kassite Babylonia*, 281–83.

42. Robert McCormick Adams, *Land behind Baghdad* (Chicago: University of Chicago Press, 1965); McCormick Adams and Hans-Jörg Nissen, *The Uruk Countryside* (Chicago: University of Chicago Press, 1972); MacGuire Gibson, *The City and Area of Kish* (Miami: Field Research Projects, 1972); Johannes Renger, *Babylon: Focus mesopotamischer Geschichte* (Saarbrücken: SDV Saarbrücker Drucherei und Verlag, 1999), 87–110.

6. THE FIRST PHASE OF THE CAMPAIGNS (745–744)

surveys point to a general decline in population, and the administration of urbanism correlated with an increase in economic and social ruralization and extensive abandonments of settlements, which were insufficiently compensated by the foundation of new sites. These developments could be due to a climatic change toward aridity or to social and political disruptions provoked by internal causes.[43] Moreover, shifts in river channels, in particular for the Euphrates, which had a variegated and complicated history, and corresponding canal realignments may have been a significant factor in Babylonian urbanism, agriculture, and trade.[44]

Whatever is the case, the lists of Aramean tribes subjugated by Tiglath-pileser provide an impressive number of tribal entities of unsubdued Arameans and vast tribal groups such as Puqudu. The Aramean groups generally had immense mobility; they migrated from one enclave to another and gave rise to interregional movements between the middle Euphrates and southern Mesopotamia. The situation depicted in Sargon's inscriptions concerning Aramean tribes moving around Babylon was probably the same as at the beginning of Tiglath-pileser's reign: "The country (of Babylon had become) desert, where passage had long since become very difficult. The way was choked and without paths. It was impossible to go where thorns, thistles, and scrub bush had taken over. Lions and jackals roamed there in packs and frisked about like lambs.... In that desert terrain, Arameans and Suteans—tent-dwellers, fugitives, thieves, and robbers—had come to dwell and had made its road desolate."[45]

The Arameans seem to have resisted the power and attraction of the prestigious Babylonian culture in spite of their repeated contacts with it.[46] Their sociopolitical organization was also particular and remained

---

43. Jehuda Neumann and Simo Parpola, "Climatic Change and the Eleventh-Tenth Century Eclipse of Assyria and Babylonia," *JNES* 46 (1987): 161–82; Wiebke Kirleis and Michael Herles, "Climatic Changes as Reason for Assyro-Aramaean Conflicts? Pollen Evidence for Drought at the End of the Second Millennium BC," *SAAB* 16 (2007): 7–37.

44. John A. Brinkman, "Reflections on the Geography of Babylonia (1000–600 B.C.)," in *Neo-Assyrian Geography*, ed. Mario Liverani (Rome: Universita di Roma "La Sapienza," 1995), 27 (with bibliography).

45. Cyril John Gadd, "Inscribed Prisms of Sargon II from Nimrud," *Iraq* 16 (1954): 192, vii, ll. 45–68; Steven W. Cole, "Marsh Formation in the Borsippa Region and the Course of the Lower Euphrates," *JNES* 53 (1994): 88; Brinkman, "Reflections on the Geography of Babylonia," 26–27.

46. Fales, "Moving around Babylon," 93–94.

unchanged. They had a kinship-based society. They had no ideology of unified leadership, but each tribe had a specific "sheikh" (*nasīku*).[47] The sheikhs were linked with institutional or geographical entities, such as lands, cities, or rivers. As a result, there was a large degree of segmentation in their territories and distinctive ethnicity. The vast tribal complexes were, beyond their self-identification, subdivided according to their specific sheikhs, who took individual courses of action. No common tribal policies are attested in the present state of documentation.[48]

The course of Tiglath-pileser's expedition in Babylonia is somewhat surprising because Nabû-nâsir (Nabonassar), king of Babylon, was never opposed to the Assyrian king's intervention and never prevented the Assyrian army from crossing and fighting in his country. Why did the Babylonian king not react when the Assyrian king seized Babylonian cities? Maybe because these cities were already controlled by Aramean tribal groups. In fact, there was a general decline in Babylonia in the first half of the eighth century.[49] The king of Babylon had to preside over a heterogeneous population, and his power was limited by independent actions of both the main cities and the tribes. He was rather weak and unable to police dissident elements, uncontrolled civil unrest, and disruption of trade routes, and he was destabilized by the problem of father-son succession. Therefore, King Nabû-nâsir probably viewed Tiglath-pileser's campaign against the Aramean tribes favorably. It is even possible that he had asked the Assyrian king for help,[50] as had been the case in 851 when the king of Babylon Marduk-zâkir-shumi I asked the king of Assyria Shalmaneser III to intervene militarily in the affairs of his country.[51] Or Tiglath-pileser's actions could be in accordance with a treaty concluded previously between Assyrians and Babylonians.[52] Either way, the Assyrians and Babylonians had a common enemy: the Aramean tribes and later the Chaldean tribes, against whom Tiglath-pileser also intervened.

One may well wonder why Tiglath-pileser decided to direct his first campaign against Babylonia and the Aramean tribes when his main adversary was the king of Urartu. Wasn't it he who represented the real danger

---

47. Fales, "Arameans and Chaldeans," 294–95.
48. Brinkman, "Reflections on the Geography of Babylonia," 26–27.
49. Brinkman, *Prelude to Empire*, 6–19.
50. Garelli and Lemaire, *Les empires mésopotamiens, Israël*, 105–7.
51. RIMA 3:30–32, A.0.102.5, iv–vi.
52. Joannès, *Dictionnaire de la civilisation mésopotamienne*, 849.

6. THE FIRST PHASE OF THE CAMPAIGNS (745–744)

for Assyria? Certainly, because the king of Urartu was setting up a Syrian-Urartian coalition. From this perspective, the campaign against Babylonia and the Aramean tribes was important because it enabled Tiglath-pileser to protect his rearguard and to control the communication routes toward Iran and the Persian/Arabian Gulf.[53] But there were probably other reasons. The Aramean tribes, often unsettled, thieving, and plundering, even in the cities, represented a factor of disorder, especially since they moved to northern Babylonia, not far from Assyria, and because they had already confronted the Assyrians in the past. The Assyrian king also intended to help the Babylonian king who was in great difficulty, particularly if the latter had asked him for help or needed it in accordance with a previous treaty of alliance. However, Tiglath-pileser's helpful intervention was probably also self-interested, since the natural extension of the Assyrian territory was southward, into southern Mesopotamia. At least, this region had to be under the control of Assyria.

Was this first campaign a success? Tiglath-pileser obtained the submission of the Aramean tribes and pacified Babylonia, which allowed him to undertake new expeditions to other borders of Assyria. However, the pacification of these regions was only provisional, and new campaigns would be necessary to complete the king's goals.

6.2. The Campaign in the Central Zagros and Media

The Eponym List mentioned one campaign for year 744: "to Namri" (*a-na* KUR.*nam-ri*).[54] The passage of the annals is detailed but much damaged: "In my second *palû*, (the god) Aššur, [my] lor[d, encouraged me and I marched against the lands Namri, …], Bīt-Zatti, Bīt-Abdadāni, Bīt-Sangi[būti."[55] The country of Namri (KUR.*nam-ri*) was the first region reached in this campaign. It was located southeast of the Diyala River, near Zamua/Mazamua, which had been an Assyrian province in the region of Sulaymaniyah since the first half of the ninth century.[56] The three following toponyms are also preceded by the determinative KUR, but their locations remain uncertain, Bīt-Sangibûti possibly being identical with Shingibutu.

---

53. Garelli and Lemaire, *Les empires mésopotamiens, Israël*, 105.
54. SAAS 2:43, 59.
55. RINAP 1:29, 6.7–8; 84, 35.i.5′–6′.
56. Radner, "Provinz. C. Assyrien," 51–52, no. 22; John Nicholas Postgate, "Assyrian Army in Zamua," 89–108; SAA 15:xxv.

Indeed, the great majority of the toponyms belonging to the Zagros and western Iran, quoted in the campaign of 744, are unknown. Their historical geography in the Neo-Assyrian period is still controversial, and the results of the proposals of locations are so contradictory on many points that they simply confirm the state of uncertainty.[57] However, it is possible to distinguish some steps of this campaign.

After his first move against Namri, Tiglath-pileser continued for a second phase into a mountainous terrain of central Zagros. The continuity is marked by the repetition of the city of Nikur (Nikkur), which was first destroyed and then rebuilt. The enemy took refuge on the high mountain peak of Halihadri.[58] The Assyrian king pursued and defeated his enemies, then captured and plundered their cities, before placing a eunuch as provincial governor over them, creating the province of Parsua. Two rulers of this region are mentioned: Kakî, possibly ruler of Bît-Zatti in western Iran, whose name could be Iranian, and Tunaku, whose name is also Iranian, possibly king of Parsua, with Nikur as his capital.[59]

There was then a third step against different rulers whom Tiglath-pileser defeated, all of them probably also in western Iran since most of them had Iranian names. Mitâki was ruler of Urshanika and Kianpal: the Assyrian king conquered his cities and took him prisoner together with his family.[60] Bâtânu was ruler of the land of Bît-Kapsi, but he submitted and was therefore allowed to keep the city of Karkarihundir (in Media).[61] Bisihadir, ruler of the city of Kishesu, was defeated, and Ramateia, ruler of the country of Araziash, probably a Mede, fled "like a centipede," and no one found his hiding place.[62] The last ruler was Tunî (Tanus?) of the country of Sumurzu in Namri at the border of Ellipi.[63] Then it is mentioned that the countries of Sumurzu and Bît-Hamban were annexed to Assyria, and a eunuch was placed as provincial governor over them. Since Tunî was a

---

57. Julian E. Reade, "Kassites and Iranians in Iran," *Iran* 16 (1978): 137–43; Reade, "Iran in the Neo-Assyrian Period Geography," in Liverani, *Neo-Assyrian Geography*, 31 (with bibliography); SAA 15:xxiv.
58. RINAP 1:29, 6.8–12; 31, 7.1–6.
59. *PNA* 2.1:594–95; 3.2:1334; SAA 15:xxv, 259.
60. *PNA* 2.2:756–57.
61. *PNA* 1.2:277; SAA 15:258.
62. *PNA* 1.2:347; 3.1:1031; Karen Radner, "An Assyrian View of the Medes," in *Continuity of Empire (?) Assyria, Media, Persia*, ed. Giovanni Battista Lanfranchi, Michael Roaf, and Robert Rollinger (Padova: S.a.r.g.o.n., 2003), 45.
63. *PNA* 3.2:1334; SAA 15:xxv, 259.

6. THE FIRST PHASE OF THE CAMPAIGNS (745–744) 81

ruler of Sumurzu, it is possible that the previously mentioned rulers were rulers of the neighboring country of Bît-Hamban.

A final step is mentioned after the creation of the province, logically independent from it. Three "city rulers" (singular: *bēl-āli*) who refused to submit had to pay "300 talents of lapis lazuli, 500 talents of..., bronze...."[64] These rulers had names of different origins: Akkadian for Mannu-kî-sâbî of the country of Bît-Abdadâni, Iranian for Uzakku of the city of [...], and uncertain origin for Mikî of the city of Halpi.[65] Mannu-kî-sâbî could have been an Assyrian official in charge of Bît-Abdadâni, possibly linked to the neighboring province of Zamua.

The annalistic text of the Iran stela provides a summary of the second campaign. After a brief report of the military operations and their results, it mentioned the different payments of the tribute (*mandattu*): "I received the payment of Taltâ/Daltâ of the land of Ellipi, the city rulers of the lands of Namri, (Bīt)-Singibūti (Bīt-Sangibūti), the Medes, (and) all the eastern mountains: horses (and) mules broken to the yoke, Bactrian camels, oxen, [and] sheep and goats, without number."[66] From the text of the annals, we know that horses were given by the city of Nikur (in Parsua) and by the ruler Ramateia, the mules by Nikur, the sheep and goats by Ramateia, and Bactrian camels by the countries of Bît-Kapsi, Bît-Sangi, and Bît-Urzakki. Ellipi was also located in central Zagros, between the region of the Medes and Elam (Luristan). Ellipi was an independent kingdom, whose ruler had the title of "king" (*šarru*) and not "city lord" (*bēl āli*). Taltâ, who became a loyal vassal of Assyria from 744, was presented in Sargon's inscriptions as "a payer of tribute and tax to the kings, my fathers, who went before."[67]

During Tiglath-pileser's return march to Nimrud, he met Taltâ of the land of Ellipi, who had heard about his heroic deeds against the city rulers of the mountain regions and was terrified. Taltâ came to the city of Sumbi, next to Assyria, kissed the Assyrian king's feet according to tradition, and offered him a great variety of horses, majestic bulls, and fattened sheep.[68] Tiglath-pileser's scribes did not give Iranzu of Mannea

---

64. RINAP 1:33, 8.10–11; on the term, cf. Giovanni Battista Lanfranchi, "Esarhaddon, Assyria and Media," *SAAB* 12 (1998): 101, n. 7.
65. RINAP 1:33, 8.11–12; *PNA* 2.2:697; 3.2:750 and 1424.
66. RINAP 1:84, 35.11'–14'. Bît-Barrûa (l. 6') was a country of Ellipi: SAA 15:257.
67. Andreas Fuchs, *Die Inschriften Sargons II. aus Khorsabad* (Göttingen: Cuvillier, 1993), Ann. 96; Prunk. 117; Elayi, *Sargon II*, 169–70.
68. RINAP 1:84, 35.i.15'–20'.

the title of king, probably ignoring the mention, contrary to Sargon's scribes who stated it.[69] The kingdom of Mannea, famous for its fine horsemanship, occupied Iranian Kurdistan, western Azerbaijan, and part of eastern Azerbaijan, northeast of the Assyrian province of Zamua. Not much else is known about Mannea, but archaeological surveys have been started at the sites of Qale Bardine, Rabat Tepe, Kul Tarike, and Qalaichi Tepe where the so-called stela of Bukân was found, bearing an Aramaic inscription dated from the end of the eighth century.[70] Mannea was, in fact, caught between the two major powers, Assyria and Urartu, and the Urartian king unceasingly tried to remove it from the Assyrian influence.

Who were the city rulers of the central Zagros defeated by Tiglath-pileser? According to Assyrian cultural attitudes, they were "bad" enemies who behaved in various evil ways toward the "good" Assyrian king.[71] Assyrian elites had ideologically oriented judgments about the nature, culture, lifestyle, and political institutions of the Zagros peoples, based on standard prejudices and factual observations. These mountain dwellers were considered as barbarians lacking any civilized character, as opposed to the inhabitants of the urbanized plain. Since they had a tribal or familial

---

69. *ARAB* 2.6; Fuchs, *Die Inschriften Sargons II. aus Khorsabad*, 90–92, 315, Ann. 55–68.

70. Hassan Rezvani and Kourosh Roustaei, "A Preliminary Report on Two Seasons of Excavations at Kul Tarike Cemetery, Kurdistan, Iran," *IrAnt* 42 (2007): 139–84; Bahman Kargar and Ali Binandeh, "A Preliminary Report of Excavations at Rabat Tepe, Northwestern Iran," *IrAnt* 44 (2009): 113–29; Youssef Hassanzadeh, "Qal'e Bardine, a Mannean Local Chiefdom in the Bukan Area, North-Western Iran," *AMI* 41 (2009): 269–82; Hassanzadeh and H. Mollasalehi, "New Evidence for Mannean Art: An Assessment of Three Glazed Tiles from Qalaichi (Izirtu)," in *Elam and Persia*, ed. Javier Alvarez-Mon and Mark B. Garrison (Winona Lake, IN: Eisenbrauns, 2011), 407–17. On the stela of Bukān, see Rassoul Bashash Kanzaq, "Lecture complète de l'inscription de Bukân," in *Recueil d'articles du 1er colloque: Langues, inscriptions et textes anciens, Shiraz 12–14 Esfand 1370 (2–4 mars 1991)* (Tehran, 1375/1996), 25–39; André Lemaire, "Une inscription araméenne du VIIIe siècle av. J.-C. trouvée à Bukân," *SIr* 27 (1998): 15–30; Lemaire, "L'inscription araméenne de Bukân et son intérêt historique," *CRAI* (1998): 293–300; Israel Eph'al, "The Bukān Aramaic Inscription: Historical Considerations," *IEJ* 39 (1999): 116–21.

71. Giovanni Battista Lanfranchi, "The Assyrian Expansion in the Zagros and the Local Ruling Elites," in Lanfranchi, Roaf, and Rollinger, *Continuity of Empire (?)*, 79–118; J. Eidem, *Zagros Studies*, Proceedings of the NINO Jubilee Conference and Other Research on the Zagros Region (Leuven: Peeters, 2020).

organization and their lifestyle was prevailingly determined by transhumant pastoralism, they were considered to be at a low level of development and to have a primitive social status that was not regulated through a structured organization. Because of their mobility and a difficult geographical context, it was impossible to impose strict control over them. Normally, when an Assyrian province was created, the Assyrian governor replaced the local king and entered into an institutional relationship with the local bureaucracy. In central Zagros, Tiglath-pileser was faced with the preexisting village structure and the local rulers connected with this structure; therefore, he was obliged to retain the local rulers. The capture of the fugitives in the mountains proved difficult as Tiglath-pileser would find out in Mount Halihadri,[72] and the efforts needed to solve such problems would have necessitated costs much greater than the expected results. Therefore, the annexations in central Zagros were not carried out with the goal of establishing a strict control but with a tolerant approach to the local polities. One can wonder why Tiglath-pileser undertook to expand his empire in this area.

The geographical location of the Median settlements is not easy to decipher. The Assyrians distinguished the Medes from other peoples living in central Zagros. Herodotus credited Deioces with uniting the six Median tribes and forming Media with Ecbatana as capital; however, the Assyrian sources fail to support Herodotus's account.[73] In 835, Shalmaneser III had already received the tribute from Median rulers.[74] The region of the Medes could be reached from Assyria via the Namri/Bît-Hamban-Parsua route, the so-called Great Khorassan road, a part of the Silk road, following the valley of the Diyala into the Zagros to the Iranian plateau.[75] The second route was difficult for large armies: along

---

72. RINAP 1:31, 8.1–2.
73. Herodotus, *Hist.* 1.95–106; Stuart C. Brown, "The Medikos Logos of Herodotus and the Evolution of Median State," in *Method and Theory: Proceedings of the London 1985 Achaemenid History Workshop*, vol. 3 of *Achaemenid History*, ed. Amélie Kuhrt and Heleen Sancisi-Weerdenburg (Leiden: Nederlands Instituut voor het Nabije Oosten, 1987–1994), 71–86; Birgit Gufler, "Deiokes, Ekbatana und das Land der Meder," *KASKAL* 13 (2016): 125 n. 74. Authors such as Jo Ann Scurlock, "Herodotos' Median Chronology Again!," *IrAnt* 25 (1990): 149–63, have tried to accommodate Herodotus's information within the chronological framework presented by the Assyrian sources.
74. *ARAB* 2.24; Radner, "Assyrian View of the Medes," 38–40.
75. Michael Roaf, "Media and Mesopotamia: History and Architecture," in *Later*

the Zab, crossing Mount Kullar, then Hubushkia, reaching Mannea and Gizilbunda. The Medes were qualified in Tiglath-pileser's inscriptions as "mighty" (*dannu*), an unexpected term since other foreign peoples were usually described with depreciatory appellations. During Tiglath-pileser's reign, the Medes and men from Bît-Sangibûti were present at the royal court of Nimrud, as attested by the Nimrud Wine Lists and the personal name *Madāyu*, "the Mede," was in fashion.[76]

For the first time, Assyria directly controlled a territory situated along the Iranian part of the Great Khorassan road.[77] What were the reasons for Tiglath-pileser's campaign to central Zagros and Media? Some scholars have assumed that the Assyrian expansion in this area was intended as a response to possible aggressions or dangers coming from the mountain peoples if they went down to the Mesopotamian plain.[78] But the Zagros ruling elites were certainly conscious that they could not seriously threaten Assyria because of the Assyrian military superiority. Another reason invoked is Assyrian economic demands, which is not true because the Zagros regions had no specific products that could be considered worth the heavy costs of annexation: no renowned wood, no precious mineral resources, no stones, and no precious stones such as lapis lazuli, imported from Afghanistan, could be obtained through trade or tribute. Cattle, sheep, and goats could be obtained through tribute and were available from elsewhere. Tiglath-pileser was probably interested in horses, which became increasingly important for his war efforts. However, he could obtain horses through tribute and trade: under his reign emerged the function of *tamkār sisē*, the royal agents who procured horses.[79] When the camel came into regular use through caravans, trade across the desert competed with the two routes across central Zagros and Media and completely changed the relationship between Assyria, Elam, and Babylonia: it resulted in the decrease of Assyrian military involvement in the Zagros

---

Mesopotamia and Iran: Tribes and Empires 1600–539 B.C.; *Proceedings of a Seminar in Memory of Vladimir G. Lukonin*, ed. John E. Curtis (London: British Museum, 1995), 56–57, fig. 22. For the excavations in Media, see Mario Liverani, "The Rise and Fall of Media," in Lanfranchi, Roaf, and Rollinger, *Continuity of Empire (?)*, 2–4 (with bibliography).

76. CTN 1, 13.r.17′; SAA 6:13, 10.r.10; 28, 29.6; SAA 15:122, 182.6′.

77. Radner, "Assyrian View of the Medes," 44–45.

78. For the different reasons proposed, see Lanfranchi, "Assyrian Expansion in the Zagros," 96–104.

79. Dalley, "Foreign Chariotry and Cavalry," 47.

6. THE FIRST PHASE OF THE CAMPAIGNS (745-744)   85

area.[80] No. The main reason for Tiglath-pileser's campaign to central Zagros and Media can be explained by political needs.[81] It is important to note that this campaign occurred just before the campaign against Urartu and its allies in 743. The most urgent need was to prevent Zagros rulers from giving military support to Urartu, especially troops and horses. If Tiglath-pileser had not conducted the campaign of 744 in central Zagros and Media, those who were already allied with Urartu would have confirmed their alliance, those who were still neutral would have entered into the Urartian sphere of influence, and those who had been loyal to Assyria would have changed their allegiance toward Urartu. In short, the campaign was a matter of strategy: Tiglath-pileser wanted to protect his rear before attacking Urartu, and this action was complementary to his action against Babylonia and the Aramean tribes. The second campaign of 744 was a success in the sense that Tiglath-pileser achieved his strategic aim and was in a position to be able to turn his army against the Syrian-Urartian coalition, having secured the southern and eastern borders of the empire.[82] However, this success was certainly provisional and more campaigns would be necessary, all the more so since the establishment of Assyrian political supremacy in central Zagros and Media would have required profound social restructuring and would have been too costly compared with the expected results.

6.3. The Creation of New Provinces

Tiglath-pileser was not only a great conqueror; he was also a good administrator. It was not possible for him to extend the borders of Assyria and to annex new territories continuously without organizing them. He knew how to administer this vast empire by using a mixture of firmness and flexibility,[83] adopting his mode of government to the various situations on a case-by-case basis. The vassal states enjoyed a great deal of liberty on

---

80. McGuire Gibson, "Duplicate Systems of Trade: A Key Element in Mesopotamian History," in *Asian Trade Routes: Continental and Maritime*, ed. Karl Reinhold Haellquist, Studies on Asian Topics 13 (London: Routledge, 1991), 36; Radner, "Assyrian View on the Medes," 52; Simonetta Ponchia, "Mountain Routes in Assyrian Royal Inscriptions: Part II," *SAAB* 15 (2006): 222–31.
81. Lanfranchi, "Assyrian Expansion in the Zagros," 98–104.
82. Garelli and Lemaire, *Les empires mésopotamiens, Israël*, 107.
83. Garelli and Lemaire, *Les empires mésopotamiens, Israël*, 110–13.

condition that they remained loyal to Assyria and that they paid the tribute and taxes. Any revolt against the tax collectors was crushed by the corps of Itueans who reestablished order. A dense net of messengers was settled throughout the whole empire, and the slightest incident was immediately reported to the court of Nimrud. This kind of organization was not completely new because it already existed under the reign of Adad-nârârî III and probably before, but what was new under the reign of Tiglath-pileser was that it was systematically extended to the whole empire. The vassal states were tightly monitored and the Assyrian provinces were administered by governors who had garrison troops at their disposal and who levied tribute. All this organization called for considerable means, both human and material, and relied necessarily on local peoples.

The administrative archives contain several general geographical lists, dealing with names of the provinces or cities.[84] Forrer based his pioneering study related to the Neo-Assyrian provincial system particularly on a multi-columned list of place names, presented by geographical sectors, possibly dated from the reign of Ashurbanipal.[85] Karen Radner has recently resumed investigations on this subject and has listed the identified and the uncertain neo-Assyrian provinces, with an attempt to give the date of their creation and their location.[86] In central Assyria, Radner listed provinces that existed before Tiglath-pileser's reign: Arbail, Arzuhîna, Assur, Isâna, Nimrud, Kilizu, Kurbail, Nêmed-Ishtar, Nineveh (Ninûa), Shimu, Talmussu, and three provinces of the high officials: commander-in-chief, treasurer, chief cupbearer (*turtānu, mašennu, rab šāqê*).[87] Then are listed the new provinces created as a result of the expansion of Assyria in the ninth century: Amedi, Arrapha, Gûzâna, Habruri, Zamua, Nasibîna, Raqamâtu, Rasappa, Shahuppa, Tillê, and Tushhan (whose capital corresponded to the modern city of Ziyaret Tepe), and in the first half of the eighth century: Hindânu, Lâqê, Lubda, Si'immê, Shibhinish, and Tamnunu.[88]

---

84. SAA 11:xiii–xv, 4–13, 1–14.
85. Forrer, *Die Provinzeinteilung des assyrischen Reiches*, 52. This text could alternatively be a lexical list: SAA 11:XIV, 4–6, 1.
86. Radner, "Provinz. C. Assyrien," 42–68.
87. Radner, "Provinz. C. Assyrien," 45–49.
88. Radner, "Provinz. C. Assyrien," 49–56. Some provinces were created after Tiglath-pileser's reign: *turtānu šumēlu* (no. 13), *mār šarri* (no. 17), Dûr-Sharrukin (no. 30), Halzi-adbâri (no. 31), Harrânu (no. 32), and Til Barsip (no. 39); John MacGinnis

6. THE FIRST PHASE OF THE CAMPAIGNS (745–744)

Tiglath-pileser enlarged the old provinces with newly conquered lands and cities and launched a massive politics of annexation, but the new provinces that he created were not always easy to identify. The king more or less followed the same procedure as in his first campaign of 745. After defeating the Aramean tribes and destroying their cities, Tiglath-pileser rebuilt the cities, annexed those areas to Assyria, placed a eunuch as provincial governor over them, imposed tax and tribute, and deported part of the population.[89] He also installed the "weapon of Assur" (*kak Aššur*) in the Assyrianized local capitals. One of these rebuilt cities was Humut east of the Tigris: "[Inside (it), I founded] a palace for my royal residence. I named it Kār-Aššur, set up the weapon of (the god) Aššur, my lord, therein, (and) settled the people [of (foreign) lands] conquered by me therein. [I] imposed upon them [tax (and) tribute], (and) considered them as inhabitants of Assyria."[90] At the same place, he erected a stela bearing his image and an account of his victories.[91] This new province (*pīhat*) was possibly the province of Lahîru east of the Tigris, between the Diyala and the Nahr al-Uzaim.[92] After defeating a second group of tribes as far distant as the Persian/Arabian Gulf, he probably created another province about which we have no information.[93]

During his second campaign, Tiglath-pileser created two new provinces, starting with Parsua: "I rebuilt [the city] of Nikur, together with the cities in its environs, settled the people of (foreign) lands conquered by me therein. [… I pl]aced [a eunuch of mine as provincial governor over them]."[94] Nikur was the capital of Parsua. The creation of this province could be explained by the political status of Parsua and by its interactions with the neighboring lands in the previous years: it had expanded its territory in countries that were allied to Assyria such as the city of Kitpattia.[95] The other new province created in 744 was Bît-Hamban, next

---

and Timothy Matney, "Archaeology at the Frontiers: Excavating a Provincial Capital of the Assyrian Empire," *Journal of Assyrian Academic Studies* 23 (2009): 3–21.

89. RINAP 1:26–27, 5.1–10.
90. RINAP 1:27, 5.3–4; 29, 6.3; Joannès, *Dictionnaire de la civilisation mésopotamienne*, 850; for the location of Humut, see RGTC 7/2-1, 237.
91. RINAP 1:29, 6.4–5.
92. Radner, "Provinz. C. Assyrien," 57, no. 44. *Lā'ir* in the Bible (2 Kgs 19:13; Isa 37:13).
93. RINAP 1:27, 5.7–8.
94. RINAP 1:31, 7.5; 84, 35.5'–10'; Radner, "Provinz. C. Assyrien," 57, no. 45.
95. Lanfranchi, "Assyrian Expansion in the Zagros," 100–102; Radner, "Assyr-

to the province of Lahîru, in the region of the Diyala.⁹⁶ The annals are explicit on this annexation: "I an[nexed] the lands of Sumurzu (and) Bīt-Ḫamban to Assyria. [(…)] I settled [the people of (foreign) lands conquered by me therein] (and) placed a eunuch of mine as provincial governor over them."⁹⁷ Tiglath-pileser had just defeated Tunî, king of Sumurzu, in a violent manner, by impaling his warriors. As Sumurzu was located in the Namri, the new province of Bît-Hamban integrated the Namri or part of it.

Other provinces were created by Tiglath-pileser after 744 during his subsequent campaigns. The provinces governed by the highest officials were important border provinces, which formed a kind of crescent protecting Assyria.⁹⁸ These governors had a significant role in administering the neighboring vassal states; information reports were sent from the vassal states directly to the king and indirectly through the high officials for a double control. Through the vassal states also passed the natural routes by which resources like timber reached heartland Assyria. Among the six provinces of the high officials, three were quoted in Tiglath-pileser's annals: the province of the "commander-in-chief" (*turtānu*), created in the ninth century and located toward the north along the Upper Euphrates as far as modern Murad-Su; the province of the "chief cupbearer" (*rab šāqê*), existing from the ninth century and located along the ridge of the Zagros Mountains, northwest of Aqra;⁹⁹ and that of the "palace herald" (*nāgir ekalli*), located east of Habruri in the western Zagros along the Urartian border and created by Tiglath-pileser.¹⁰⁰ A letter from Nergal-uballit,

---

ian View of the Medes," 57 and table 7. Forrer, *Die Provinzeinteilung des assyrischen Reiches*, 94, erroneously situated in Parsua the *rab-ša-rēši* province, followed by Florence Malebran-Labat, *L'armée et l'organisation militaires de l'Assyrie d'après les lettres des Sargonides trouvées à Ninive* (Geneva: Droz, 1982), 156.

96. Radner, "Provinz. C. Assyrien," 57, no. 41.
97. RINAP 1:32, 8.6–7.
98. SAAS 11:138–39.
99. Forrer's location in the Kashieri Mountains (*Die Provinzeinteilung des assyrischen Reiches*, 107–10) was contested by Karlheinz Kessler, *Untersuchungen zur historischen Topographie Nordmesopotamiens* (Wiesbaden, 1980), 123–25; Shigeo Yamada, "Ulluba and Its Surroundings: Tiglath-pileser III's Province Organization Facing the Urartian Border," in *Neo-Assyrian Sources in Context: Thematic Studies of Texts, History, and Culture*, ed. Shigeo Yamada (Helsinki: Neo-Assyrian Text Corpus Project, 2018), 22–26.
100. RINAP 1:27, 5.10; Radner, "Provinz. C. Assyrien," 48–49, no. 12, 15, 16;

6. THE FIRST PHASE OF THE CAMPAIGNS (745–744) 89

governor of Ahi-zuhina, to Tiglath-pileser provides information on the location of *bēt sartinni* and *bēt sukalli*, south of the province of Ahi-zuhina.[101] These were probably lands owned by the *sartinnu* and the *sukkallu* in the province of Ahi-zuhina, not administrative units in their charge.[102]

The province of Barhalzi was first mentioned in Tiglath-pileser's inscriptions of the campaign of 745. It was located in heartland Assyria, northwest of Nineveh.[103] The Assyrian king had created the province of Ulluba (Ashur-Iqîsha, later Birtu) in 739 in northern Mesopotamia on the Urartian border and probably the province of Halzi-adbari, northwest of the province of Ulluba.[104] The province of Arpad in north Syria was created in 740, after the fall of the city.[105] Tiglath-pileser created the province of Damascus in 732.[106] In 738, he created the province of Hatarikka, east of the province of Simirra.[107] The province of Haurâna (Hauranu) must not be confused with the province of Harrân; it was probably located in the present Syrian region of Hauran (Jabal al-Druze massif) and may have been created in 732.[108] The province of Kullania (Unqi), located in north Syria in the loop of the Orontes, was created in 738.[109] The province of Magiddû (Megiddo) was created by Tiglath-pileser, possibly in 732 accord-

---

SAAS 11:137–39. The existence of this province under Tiglath-pileser has been questioned by John Nicholas Postgate, "Assyria: The Home Provinces," in Liverani, *Neo-Assyrian Geography*, 8.

101. SAA 19:93, 89.16–20; SAAS 11:81–82, 97–99.

102. Postgate, *Taxation and Conscription*, 38.

103. RINAP 1:25, 5.10; SAA 19:62, 56.r.6; 57.6; Radner, "Provinz. C. Assyrien," 53–54, no. 29.

104. RINAP 1:43, 13.12; 98, 39.25, 28; 103, 41.27', 29'; 121, 47.43; 130, 49.6'–7'; SAA 19:68, 65.8; Radner, "Provinz. C. Assyrien," 39–40, no. 40; 54, no. 31; Mikko Luukko, "The Governors of Halzi-atbari in the Neo-Assyrian Period," in *Studies in Honour of Nicholas Postgate*, ed. Yağmur Heffron, Adam Stone, and Martin Worthington (Winona Lake, IN: Eisenbrauns, 2017), 321–33.

105. RINAP 1:39, 12.2'; 109, 43.i.25; SAA 19: 3, 47.r.11; 57, 52.i.2; 63, 57.15; Radner, "Provinz. C. Assyrien," 58, no. 46.

106. RINAP 1:38, 11.4'; 59, 20.17'; 87, 35.iii.4; SAA 19:6, 3.s.3; 50, 44.r.4; 51, 45.8; Radner, "Provinz. C. Assyrien," 58, no. 48.

107. RINAP 1:42, 13.7; 74, 30.3; 105, 42.1'; 109, 43.ii.16; 131, 49.r.1; 134, 50.r.1; Radner, "Provinz. C. Assyrien," 58, no. 50.

108. RINAP 1:109, 43.ii.1; 140, 53.14; Radner, "Provinz. C. Assyrien," 58, 61, no. 51.

109. RINAP 1:40, 12.5'; 46, 14.5; 68, 26.3; 109, 43.ii.15; 115, 46.20; 131, 49.26'–27'; 134, 50.1'–2'; SAA 19:99, 96.3; Radner, "Provinz. C. Assyrien," 61, no. 61.

ing to the Bible.[110] The province of Mansuate, in north Syria between the Orontes and the province of Simirra, was created in 732.[111] The province of Qarnîna (Qarnê), located east of the Jordan and above the Yarmuk River, was possibly created by Tiglath-pileser in 732; it corresponded to the biblical Karnaim, now Sheikh Saad.[112] The Phoenician city of Simirra (Sumur) was first added to the province of the chief cupbearer and then turned into an Assyrian province in 738.[113] The province of Tu'ammu is first mentioned in Tiglath-pileser's inscriptions as a province or provincial capital; it can be located at Al-Tawwâma, 29 km west of Aleppo.[114]

The province of Subutu would have been created in 732; it would have been the ancient Aramean kingdom, absorbed by the Aramean kingdom of Hamath in the first half of the eighth century, situated in the Lebanese Beqa'.[115] Was there a province of Hamath? It depends on the interpretation of the following passage concerning the campaign of 738: "I annexed to Assyria (those) nineteenth districts of the city Hamath.... I placed two eunuchs of mine as provincial governors over them." These districts were constituted as two provinces, possibly integrated into the provinces of Simirra and Hatarikka.[116] Du'ru (biblical Dor) was maybe not constituted as a province but integrated into the province of Megiddo and possibly established as an Assyrian *kāru*.[117] In 732, according to the Bible, Tiglath-

---

110. 2 Kgs 15:29; Radner, "Provinz. C. Assyrien," 61, no. 53; Peter Zylberg, "The Assyrian Provinces of the Southern Levant: Sources, Administration, and Control," in *The Southern Levant under Assyrian Domination*, ed. Shawn Zelig Aster and Avraham Faust (University Park, PA: Eisenbrauns, 2018), 56–88.

111. SAA 19:46, 40.8; Radner, "Provinz. C. Assyrien," 61, no. 54.

112. RINAP 1:85, 35.ii.7'; SAA 19:48, 41.r.2; Radner, "Provinz. C. Assyrien," 61–62, no. 56.

113. RINAP 1:98, 39.30; 114, 46.18; 130, 49.14'; SAA 19:49, 43.r.11, 15–16; Radner, "Provinz. C. Assyrien," 62, no. 60.

114. Radner, "Provinz. C. Assyrien," 62–63, no. 61; Lipiński, *Aramaeans*, 344–45.

115. RINAP 1:46, 14.8; 70, 27.1; 86, 35.ii.14'; Radner, "Provinz. C. Assyrien," 63, no. 63; Lipiński, *Aramaeans*, 203.

116. RINAP 1:76, 31.5–8; SAA 19:50, 44.r.5; Radner, "Provinz. C. Assyrien," 66, no. 83; Lipiński, *Aramaeans*, 314–15.

117. Radner, "Provinz. C. Assyrien," 66, no. 81; Nadav Na'man, "Did the City of Dor Serve as the Capital of an Assyrian Province?," *ErIs* 29 (2009): 310–17; Ayelet Gilboa and Ilan Sharon, "The Assyrian *kāru* ar Dor (Ancient Du'ru)," in *The Provincial Archaeology of the Assyrian Empire*, ed. John MacGinnis, Dirk Wicke, Tina Greenfield, and Adam Stone, McDonald Institute Monographs (Cambridge: McDonald Institute for Archaeological Research, 2016), 241–52.

6. THE FIRST PHASE OF THE CAMPAIGNS (745-744) 91

pileser annexed the territories of Gilead and Galilee, but we do not know whether he integrated them into a neighboring province.[118] We have listed seventeen (or twenty?) new provinces created by Tiglath-pileser, out of a total of around thirty-one provinces existing before his reign. This number is high, but he probably created even more.

Some governors in charge of provinces during Tiglath-pileser's reign are known by name: those of the ancient provinces such as Nabû-belu-uṣur governor of Arrapha (then of Simme?), Bêl-Dân governor of Nimrud, Adad-bêlu-ka"in governor of Assur, Bêl-êmuranni governor of Rasappa, Ninurta-ilâya governor of Nisibîna, Ashur-shallimanni governor of Arrapha, Ashur-da"inanni governor of Zamua, Bêl-lû-dâri governor of Tillê, Liphur-ilu governor of Habruri, Dur-Ashur governor of Tushhan, and Shamash-bunaya, prefect and possibly governor of northern Babylonia.[119] The governors of the new provinces included Nergal-uballit governor of Ahi-zuhina, Ashur-remanni governor of Kullania, Bêl-duri (?) governor of Damascus, Ninurta-bêlu-usur governor of Arpad, Qurdi-ashur-lâmur governor of Simirra, Sulaya governor of Tu'imme (?), and Shamash-ahu-iddina (?) governor of Subutu. It is important to note that Tiglath-pileser systematically reported (about forty times) that he appointed his eunuchs as provincial governors, but he never mentioned their names.[120] This means that Tiglath-pileser was extremely cautious in the choice of men for administering the new annexed territories, opting for those who were supposedly the most loyal. The fact that the eunuchs were nameless in the royal inscriptions could prevent them from becoming over-ambitious. However, in correspondence exchanged with Tiglath-pileser, the governors who were probably eunuchs, or at least some of them, were obliged to mention their names, for example: "To the king, my lord: your servant Bêl-duri. Good health to the king, m[y] lord!"[121]

---

118. RINAP 1:13; 2 Kgs 15:29; Zvi Gal, "The Lower Galilee between Tiglath-pileser III and the Beginning of the Persian Period," *ErIs* 29 (2009): 77-81.
119. SAAS 2:59; SAA 19:xvii-xviii.
120. May, "Administrative and Other Reforms of Sargon II and Tiglath-pileser III," 107; RINAP 1:27, 31-32, 40, 43-45, 53, 76, 83-84, 92, 97-98, 100, 102-3, 105, 113-5, 118-19, 121, 130-31, 134, 136, 138.
121. SAA 19:174, 172.1-3.

6.4. A New Deportation Policy

The creation of numerous provinces was linked to a new policy of mass deportations in Tiglath-pileser's global strategy. Tiglath-pileser was certainly not the first Assyrian king to employ the technique of mass deportations. Before him, several kings carried out mass deportations of civilians in conquered regions. Some minimal figures can be calculated based on the royal inscriptions: 12,900 for Ashurnasirpal II; 167,500 for Shalmaneser III; and 32,200 for Shamshî-Adad V.[122] The use of deportations to relocate prisoners of war was not only an Assyrian practice but also a practice throughout the Near East and Egypt since the third millennium.[123] However, Tiglath-pileser was the first to use the technique of deportation on such a scale and as part of a deliberate program of political and economic expansion. He was also the initiator of crossed deportations, in which a conquered region was partly emptied of its inhabitants and repopulated by deportees coming from a remote region.[124] The minimal figures of deportees calculated for his reign were 368,543 + 25,055.[125] Tiglath-pileser's strategy of deportations was applied right from his very first campaign: "[From] those [Ara]means whom I deported, [I distribut]ed (and settled [… thousand to the province of the commander-in-chief, 10,000 (to) the province of the palace herald, […] thousand (to) the province of the chief cupbearer, [… thousand (to) the province of the land] of Barḫa(l)zi, (and) 5,000 (to) the province of the land of Zamua."[126] Tiglath-pileser's aim was clearly to move the deportees as far away as possible from their countries of origin to the borders of the empire and to scatter them in countries distant one from the other. In fact, the province of the commander-in-chief was located in the northwest, the provinces of the chief cupbearer and of Barhalzi were north of heartland Assyria, and the provinces of the palace herald and of Zamua were in the eastern border.[127]

---

122. Bustenay Oded, *Mass Deportations and Deportees in the Neo-Assyrian Empire* (Wiesbaden: Reichert, 1999), 20; Daniel Sarlo, "The Economics of Mass Deportations in the Neo-Assyrian Period under Tiglath-Pileser III (744–727 BCE)," *NMC* 1020 (2013): 1.

123. Oded, *Mass Deportations and Deportees*, 42 (with bibliography).

124. Joannès, *Dictionnaire de la civilisation mésopotamienne*, 227–30; Sarlo, "Economics of Mass Deportations," 1–21.

125. Oded, *Mass Deportations and Deportees*, 20.

126. RINAP 1:27, 5.9–10.

127. Radner, "Provinz. C. Assyrien," 42–68.

6. THE FIRST PHASE OF THE CAMPAIGNS (745–744) 93

What were Tiglath-pileser's reasons for adopting this strategy of mass deportations? Deportation was first of all a punishment for populations who had not accepted the Assyrian yoke and who had revolted, such as the Aramean tribes.[128] Thus, deportees are represented as prisoners, who, along with cattle, are led away from a Babylonian city on a relief in Tiglath-pileser's palace.[129] The fact that people were expelled from their homes and their homeland was a very severe punishment. Deportation was also a deterrent to prevent rebellion. For example, the Assyrian king carried off the royal family of Hanunu of Gaza to Assyria as hostages before returning Hanunu to his position as king, so that he would not dare to revolt again.[130] Mass deportations were performed in recalcitrant states and sources of potential danger, such as Arpad, Hamath, or Damascus. The uprooting of the inhabitants weakened their link with their homeland and reduced the possibility of a national revival. Their dispersal in various places was a way of breaking up nationalistic entities. As the deportees formed a minority group in their new communities, they had no other choice than to be loyal to the Assyrian king who became their only protector. That is why many deportees were settled in border towns and sensitive border areas, in order to provide a kind of buffer against hostile states. Conversely, their deportation created space for Assyrians to set up a permanent and efficient administrative and military organization in the occupied areas, the homeland of the deportees. Tiglath-pileser used the deportees in his defense policy: they were integrated into the army, in particular in the infantry. This was a means to enlarge the Assyrian army, which became more and more a necessity because of the continuous expansion of the empire. These conscripted deportees had no sentimental attachment to the country where they were employed, which was usually far from their homeland. Thus, the Assyrian army became multiethnic. Mass deportation was also a source of skilled professional workers and craftsmen, often brought to the heartland of Assyria to work for the king. These workers were distributed as needed; for example, they could be sent to newly founded cities to work on building projects, such as palaces and temples.[131] Another objective of mass

---

128. Oded, *Mass Deportations and Deportees*, 41–74; Sarlo, "Economics of Mass Deportations," 3–13.
129. Barnett and Falkner, *Sculptures*, 52–53, pls. V–VI (BM 118882).
130. RINAP 1:127, 48.14′–18′.
131. Max E. L. Mallowan, *Nimrud and Its Remains*, vol. 1 (London: Collins, 1966), 75–76; Melanie Gross, "Craftsmen in the Neo-Assyrian Empire," in *What's in a Name?*

deportation was demographic: to populate older cities as new and rebuilt cities and as strategic cities. When Tiglath-pileser destroyed a city, he usually sent deportees there to rebuild it and resettle the land. For example, in his first campaign, he rebuilt Humut, calling it Kâr-Assur, settled people there from conquered foreign lands, and imposed tax and tribute upon them as inhabitants of Assyria.[132]

Another objective was to repopulate abandoned or desolate regions and to employ the deportees for agricultural labor. A letter from Tiglath-pileser to Ninurta-bêlu-usur referred to this kind of deportee: "this cornfield that is under cultivation is for the deportees who are coming. When they come from Damascus, there are 100 (homers of) wheat and 20 (homers of) barley to send them from Orontes."[133] In a damaged passage of the annals, the Assyrian king probably used the Aramean deportees for cultivating "the abandoned settlements on the periphery of my [land] that had bec[ome] desolated [during the reign(s) of (previous) kings], my [ancestor]s, ..."[134] Expanding the empire not only had political interests for the Assyrian king, but also economic interests. Tiglath-pileser replaced the old technique of pillaging and destroying cities with a strategy that was more economically sensible and sustainable. Exploiting rather than killing the prisoners was certainly a more profitable operation. That is why the king also used deportees for securing trade routes leading to the resources that he needed and reestablishing long distance trade, in particular for metals such as silver, tin, copper, and iron.[135] Apart from skilled craftsmen, Tiglath-pileser also required unskilled laborers. The deportees were brought to the heartland of Assyria to produce grain for important cities such as Nimrud, Assur, and Nineveh. Archaeological discoveries have shown that specialized sites serving as satellite farms sur-

---

Terminology Related to the Work Force and Job Categories in the Ancient Near East, ed. A. Garcia-Ventura, AOAT 440 (Münster: Ugarit-Verlag, 2018), 369–95.

132. RINAP 1:27, 5.3–4.
133. SAA 19:6, 3.s.1.
134. RINAP 1:27–28, 5.11–12.
135. N. B. Jankowska, "Some Problems of the Economy of the Assyrian Empire," in *Ancient Mesopotamia: Socio-economic History*, ed. Igor Mikhailovich Diakonoff (Moscow: Nauka, 1969), 253–76; Frederick Mario Fales, "Palatial Economy in Neo-Assyrian Documentation: An Overview," in *Palatial Economy in the Ancient Near East and in the Aegean First Steps towards a Comprehensive Study and Analysis*, ed. Pierre Carlier, Francis Joannès, François Rougemont, and Julien Zurbach (Rome: Fabrizio Serra Editore, 2017), 171–294.

rounded these cities.[136] It was cheaper to use deportees than to hire native Assyrians as farmers.

Tiglath-pileser's economic strategy is also revealed by his decision not to deport populations when this was deemed more beneficial. A wealthy city posing no threat to the empire provided an alternative source of wealth: tribute and tax. If this exceeded the value of deportation and resettlement, the Assyrian king preferred the option of leaving the city autonomous, as was the case, for example, for most of the Phoenician and Philistine cities. To accompany and safeguard this option, Assyrian spies were responsible for monitoring the loyalty of Assyrian vassals.[137] In brief, the use or nonuse of mass deportation by Tiglath-pileser was highly innovative and contributed to the foundation of the Assyrian Empire.

The numerous deportations that Tiglath-pileser decided to carry out during his campaigns to the different borders of the empire[138] seem, most of the time, to have been carefully planned and, in so doing, provide answers to the following questions: is it beneficial to deport such-and-such population? What inhabitants must be chosen to become deportees? To which country should they be deported? What other deportees have to be settled in place of them? Even if the journey of the deportees was well organized by the Assyrians, who authorized them to take their family with them, together with their cattle and their goods, the conditions of the displacement were very harsh due to exhaustion, the difficulty in finding supplies, and epidemics linked with the volumes of the transferred populations. The death rate during the journey could reach between 5 and 20 percent.[139] When the deportees arrived at their destination, they were suitably welcomed and settled in their new homes. Tiglath-pileser repeated several times in his annals that he wanted to integrate the deportees, treating them exactly as Assyrians, with the same rights and duties. For example, when he settled 555 captive highlanders from Bît-Sangibûti in the city of Til-karme, he wrote: "I considered [them] as inhabitants of Assyria, (and [imposed upon

---

136. Bradley J. Parker, "Archaeological Manifestations of Empire: Assyria's Imprint on Southeastern Anatolia," *AJA* 107 (2003): 541.

137. Villard, "Quelques aspects du renseignement militaire dans l'empire néo-assyrien," 87–97.

138. RINAP 1:27, 43–44, 46, 53, 55, 59, 61–63, 65, 68, 70, 97, 100, 102, 119, 121; Oded, *Mass Deportations and Deportees*, 116–35.

139. Joannès, *Dictionnaire de la civilisation mésopotamienne*, 228–29.

them the corvée labor like that of the Assyrians]."[140] At the same time, Tiglath-pileser allowed the deportees to retain their distinctive culture. The socioeconomic and legal status of the deportees was not uniform; their conditions were not identical but depended on their occupations, on their employers, on their personal ability, and on where they lived.[141] Anyway, the consequences of the mass deportation conducted by Tiglath-pileser were an enormous mixing of populations, an increase in the multi-ethnicity of the Assyrian Empire, and the acceleration of the diffusion of Aramaic as the common language of the empire.

---

140. RINAP 1:70, 27.1–2.
141. Oded, *Mass Deportations and Deportees*, 75–115.

7
THE SECOND PHASE OF THE CAMPAIGNS (743–738)

7.1. The Campaigns against the Coalition of Syria and Urartu

After having provisionally secured the southern and eastern borders, Tiglath-pileser observed a respite before attempting to deal with Assyria's worst enemy: Urartu. The timing of the campaign was probably part of Tiglath-pileser's overall strategy, but he was also forced to intervene against a coalition that was forming against Assyria. Therefore, between 743 and 740, Assyrian campaigns focused on Urartu and the unruly states of north Syria. In 746 or possibly in 744, Sarduri II, king of Urartu, conquered Kummuhu and subdued its king Kushtashpi, as reported in his annals: "The gods opened [for] me the road. Hastily, I marched against the land of Qumaha. Uita, a royal city, a fortified one, I conquered in battle. Halpa, a royal city, located on a lake, I conquered."[1] Since the Urartian annals for the years following the conquest of Kummuhu are missing, the date of the conquest is debated. An approximate date circa 750 was suggested by Trevor Bryce.[2] The date of 746 or 744 was proposed by Dan'el Kahn and is more probable than that of 743 (proposed by Mirjo Salvini), because the events in Kummuhu could not be so condensed.[3] Now, the Assyrian kings had never relinquished their claims to the states of north Syria. Adad-nârârî III had restored Assyrian sovereignty over them, but it

---

1. HchI, 124, 103, §9.IV; CTU 1, 424–426, A.9-3.IV; Krzysztof Hipp, "Sarduri II: One of the Most Unfortunate Rulers of the Eighth Century B.C.E.," *Recherches archéologiques* NS 5–6 (2014): 87–100.
2. Bryce, *World of the Neo-Hittite Kingdoms*, 114.
3. Astour, "Arena of Tiglath-pileser III's Campaign," 5; Mirjo Salvini, *Geschichte und Kultur der Urartäer* (Darmstadt: Wissenschaftliche Buchgesellschaft, 1995), 72–76; Dan'el Kahn, "The Kingdom of Arpad (Bīt-Agūsi) and 'All Aram': International Relations in Northern Syria in the Ninth and Eighth Centuries BCE," *ANES* 44 (2007): 83.

was lost under his weak successors. In 754, Ashur-nârârî V reimposed a treaty of vassalage on Mati'-ilu, king of Arpad (Bît-Agusi). But Sarduri II was expanding the kingdom of Urartu and invaded north Syria. His target was the Neo-Hittite kingdom of Qumaha (Kummuhu in Akkadian; later known as the Greco-Roman Commagene).

The kingdom of Qumaha was situated north of the present border between Syria and Turkey. It was encircled to the east by the bend of the Euphrates and separated by a mountain range from the northern kingdom of Melid.[4] Its capital city, which bore the same name (Kummuhu), has been identified with the modern city of Samsat (classical Samosata). The site has been lost in modern times, having been flooded by the waters of the Atatürk dam, and only preliminary reports of excavations of this site have been published.[5] The remains of the later kingdom of Commagene (163 BCE–72 CE) are better known (in particular, the ruins of the mountaintop sanctuary of Nemrud Dag). The Malpinar rock inscription (first half of the eighth century), composed in Luwian hieroglyphics, mentions the "city of Kumaha."[6] Generally, Kummuhu's rulers remained loyal to the Assyrian kings and received some support from them in their conflicts with other states west of the Euphrates, at least until Kushtashpi was forced to break his Assyrian allegiance to become a tributary of Urartu. Tiglath-pileser conquered Kummuhu in 743, forgave Kushtashpi, and allowed him to resume his throne as an Assyrian loyal vassal. Consequently, during the long conquest of Syria, the Assyrian king incorporated Kummuhean troops as part of his army. In 732, when Damascus became an Assyrian province, two thousand warriors of the king of Kummuhu were listed as part of the Assyrian forces in the province.[7]

The Syrian-Urartian coalition of 743 was fomented either by Sarduri of Urartu[8] or by Mati'-ilu of Arpad, according to the different royal inscriptions:

---

4. John David Hawkins, "The Political Geography of North Syria and South-East Anatolia in the Neo-Assyrian Period," in Liverani, *Neo-Assyrian Geography*, 92.

5. Machteld Mellink, "Archaeology in Asia Minor," *AJA* 84 (1980): 501–18; Jörg Wagner, ed., *Gottkönige am Euphrat: Neue Ausgrabungen und Forschungen in Kommagene* (Mainz: von Zabern, 2000), 74, fig. 99.

6. Mustafa Kalaç and John David Hawkins, "The Hieroglyphic Luwian Rock-Inscription of Malpinar," *AnSt* 39 (1989): 107–12.

7. SAA 1:135, 172.27–28.

8. RINAP 1:98, 39.20; 103, 41.17'; 122, 47.47 (Sarduri).

7. THE SECOND PHASE OF THE CAMPAIGNS (743–738)

In my third *palû*, Matiʾ-ilu, [the son of A]ttaršumqa (Attar-shumkî), fomented a rebellious insurrection against Assyria and violated (his loyalty oath). [He sent] hostile messages about Assyria [to] the kings ... of the land of Ḫatti (and) ... the land of Urarṭu and (thus) caused en[mity] in all (those) lands. Sarduri of the land of Urarṭu, [Sulum]al of the land of Me[lid], (and) Tarqularu (Tarḫulara) of the land of Gurgum [came] to [his] aid.[9]

Besides Matiʾ-ilu and Sarduri, the coalition was joined by Sulumal of Melid, Tarhulara of Gurgum, and Kushtashpi of Kummuhu.[10] Melid was another Neo-Hittite kingdom, classical Melitene, identified with modern Arslantepe, 7 km northeast of Malatya.[11] The extent of its territory is defined by the Luwian hieroglyphic inscriptions, centered in the plain of Malatya on the west bank of the Upper Euphrates, below the junction of the Kara-Su and Murad-Su branches. The kingdom extended westward along the routes to Anatolia and into the plain of Elbistan. In the ninth century BCE, Melid was known from Urartian and Assyrian inscriptions to have been a strategic kingdom and a flourishing cultural center.[12] But during the first half of the eighth century, Assyrian pressure was replaced by Urartian pressure: Khilaruata, the ruler of Melid, was defeated and forced to pay tribute to Urartu.[13] The ceremonial hall excavated in Melid has been dated to ca. 750–710 and probably corresponds to the period of Assyrian domination after 743.[14]

---

9. RINAP 1:84, 35.i.21′–24′.
10. RINAP 1:122, 47.46; PNA 2.2:745; 3.1:1157; 3.2:1315; 2.1:644.
11. John Garstang and O. R. Gurney, *The Geography of the Hittite Empire* (London: British Institute of Archaeology at Ankara, 1959), 47; Simo Parpola and Michael Porter, *The Helsinki Atlas of the Near East in the Neo-Assyrian Period* (Helsinki: Neo-Assyrian Text Corpus Project, 2001), 17; Hawkins, "Political Geography of North Syria and South-East Anatolia," 88–90, finds it best placed in the plain of Elbistan; Bryce, *World of the Neo-Hittite Kingdoms*, 98–110.
12. Marcello Frangipane and Mario Liverani, "Neo-Hittite Melid: Continuity or Discontinuity?," in *Across the Border: Late Bronze-Iron Age Relations between Syria and Anatolia*, ed. K. Alishan Yener, ANESSup 42 (Leuven: Peeters, 2013), 359–60.
13. Mario Liverani, "Melid in the Early and Middle Iron Age, Archaeology and History," in *The Ancient Near East in the Twelfth–Tenth Centuries BCE, Culture and History: Proceedings of the International Conference Held at the University of Haifa, 2–5 May 2010*, ed. Gershon Galil et al. (Münster: Ugarit-Verlag, 2012), 340–41 (with bibliography); PNA 1.1:129–130.
14. Frangipane and Liverani, "Neo-Hittite Melid," 360.

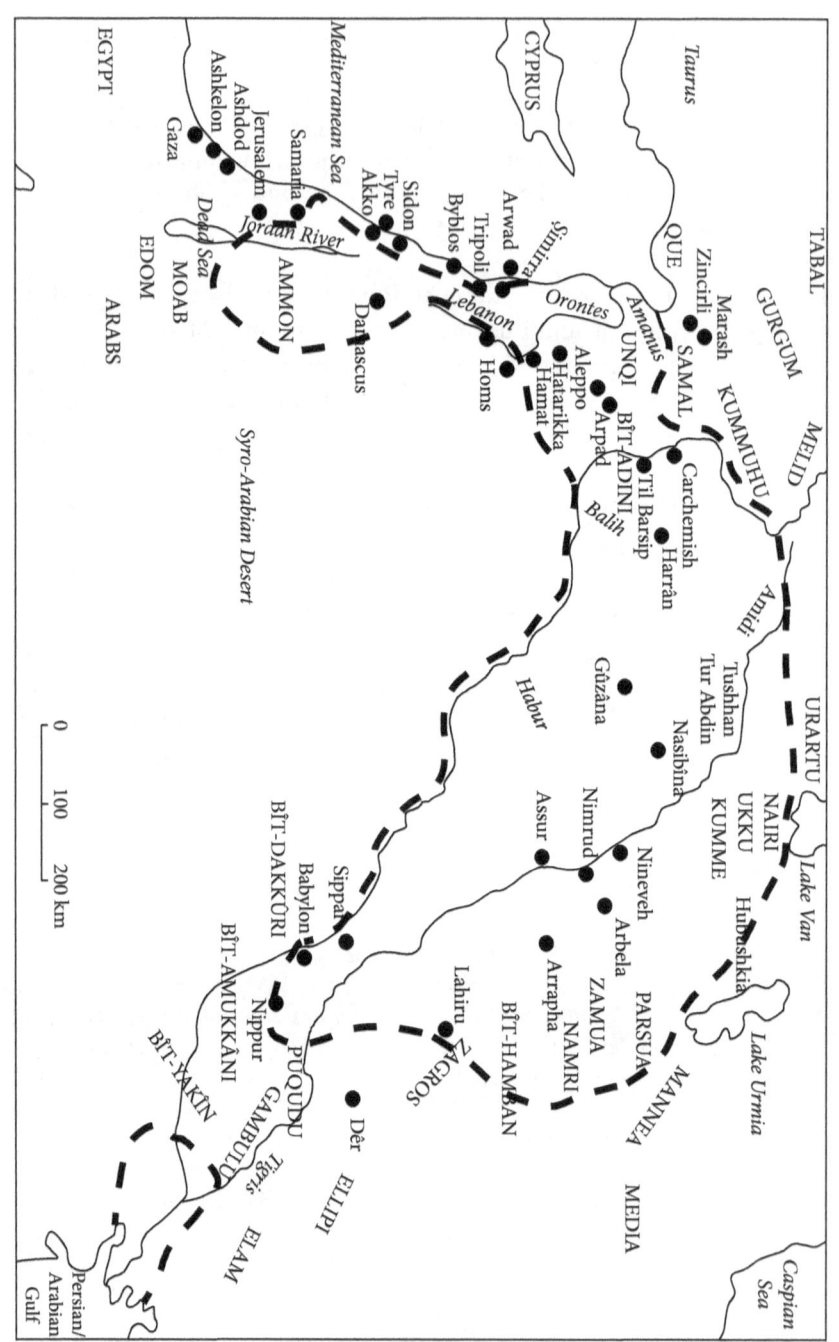

Fig. 3. The Assyrian Empire ca. 727 BCE

7. THE SECOND PHASE OF THE CAMPAIGNS (743-738) 101

Gurgum was the other Neo-Hittite kingdom that joined the anti-Assyrian coalition. Its capital was Markasi/Markasa (modern Marash); it was located west of Tabal and about 120 km northwest of Carchemish. The kingdom included principally the plain of Marash on an upper stretch of the Ceyhan River where it is joined by the Aksu River coming down from Pazarcik.[15] To the north, the kingdom was separated from the plain of Elbistan by high mountains. There was a rift valley running southward down to the east side of the Amanus to the Amuq plain. A relatively large number of Luwian hieroglyphic inscriptions were found at or in the vicinity of Marash.[16]

The identity of the leader of the anti-Assyrian coalition is contradictory in the Assyrian inscriptions. The Iran stela, which is dated from 737 and is the earliest account of the episode, refers to Mati'-ilu as leader. With this being the most reliable source, Urartian involvement in north Syria cannot be explained by an Urartian expansion and policy to control north Syria. Sarduri was somewhat encouraged to take part in the coalition at the request of Mati'-ilu.[17] Although Mati'-ilu was linked to Assyria by his treaty with Ashur-nârârî V, he apparently took advantage of the king of Assyria's death to break his treaty and to foment a rebellion along with the north Syrian and Anatolian states against Assyrian rule.[18] Tiglath-pileser responded by attacking the anti-Assyrian forces in 743. He labored to reach the point of confrontation, employing forced marches, all day and night, to do so. He did not allow his soldiers to rest; he gave them no water to drink and did not allow them to pitch camp or bivouac. Even if the account is exaggerated, it showed Tiglath-pileser's determination to crush the coalition. According to his annals, the battle was easily and quickly won: "I fought [with th]em, defeated them, (and) took their camp(s) away from them."[19]

The account of this episode reported in the Assyrian inscriptions is clear, in spite of some lacunae:

---

15. Wolfgang Röllig, "Maraş," *RlA* 3 (1957-1971): 703-4; John David Hawkins, "Marqas," *RlA* 7 (1990): 352-53; Hawkins, "Political Geography of North Syria," 93-94 (with bibliography); 101, fig. 1; Lorenzo d'Alfonso, "Tabal, an 'Out-Group' Definition in the First Millennium BCE," in Battista Lanfranchi et al., *Leggo!*, 173-94.
16. Bryce, *World of the Neo-Hittite Kingdoms*, 122-28.
17. Kahn, "Kingdom of Arpad (Bīt-Agūsi) and 'All Aram,'" 83-84.
18. SAA 2:8-13, 2; Lipiński, *Aramaeans*, 595-97; Bryce, *World of the Neo-Hittite Kingdoms*, 167-68.
19. RINAP 1:85, 35.i.27'-31'.

Bet]ween the lands of Kištan and Ḫalpi, districts of the land of K[ummuḫu, I (utterly) defeated them.... With the blood of] their [warr]iors [I dyed] the Sinzi River as red as dyed wool. I defeated him [Sarduri] and took his entire camp away from him. He became frightened of the terrifying radiance of my weapons and fled alone in order to save his life.[20]

The battle took place in the kingdom of Kummuhu, but the exact location remains imprecise: near the Sinzi River and mountain gorges,[21] between the "countries" (singular *mātu*) of Kishtan and Halpi, which were "districts" (singular *nagiu*) of the "city" (*ālu*) of Kummuhu. There is some debate regarding the location of the battle: Astour examined all the propositions and suggested identifying Kishtan with modern Keysun and Halpi as an ancient mount on the eastern shore of Lake Gölbaşi.[22] In an inscription reporting both Assyrian campaigns of 743 and 735 against Urartu, Sarduri is said to have escaped during the night, mounting a mare and fleeing to Mount Sizir (probably modern Malatya Dağlari). This episode is possibly related to Sarduri's defeat in 743.[23] According to the annals, Tiglath-pileser pursued Sarduri to the bridge or causeway (*titurri*) crossing the Euphrates.[24] This was probably a floating bridge, situated next to the fortress of Tumeshki, an Urartian advanced base, where the river is calm and relatively narrow.[25] The bridge was probably destroyed just after the passage of Sarduri and his troops. In order to compensate for the fact that he had not captured Sarduri, the Assyrian king described in detail the booty collected in his camp: his pavilion, his royal tent, the bed that he offered to Ishtar, his processional chariot, his royal chariot, the cylinder seal that hung around his neck, his necklace, and many other items.[26]

Tiglath-pileser's battle against the Syrian-Urartian coalition was also briefly mentioned in the Eponym List, but the events of year 743 are difficult to understand: *ina* URU.*ar-pa-da* [*d*]*i-ik-tú ša* KUR.*ur-ar-ṭi di-*

---

20. RINAP 1:122, 47.47–49; 98, 39.21–23.
21. RINAP 1:34, 9.7'; 122, 47.48.
22. Astour, "Arena of Tiglath-pileser III's Campaign," 9–14.
23. RINAP 1:129, 49.1'–2'; on Mount Sizir, see Ariel M. Bagg, *Die Assyrer und das Westland: Studien zur historischen Geographie und Herrschaftspraxis in der Levante im 1. Jt.v.u.z.*, OLA 216 (Leuven: Peeters, 2011), 78.
24. RINAP 1:35, 9.10'–12'.
25. Astour, "Arena of Tiglath-pileser III's Campaign," 15.
26. RINAP 1:35, 9.11'–12', 14'–16'.

7. THE SECOND PHASE OF THE CAMPAIGNS (743-738)

kat.[27] This sentence has been translated differently by Millard, "In Arpad; defeat of Urartu made," and by Tadmor, "The land Urarṭu [was defea]ted at the city Arpad."[28] Since Arpad was besieged for a period of three years, it would have been impossible to enter the city in 743.[29] The entry of 743 is problematic. Anyway, there were probably two different sentences concerning Arpad and Urartu. The scribe could have made a mistake: "in" (*ina*) Arpad, instead of "to" (*ana*) Arpad, as it was written in the entries for the following three years (742–740).

After the battle against the coalition, Tiglath-pileser conquered one hundred cities of the land of Gurgum. He forced king Tarhulara into submission, but he accepted the defeated king's plea to spare his royal capital. Tarhulara was also allowed to retain his throne as an Assyrian vassal.[30] Tarhulara is subsequently attested as an Assyrian tributary in 738 and 732 and continued to occupy his kingdom's throne until circa 711.[31] Sulumal of Melid and Kushtashpi of Kummuhu were also allowed to retain their thrones as they are attested among the tributaries in 738 and 732.[32] How can this conciliatory policy of Tiglath-pileser be explained? It was certainly more beneficial for him that these Neo-Hittite states became his Assyrian vassals, rather than to annex them. Tiglath-pileser defeated Sarduri, but he could not do more since he never caught up with him. However, after a long interval, Tiglath-pileser reestablished a minimal Assyrian political presence in the region. Thus ended the short-lived Urartian interference in north Syria.

7.2. The Fall of Arpad and Its Consequences

Only one member of the Syria-Urartian coalition was treated differently by Tiglath-pileser: Mati'-ilu, king of Arpad. How was he treated and why? This episode is not mentioned in the preserved annals, but it was no doubt included in a section that is now missing. The only source is

---

27. SAAS 2:43, 59.
28. SAAS 2:59; RINAP 1:17.
29. Kahn, "Kingdom of Arpad (Bīt-Agūsi) and 'All Aram,'" 84–85.
30. RINAP 1:85, 35.i.32′–42′.
31. RINAP 1:70, 27.5; 122, 47.r.8′; Bryce, *World of the Neo-Hittite Kingdoms*, 128.
32. RINAP 1:38, 11.7′: 70, 27.5; 122, 47.r.8′; Bryce, *World of the Neo-Hittite Kingdoms*, 109, 114.

therefore the Eponym List.³³ Tadmor considered as problematic the fact that Arpad was mentioned four times in the years 743, 742, 741, and 740 and that its siege was said to have lasted three years.³⁴ But Kahn partly solved this problem by proposing that actions against Arpad were undertaken over a three year period, from 743 to 741, and that after the capture of the city in 741, the following year (740) was used to complete the deportations and the reorganization of Arpad as an Assyrian province.³⁵ To totally solve the problem, I would add that 743 was the first year of the campaign "against" Arpad and not "in" Arpad, as it was written erroneously by the scribe.

There is no information on the course of the siege or on the capture of the city. After the city fell, we do not know whether Mati'-ilu escaped and took refuge in the mountains as other fugitives from Assyrian authority had done or whether he was captured and then deported or executed. In any case, the kingdom of Arpad was turned into an Assyrian province, the first of the western states to be brought directly under Assyrian control during Tiglath-pileser's reign. Even if there is no account of this event, mention is made of an Assyrian governor, probably a eunuch, being installed in the capital of this new province. Part of the population of Arpad was deported, and they were replaced by settlers brought in from other parts of the Assyrian Empire.³⁶ The first mention of Arpad after its fall was in 738, when Tiglath-pileser received tribute from this city, but the text is too damaged to identify who the tributaries were.³⁷

Now what were the reasons for such a treatment being inflicted on Mati'-ilu? Unlike the other north Syrian kings of the coalition who were forgiven, Mati'-ilu of Arpad was bound to Assyria by a treaty, and he had violated it. Tiglath-pileser could not accept such a betrayal. There was another reason: Tiglath-pileser had decided to conquer the kingdom of Arpad. The difficulties experienced by the Assyrian kings in subjugating the territories across the Euphrates were mainly due to the interference of Arpad, which had become a major power in north Syria during the

---

33. SAAS 2:43–44, 59.

34. Hayim Tadmor, "Azriyau of Yaudi," in *Scripta Hierosolymitana 8: Studies in the Bible*, ed. Christian Rabin (Jerusalem: Magnes Press, 1962), 254.

35. Kahn, "Kingdom of Arpad (Bīt-Agūsi) and 'All Aram,'" 84–85.

36. Bryce, *World of the Neo-Hittite Kingdoms*, 261–63.

37. RINAP 1: 39, 12.1'–2'. Text no. 12 possibly continued text no. 11 as Tadmor has suggested, but it is incomprehensible why line 1' (no. 12) repeated line 10' (no. 11).

7. THE SECOND PHASE OF THE CAMPAIGNS (743-738) 105

ninth century.[38] This kingdom was engaged in several confrontations with the Assyrians and had acted as a focus for anti-Assyrian activities in the region. In the eighth century, Arpad had probably received the support of Urartu, which was seeking to extend its authority beyond the Euphrates into north Syria and southeastern Anatolia, in concurrence with Assyria. After 755, Matiʾ-ilu probably expanded his authority southward and subjugated the kingdom of Hamath.[39] Ashur-nârârî V's campaign against Arpad in 754 is only attested in the Eponym List and Sarduri's annals.[40] Yet, even if there is no evidence of the victory claimed by Sarduri, Ashur-nârârî decided to neutralize the alliance between Arpad and Urartu by signing a treaty, which he drew up with Matiʾ-ilu, king of Arpad. His aim was to isolate Matiʾ-ilu from Urartu and to ensure that he remained separate from states such as Damascus. Peace for the Assyrians lasted only a few years until Ashur-nârârî's death when Matiʾ-ilu broke his treaty. Tiglath-pileser's strategy consisted of conquering the nearest kingdoms and annexing them to Assyria, and the first kingdom in the west to be affected by this decision was Arpad. This conquest was a springboard to further conquests westward into Syria. The crushing of the Syrian-Urartian coalition and in particular the fall of Arpad had considerable international consequences. It prompted several western rulers to pledge allegiance to the Assyrian king by sending tribute when Tiglath-pileser was still in Arpad. Thus, Rahiânu (biblical Rezin) of Damascus sent three talents of gold (111 kg) and three hundred talents of silver (742 kg); other western rulers mentioned alongside him include Kushtashpi of Kummuhu, Ittobaʿal (Tubaʾil) of Tyre, Uriakki (Urikki) of Que, Pisîris of Carchemish, and Tarhulara of Gurgum.[41]

7.3. The Campaign against Ulluba

Tiglath-pileser might have thought that, with the fall of Arpad and the allegiance of several western rulers, the situation in the west was under control, at least provisionally. That is why, in 739, he undertook a campaign

---

38. Lipiński, *Aramaeans*, 195–219; Kahn, "Kingdom of Arpad (Bīt-Agūsi) and 'All Aram,'" 66–89; Bryce, *World of the Neo-Hittite Kingdoms*, 256–59.
39. Kahn, "Kingdom of Arpad (Bīt-Agūsi) and 'All Aram,'" 82.
40. SAAS 2:59; HchI, 116, 102.r.I; *PNA* 1.1:208.
41. RINAP 1:38, 11.1ʹ–10ʹ; 39, 12.1ʹ–2ʹ.

against Ulluba.⁴² The country of Ulluba, which was probably the wide plain across which the Lesser Habur flows, represented an immediate danger for Assyria because it was located only about 100 km north of Nineveh, it was under Urartian influence, and it had rebelled.⁴³ This Assyrian campaign is reported at length, with many details provided, particularly in the Mila Mergi inscription. Even though the inscription is damaged, the various steps of the campaign can be deduced.⁴⁴ The people of Ulluba, as well as the Ahlamû, "had not regularly done obeisance" to the previous kings; they did not bring gifts to Tiglath-pileser and did not recognize his authority. Instead, they planned evil, spoke belligerently against Assyria, and continuously committed sinful deeds. The Assyrian king ordered his troops to march first to Halziatbar, a rebellious land located on the road to Urartu in difficult mountains, in the region of Dohuk in today's Iraqi Kurdistan.⁴⁵ Mount Ilimeru has been identified with Zaw-e Dağ, southwest of Čiyâ Bêhêr (Mount Nal).⁴⁶ The account of this episode was engraved in the Mila Mergi rock inscription, northwest of Dohuk.

Now Amadînu must not be confused with the province of Amidi (Nairi), which was created by Ashurnasirpal II and was situated next to the province of Tushhan.⁴⁷ Most of the twenty-nine cities of Ulluba captured and plundered by the Assyrian army cannot be identified, as several names are damaged. The people of these cities, terrified, fled to a fortress situated in the treacherous terrain of Mount Ilimeru. Apparently, the fortress was seized, and the country was turned into the Assyrian province of Ulluba or Ashur-iqîsha, referred to later as Birtu from the word for "fortress": "I [re]organized those cities in their entirety (and) settled there the people of (foreign) lands conquered by me. [I placed] a eunuch [of mine as provincial governor over them] (and thereby) I annexed those (areas) [to] Assyria."⁴⁸ Tiglath-pileser erected a monument on Mount Ilimeru; the

---

42. SAAS 2:59.
43. RGTC 7/2-2, 625–26; Joannès, *Dictionnaire de la civilisation mésopotamienne*, 850; Yamada, "Ulluba and Its Surroundings," 11–40.
44. RINAP 1:36, 10.1′–8′; 91–92, 37.16–54.
45. RGTC 7/2-1, 201–2.
46. RGTC 7/2-1, 244; 7/2-2, 445–46.
47. RINAP 1:36, 10.7′; RGTC 7/2-1, 42.
48. RINAP 1:92, 37.43–44; Radner, "Provinz. C. Assyrien," 56–57, no. 40; Yamada, "Ulluba and Its Surroundings," 27–29. Deportees from Ulluba were probably entrusted to Ninurta-ilâya, governor of Nasibîna, according to a letter of Nabû-êṭiranni (SAA 19:65).

monument bore an inscription and his royal image engraved on it. The king addressed the usual curse against the one who would obliterate or destroy the inscription and gave a blessing to a future ruler who would "read aloud] this inscription, [wash (it) with water], anoint (it) with oil, (and) [make an offering]."[49] This inscription was probably the Mila Mergi inscription, which was engraved during, or immediately after, the campaign against Ulluba and is its principal historical source. Later, maybe in 736, Tiglath-pileser built Ashur-iqîsha, the new capital of the province of Ulluba, in order to reinforce Assyrian control on the border of Urartu. After the creation of the province of Ulluba, he probably created the province of Halzi-adbari, northwest of Ulluba, presumably in the Cizre-Şirnak zone, east of the Tigris.[50]

7.4. The Second Campaign to the West

In spite of the fall of Arpad and the allegiance of several western rulers, other western states obstinately carried on with their revolt against Assyria, with the result that just two years later, in 738, Tiglath-pileser was obliged to undertake a second campaign to the west, a large-scale one. He marched to north Syria, first to Unqi (ancient Patin) in the Amuq plain. Unqi's capital was Kullania (Kunalîa, Kinalîa), which is probably to be identified with Tell Tayinat.[51] The kingdom of Unqi seems to have remained submissive to Assyria since the reign of Salmaneser III, that is, if it is possible to judge from the absence of any reference to it in the Assyrian inscriptions. In 738, "[Tutammû, king of the land Unqi], neglected [the loyalty oath (sworn by) the great gods] (and thereby) disregarded his life. *On my campaign* [... he did not con]sult me."[52] Tiglath-pileser was furious; he deposed the rebellious king, deported him with his nobles, and captured his royal city of Kullania. In a letter addressed to the Assyrian king, Ninurta-ilâya, possibly governor of Nasibîna, reported that Tutammû would come with his eunuchs before the king.[53] The Assyrian king boasted by having installed

---

49. RINAP 1:92, 37.51–53.
50. RINAP 1:91, 37.23; Radner, "Provinz. C. Assyrien," 54, no. 31; Luukko, "Governors of Halzi-atbari," 321–33; Yamada, "Ulluba and Its Surroundings," 29–27, 34.
51. John David Hawkins, "Cilicia, the Amuq, and Aleppo," *NEA* 72 (2009): 171; Bryce, *World of the Neo-Hittite Kingdoms*, 130–33.
52. RINAP 1:39, 12.3′–4′.
53. SAA 19:61, 55; *PNA* 2.1:550; 3.2:1337.

his throne in Tutammû's palace.⁵⁴ He distributed his possessions, in particular mules, sheep, and goats among the Assyrian army, and he carried off booty from the palace: twenty talents of gold, three hundred talents of silver, battle equipment, multi-colored garments, linen garments, and all types of aromatics. Then he reorganized Kullania, subdued all the land of Unqi, and placed his eunuchs as governors over it. If there was only one province, it did not need multiple governors, but as the text is damaged, another province was probably mentioned in a missing line. In another passage, two governors are mentioned for the provinces of Unqi and Arpad, and in still another, only one governor is mentioned for the province of Unqi.⁵⁵ Then Tiglath-pileser settled 600 captives from the city of Amlatu of the tribe of Damunu and 5,400 captives from the city of Dêr in Kullania and other cities of Unqi. In the meantime, while Tiglath-pileser was campaigning in the west, the governor of Nairi (Amidi) captured the city of Supurgillu (yet unidentified) and other cities in the environs, continuing the military operation of the previous year along the Upper Tigris. The governor of Zamua captured cities located "behind the fortress of the Babylonians."⁵⁶ While the passage is very badly damaged, these governors or Shiqilâ, a fortress commander, brought the booty to the Assyrian king in Unqi.⁵⁷

Tiglath-pileser then marched to Hatarikka, east of the Orontes.⁵⁸ The ancient kingdom of Luash had been incorporated into the kingdom of Hamath by 800 at the latest, perhaps by an Aramean king of Hamath named Zakkur, whose stela has been found at Tell Afis, a fortified urban center in northwestern Syria. Hatarikka would have served as Luash's capital.⁵⁹ Hatarikka is quoted along with Nuqudina in a text that reflects the provincial administration of the land of Hamath and where defined borders between and within states were firmly established in the local tradition.⁶⁰ The king of Assyria violently criticized Azariyau, the king of

---

54. RINAP 1:40, 12.7′–8′, 11′–12′; 131, 49, 26′–27′.
55. RINAP 1:115, 46.20–21; 131, 49.26′–27′; 134, 50.1′–2′.
56. RINAP 1:45–46, 14.1–4; 68, 26.1–3; 43–44, 13.14–20.
57. *PNA* 3.2:1267.
58. Hawkins, "Neo-Hittite States in Syria and Anatolia," 389.
59. Bryce, *World of the Neo-Hittite Kingdoms*, 133–34.
60. RINAP 1:42, 13.7; 74, 30.3; 105, 42.1′; 109, 43.ii.16; 131, 49.1; 134, 50.r.1; Tadmor, *Inscriptions of Tiglath-pileser III*, 60–61 n. 7; Radner, "Provinz. C. Assyrien," 58, no. 50.

7. THE SECOND PHASE OF THE CAMPAIGNS (743–738) 109

Hatarikka, who had "criminally and sinfully seized" nineteen districts of the city of Hamath.[61] The annexation of Hatarikka was not described in as much detail as that of Unqi, but it was mentioned together with the creation of other provinces in this area, especially the province of Simirra.[62]

In 738, Tiglath-pileser received the tribute of Panammû, king of Sam'al, and decided that it was not necessary to annex his kingdom.[63] Thus, the province of Sam'alla (Sam'al) was not created by Tiglath-pileser but by his successors.[64] Panammû is to be identified with Panamuwa II, son of Barsur, a loyal vassal whom Tiglath-pileser had saved from a palace conspiracy, then installed on the throne between 743 and 740. Panammû also personally participated in Assyrian campaigns to Syria.[65] Archaeological remains that were discovered at the capital of Zincirli (modern Höyuk in Turkey) are mainly attributed to his son Bar-Rakib.[66]

The city of Hamath, located on the Orontes, was the capital of a large and important kingdom of the same name in the tenth–ninth century. It is frequently attested in Assyrian and biblical sources.[67] In 738, the political influence of Hamath extended not only to the coastal cities in the region of Latakia, such as Ushnû, Gubla, and Siyân, but also to Simirra, Arqâ, and Kashpûna.[68] However, rather than turning Hamath into an Assyrian province,[69] Tiglath-pileser dismantled major parts of its territory and integrated them into different provinces. Beforehand, he recuperated the nineteen districts of Hamath seized by Azariyau

---

61. RINAP 1:42, 13.1–3; 76, 31.7–8; *PNA* 1.1:240.
62. RINAP 1:105, 42.1'–5'.
63. RINAP 1:47, 14.12; 70, 27.4; 77, 32.4; 87, 35.iii.17; 122, 47.r.8'.
64. Radner, "Provinz. C. Assyrien," 62, no. 58.
65. John C. L. Gibson, *Aramaic Inscriptions*, vol. 2 of *Textbook of Syrian Semitic Inscriptions* (Oxford: Clarendon, 1975), 79, no. 14.7; *KAI* 223, 215.7; Hélène Sader, *Les États Araméens de Syrie depuis leur fondation jusqu'à leur transformation en provinces Assyriennes* (Beirut: In Kommission bei Franz Steiner Verlag, 1987), 176–93; Lipiński, *Aramaeans*, 243–44; *PNA* 3.1:983.
66. J. D. Schloen and A. S. Fink, "New Excavations at Zincirli Höyuk in Turkey (Ancient Sam'al) and the Discovery of an Inscribed Mortuary Stele," *BASOR* 356 (2009): 7–10; Bryce, *World of the Neo-Hittite Kingdoms*, 169–75.
67. 2 Sam 9–10; 1 Chr 18:9–10; 2 Kgs 14:28; Sader, *Les États Araméens de Syrie*, 194–226; Bryce, *World of the Neo-Hittite Kingdoms*, 133–38.
68. Lipiński, *Aramaeans*, 286–87.
69. Radner, "Provinz. C. Assyrien," 66, no. 83.

of Hatarikka.⁷⁰ Other parts of the territory of Hamath were possibly incorporated into the neighboring provinces of Hatarikka and Simirra.⁷¹ Eni'ilu remained king but now in a reduced kingdom of Hamath.⁷² Eni'ilu is mentioned as having made an appeal to the commander-in-chief in an undated letter addressed to Tiglath-pileser by Shamash-ahu-iddina, chief eunuch active in the west.⁷³ Eni'ilu paid tribute in 738 with other western rulers: Menahem of Samaria, Hiram II of Tyre (the successor of Ittoba'al II), Sibitti-bi'il (Shipitba'al II) of Byblos, Panammû of Sam'al, Sulumal of Melid, Dadîlu of Kaska, Uassurme of Tabal, Ushitti of Tuna, Urballâ of Tuhana, Tuhamme of Ishtunda, Urimmi of Hubishna, and Zabibe queen of the Arabs.⁷⁴

The Syrian coast, from the Djebel al-Aqra (Mount Ba'ali-sapûna) to the foot of Mount Lebanon and Ammanâna (Anti-Lebanon), and its hinterland were incorporated into the Assyrian Empire in 738. The inscriptions relating this episode are much damaged, and it is difficult to know the names of all the conquered cities and the number and names of provinces created. It was the first time that Phoenician cities were subdued by the Assyrians.⁷⁵ However, this was not Tiglath-pileser's aim but a consequence of the submission of the hinterland. The identifiable cities conquered were Rêshi-sûri, Maarabâ, Ahtâ, Gubla, Usnû, Siannu, Arqâ, Kashpûna, Zimarra, and Simirra. The city of Rêshi-sûri, situated between Mount Lebanon and Mount Sapûna (Saphon), was annexed to Assyria.⁷⁶ Rêshi-sûri could be Râs Ibn Hânî, located 9 km northwest of Latakia, or Qalaat ar-Rûs, located 14 km southeast of Latakia.⁷⁷ The city of Maarabâ, whose name must be partially restored, could be identified with *Ma'araba(y)*, an important settlement mentioned in many texts from Late Bronze Age Ugarit.⁷⁸ The city of Ahtâ, "the emporium(s)" (*bēt kāri*) on the seashore,

---

70. RINAP 1:43, 13.10–11; 76, 31.6–8; 85, 35.ii.9'; 109, 43.ii.20.
71. Radner, "Provinz. C. Assyrien," 66, no. 83.
72. RINAP 1:46, 14.12; 70, 27.4; 77, 32.4; 122, 47.r.8'; PNA 1.2:397.
73. SAA 19:42, 37.12–17; PNA 3.2:1189.
74. RINAP 1:46–47, 15.10–12; 70, 27.2–7; 77–78, 32.1–12.
75. Elayi, *History of Phoenicia*, 146–47.
76. RINAP 1:86, 35.ii.11'–12'; 105, 42.3; 109, 43.ii.19.
77. Lipiński, *Aramaeans*, 291.
78. RINAP 1:105, 42.3'; PRU 3:266b (index); Florence Malbran-Labat and Pierre Bordreuil, *Une bibliothèque au sud de la ville*, Ras Shamra-Ougarit 7 (Paris: La Mission Archéologique Française de Ras Shamra-Ougarit, 1991), no. 4, 24; Lipiński, *Aramaeans*, 290.

7. THE SECOND PHASE OF THE CAMPAIGNS (743–738) 111

was perhaps located at Râs al-Bassit, 50 km north of Latakia.[79] The city of Gubla, while easily confused with Byblos, must not be equated with that Phoenician city. It should rather be identified with Gabala (modern Jeble), located 20 km south of Latakia.[80] The city of Usnû would correspond to Tell Darûk, southeast of Jeble.[81] Siannu was located 8 km east of Jeble, corresponding to Tell Sianû, which was excavated by Adnan Bounni and Michel Al-Maqdissi.[82] The city of Arqâ, today Tell Arqâ, is a large tell situated 17 km north of Tripoli in Lebanon, in the plain of Akkar; the break between Levels 10 and 9 corresponding to the annexing of the site is characterized by the disappearance of the city walls, the rarity of fine ware, and imported ware.[83] The city of Kashpûna has been traditionally identified with Kûsbâ, some 12 km inland, between Tripoli and Batrûn.[84] However, Lipiński has contested this identification under the pretext that

---

79. RINAP 1:85, 35.ii.12′; Lipiński, *Aramaeans*, 291–92; Paul Courbin, *Fouilles de Bassit: Tombes du Fer* (Paris: Recherche sur les civilisations, 1993).

80. RINAP 1:105, 42.2′; 109, 43.ii.16; Josette Elayi, "Studies in Phoenician Geography during the Persian Period," *JNES* 41 (1982): 86–92; Elayi, "Les sites phéniciens de Syrie au Fer III/Perse: Bilan et perspectives de recherche," in *Essays on Syria in the Iron Age*, ed. Guy Bunnens (Leuven: Peeters, 2000), 337–38; John Lund, "The Northern Coastline of Syria in the Persian Period: A Survey of Archaeological Evidence," *Trans* 2 (1990): 13–36.

81. RINAP 1:42, 13.3′; 46, 14.6; 68, 26.5; 105, 42.3′; 109, 43.ii.18; Elayi, "Les sites phéniciens de Syrie au Fer III/Perse," 335; Edward Lipiński, *Dictionnaire de la civilisation phénicienne et punique* (Turnhout: Brépols, 1992), 488; Valentina Melchiorri and Paolo Xella, *Historical Characters*, vol. 1 of *Encyclopedic Dictionary of Phoenician Culture* (Leuven: Peeters, 2018).

82. RINAP 1:42, 13.5; 46, 14.6; 68, 26.5; 85, 35.ii.10′; 105, 42.3′; 109, 43.ii.18; Adnan Bounni and Michel Al-Maqdissi, "Compte-rendu de la cinquième campagne de fouilles à Tell Sianū sur la côte syrienne," *AoF* 25 (1992): 257–64; Al-Maqdissi, "Notes d'archéologie levantine VIII: Stratigraphie du chantier de Tell Sianu (plaine de Jablé)," *Syria* 83 (2006): 229–46.

83. RINAP 1:46, 14.6; 68, 26.5; 105, 42.2′; 109, 43.ii.17; 115, 46.22; 131, 49.r.1; 134, 50.r.1; Jean-Paul Thalmann, "Tell 'Arqa de la conquête assyrienne à l'époque perse," *Trans* 2 (1990): 51–57; Lipiński, *Aramaeans*, 288; Anis Chaaya, "L'évolution et le changement culturel à Tell 'Arqa après l'invasion de Tiglath-pileser III (Niveaux 10-9)," in *Proceedings of the First International Congress on the Archaeology of the Ancient Near East (Rome, May 18th–23rd 1998)*, ed. Paolo Matthiae et al. (Rome: Dipartimento di Scienze Storiche, Archeologiche e Antropologiche dell'Antichità, Univ. degli Studi di Roma "La Sapienza," 2000), 213–19.

84. RINAP 1:42, 13.5; 105, 42.51; 115, 46.22; 126, 48.8′; 131, 49.r.1; 134, 50.r.1; Hayim Tadmor, "'Rashpuna'—A Case of Epigraphic Error," *ErIs* 18 (1985): 180–82;

the city was described as being on the seacoast.[85] His objection cannot be accepted since Arqâ and Siannu, also inland, were said to be on the coast, but the Assyrian scribes failed to apply precise details to the geography of this new region. The city of Zimarra can best be identified with *Zi-im-ma-ri*, a city mentioned in the Ugaritic texts and possibly located near the marshes of the Ghâb.[86] (For Simirra, see below.) Tiglath-pileser did not conquer the neighboring cities: northward, Al-Mina at the mouth of the Orontes, southward, Tell Sukas south of Jeble, and the Phoenician city of Arwad due south of Tell Sukas. Arwad was left independent because it was located on an island 2.5 km off the Syrian coast and therefore difficult to capture.[87] It is uncertain whether some of the cities conquered by Tiglath-pileser belonged to the continental territory of Arwad.

As usual, the Assyrian king carried out deportations from these cities: "I settled [...] captive highlanders of the land Bīt-Sangibūti, 1,200 people of the (tribe) Illiku, (and) 6,208 people of the (tribes) Nakkabu (and) Būdu [in the cities..., Ṣi]mirra, Arqâ, Usnû, (and) Siannu, (cities) on the seacoast."[88] The organization of the cities is problematic. In particular in a lacunary passage mentioning Hatarikka and Simirra and noting where Tiglath-pileser exercised authority, the scribe states: "I placed six eunuchs [of mine as provincial governors over] them."[89] The figure six poses a problem because, although the reading is clear, the figure is mentioned only in this passage and only two provinces are named in the preserved toponyms. It is difficult to imagine that Tiglath-pileser created four other provinces, besides Hatarikka and Simirra, in this area. Since "provincial governors" is itself a restoration, I would propose restoring a different Assyrian official, such as the *qêpu*, "representative," who was in charge of controlling Samsi, queen of the Arabs.[90] On the other hand, we know from another text that Arqâ and Kashpûna were joined to the province of Simirra: they

---

Nadav Na'man, "Looking for KTK," *WdO* (1977–1978): 230–31; Lipiński, *Dictionnaire de la civilisation phénicienne et punique*, 243.

85. See below in chapter 9.
86. RINAP 1:105, 42.2′; Lipiński, *Aramaeans*, 290 (with bibliography).
87. Josette Elayi and Alain G. Elayi, *Arwad, cité phénicienne du nord* (Pendé: Gabalda, 2015), 94–95.
88. RINAP 1:68, 26.4–5; 114, 46.5–6.
89. RINAP 1:105, 42.4′.
90. RINAP 1:107, 43.26.

7. THE SECOND PHASE OF THE CAMPAIGNS (743–738) 113

were "placed under the authority of a eunuch of mine, the provincial governor of the city Si[mirra]."[91] The city of Simirra (Sumur) is usually identified with Tell Kazel, 20 km from Tartus, on the right bank of the Nahr al-Abrash, 3.5 km from its mouth.[92] The creation of this new province is mentioned several times in Tiglath-pileser's inscriptions, together with the deportations.[93] Nothing is said about the circumstances surrounding the creation of this province, but it was probably formed following a revolt and a harsh repression.[94] Arwad, the great northern Phoenician city, was surrounded by Assyrian territories, and the transformation of its neighboring Phoenician city of Simirra into an Assyrian province was a major change in the region.[95] Tiglath-pileser probably counted on the strategic importance of the fortified city of Simirra, rich and powerful as it was, to control the Phoenician cities, starting with the unsubdued city of Arwad, and to supervise trade in the western Mediterranean. However, the change of status of Simirra is not visible in the archaeological remains. It maintained the same architectural and handicraft traditions and pursued its trading activities without any significant change, except for the luxury products that had all but disappeared.[96] The main beneficiary of the annexation of Simirra was Arwad, which remained independent and secure on its island. Its king, possibly Mattanbaʿal II,[97] succeeded in resisting the Assyrian conquest.

---

91. RINAP 1:115, 46.22–24; 126, 48.8′–9′; 131, 49.r.1–2; 134, 50.r.1–2.
92. Even if it is sometimes presented as being on the seashore. Leila Badre et al., "Tell Kazel (Syrie): Rapport préliminaire sur les 4ᵉ–8ᵉ campagnes de fouilles (1988–1992)," *Syria* 71 (1994): 259–359; Emma Capet and Éric Gubel, "Tell Kazel: Six Centuries of Iron Age Occupation (c. 1200–612 B.C.)," in *Essays on Syria in the Iron Age*, ed. Guy Bunnens (Leuven: Peeters, 2000), 425–57; Lipiński, *Aramaeans*, 287 (with bibliography).
93. RINAP 1:46, 14.6; 68, 26.5; 86, 35.ii.11′; 105, 42.2′; 109, 43.ii.17; 115, 46.22; 126, 48.9′, 131, 49.r.1; 134, 50.r.1.
94. Forrer, *Die Provinzeinteilung des assyrischen Reiches*, 59; Bustenay Oded, "Phoenician Cities and the Assyrian Empire in the Time of Tiglath-pileser III," *ZDPV* 90 (1974): 42–45; Karlheinz Kessler, "Die Anzahl der assyrischen Provinzen des Jahres 738 v. Chr. in Nordsyrien," *WdO* 8 (1975): 54, 59–61; Nadav Naʾaman, "Borders and Districts in Descriptions of the Conquest of the West in Tiglath-pileser III's Inscriptions and in Biblical Historiography," *SAAB* 16 (2007): 42–48.
95. Elayi and Elayi, *Arwad, cité phénicienne du nord*, 94–95.
96. Leila Badre and Éric Gubel, "Tell Kazel Syria, Excavations of the AUB Museum, 1993–1998: Third Preliminary Report," *Berytus* 44 (1999-2000): 170–92, 198.
97. Elayi, *History of Phoenicia*, 296.

The second campaign of Tiglath-pileser to the west was a success, at least for a few years. He had crushed the western rebellions and established the new organization of the empire by restructuring the region with Assyrian provinces and tributary vassals. His campaign was also fruitful because he henceforth had access to the riches of the western states and to the Mediterranean trade. He also had access to the abundant forests of Mount Amanus, Mount Lebanon, and Mount Ammanâna, which he called "the boxwood mountain."[98]

7.5. Treaties and Loyalty Oaths

Treaties and loyalty oaths were instruments of Neo-Assyrian imperialism. The distinction between the two categories is somewhat arbitrary. From the early first millennium, the Assyrians used treaties to establish peaceful relations with their neighbors, thereby maintaining the established world order.[99] Treaties were generally concluded with other states or powerful tribes, and partners of the treaties were highly influential and charismatic leaders. The main point of contact between treaties and loyalty oaths is the invocation of the seal of Assur.[100] The seal, marked on these documents, implied solemn undertakings, founded on the highest possible authority. Another point of contact between the treaties and the oaths is the curses directed against whoever might break the agreement. The typical curse called on many deities to inflict dire punishments on the offender. Treaties and loyalty oaths both apparently involved an oath. However, some of them were bilateral agreements between rulers and were hence similar to treaties in the modern sense of the word. The genre of the treaty comprised several different types of pacts concluded for different purposes. Among others, these included bilateral and unilateral treaties, nonaggression pacts, peace and friendship treaties, mutual assistance pacts, and alliance treaties.[101] Treaties

---

98. RINAP 1:42, 13.5–6.
99. SAA 19:xxxix–xl; Karen Radner, "Neo-Assyrian Treaties as a Source for the Historian: Bonds of Friendship, the Vigilant Subject and the Vengeful King's Treaty," in *Writing Neo-Assyrian History: Sources, Problems, and Approaches*, ed. Giovanni Battista Lanfranchi, Raija Mattila, and Robert Rollinger (Helsinki: The Neo-Assyrian Text Corpus Project, 2019), 309–28.
100. SAA 12:xx, 4.
101. SAA 2:xv–xx.

7. THE SECOND PHASE OF THE CAMPAIGNS (743–738) 115

and loyalty oaths were designated from the second quarter of the eighth century by the same word, *adê*, which was borrowed from the Arameans.[102] On the other hand, the parity treaties concluded in earlier times, for example, between kings of Assyria and kings of Babylonia, used the traditional Akkadian terminology and probably followed a Babylonian pattern.[103] However, the Aramaic word '*dy* was already employed in a private document dating to the mid-thirteenth century, under the reign of Shalmaneser I.[104] This Aramaic loanword can only be explained by contacts with Aramaic tribes.[105]

In 743, Mati'-ilu, king of Arpad, "fomented a rebellious insurrection against Assyria and violated (his loyalty oath)."[106] The violated oath was a treaty concluded between him and Ashur-nârârî V, which has been preserved, except for the beginning of the obverse and a passage on the reverse.[107] There is no account of the circumstances that led to the conclusion of this treaty, but it can be assumed that the treaty was the result of the political surrender of Mati'-ilu in the face of the Assyrian troops. The treaty would have represented a favor granted to the king of Arpad, possibly at his request.[108] Ashur-nârârî was the superior partner in the pact, and Mati'-ilu had the status of inferior subject. The kind of oaths sworn remains unknown, but it is clear that they bound Mati'-ilu with unconditional loyalty to his Assyrian overlord and forbade him to form alliances with any other states. This Assyrian treaty presents similarities with three Aramaic treaties found at Sfire near Aleppo, concluded between the same king of Arpad and Bar-Ga'yah of *KTK* (see above).[109] There are affinities between the ceremonial acts, the curses, some details of formulation, and the general structure of the texts.

---

102. Lipiński, *Aramaeans*, 595–96.
103. SAA 2:xviii; Simonetta Ponchia, "Notes on the Legal Conventions and on the Practice of the *adê* in the Early Neo-Babylonian Letters from Nippur," *SAAB* 14 (2002–2005): 133–67; Jacob Lauinger, "The Neo-Assyrian adê: Treaty, Oath, or Something Else?," *ZAR* 19 (2013): 99–116.
104. Erich Ebeling, *Keilschrifitexte aus Assur juristischen Inhalts*, MVDOG 50 (Leipzig: Hinrichs, 1927), no. 83.14–18; John Nicholas Postgate, "More Assyrian Deeds and Documents," *Iraq* 32 (1970): 147.
105. Lipiński, *Aramaeans*, 597.
106. RINAP 1:84, 35.i.21'–22'.
107. SAA 2:8–13, 2.
108. SAA 2:xxvii.
109. *KAI* 264–274, 224.

During his reign, Tiglath-pileser imposed a treaty on Merodach-baladan of Bît-Yakîn, which is known from a Babylonian letter clearly twice mentioning the "treaty tablet [*ṭup-pi a-de-e*] of the son of Yakin."[110] A similar treaty was probably sworn by Balâssu of the Bît-Dakkûri and Nâdinu of Larak, both of whom were leaders of the most powerful Chaldean tribes in Babylonia.[111] In another Babylonian letter, Hamapi, possibly a tribal leader, emphasized the importance of adhering to the Assyrian treaties: "By that very command, whoever transgresses your word (or) alters your treaty, will be consigned into your hands."[112] Tiglath-pileser possibly also imposed a treaty on the king of Ashdod. According to a damaged letter of Qurdi-ashur-lâmur, it reports that the Ashdodite king had made an appeal to the Assyrian king because of a treaty.[113]

Some loyalty oaths, which seem to be sworn by vassals, are mentioned in Tiglath-pileser's inscriptions. The less influential tribal leaders had an obligation to conclude loyalty oaths with the king of Assyria. Zaqiru, leader of the Chaldean tribe of Bît-Sha'alli, violated his oath and was captured by the Assyrians: "(he) neglected the loyalty oath (sworn by) the great gods and [conspir]ed with [my enemies]."[114] Tutammû, king of Unqi, likewise neglected his loyalty oath and was severely punished.[115] Mitinti, king of Ashkelon, also discarded the loyalty oath, revolted, and was deposed.[116] Samsi, queen of the Arabs, "had transgressed her oath (sworn by) the god Šamaš" and was defeated by the Assyrians.[117] Here, Shamash replaced the great gods, and a word other than *adê* is used: *mamîtu*. Loyalty oaths, which were only mentioned in Tiglath-pileser's inscriptions when they had been broken, were probably a means of government largely used by him. They became systematic under his successors in the seventh century as a means of obligating every Assyrian to accept and protect the ruling king.

---

110. SAA 19:135–136, 133.
111. SAA 19:xl; SAA 10:112.r.27–29.
112. SAA 19:140.r.5–6.
113. SAA 19:35, 28; Shigeo Yamada, "Qurdi-Assur-lamur: His Letters and Career," in *Treasures on Camels' Humps*, ed. Mordechai Cogan and Dan'el Kahn (Jerusalem: Magnes, 2008), 296–311.
114. RINAP 1:119, 47.19.
115. RINAP 1:39, 12.3′.
116. RINAP 1:61, 21.12′; 63, 22.8′.
117. RINAP 1:59, 20.18′.

8
THE THIRD PHASE OF THE CAMPAIGNS (737–735)

8.1. A Second Campaign against Media

Tiglath-pileser took advantage of the fact that the Assyrian Empire was provisionally stabilized to undertake a second campaign against Media. He did not indicate the reason for this campaign: "In my ninth *palû*, (the god) Aššur, my lord, encouraged me and I marched against the lands of Bīt-Kap[si, Bīt-Sangi], Bīt-Urzakki, Media, Bīt-Zualzaš, Bīt-Matti, (and) Tupliaš."[1] As usual, Tiglath-pileser's action was violent, capturing, plundering, destroying, devastating, and burning many cities. The total count, based on the names cited (excluding those that are damaged), amounts to seventy-two cities and countries. Among the identifiable names, eleven of them were already mentioned in the accounts of the first Median campaign: Bît-Kapsi, Bît-Zatti, Bît-Abdadâni, Bît-Sangibûti, Bît-Sangi, Bît-Urzakki, Mannea, Namri, Parsua, Sumurzu, and Ellipi. The total number of names quoted for the first campaign was twenty. The names of some of the rulers of these cities and countries are also repeated, sometimes in association with a different city: Taltâ of Ellipi, Iranzu of Mannea, and Ra/umateia of Araziash (or Kazuqinzani).[2]

The recapture of the same places, even Parsua, which was an Assyrian province, means that, after having been captured in 744, they had rebelled again. The new troubles in the Zagros in western Iran necessitated a second campaign on a larger scale in 737. However, some of the cities and countries quoted, such as Ellipi and Mannea, were not captured; their rulers made allegiance to Tiglath-pileser. Reference is made to Mount Silhazu, a mountain

---

1. RINAP 1:48, 15.5–6.
2. RINAP 1:32, 8.1; 84, 86, 35.i.11′ and 15′; ii.36′; iii.24–25; 88, 36.6; 118, 47.7; Ina N. Medvedskaya, "Media and Its Neighbours I: The Localization of Ellipi," *IrAnt* 34 (1999): 53–70; *PNA* 1.2:373 (Taltâ); 2.1:563 (Iranzu); 3.1:1031 (Ramateia).

peak in Media, "which they called the fortress of the Babylonian(s)," but the location has not been identified.[3] It is also uncertain as to why the mountain of Shikrakki was called "the Assyrian mount" and "the land of gold" in two different passages.[4] One of the Median rulers, Upash of Bît-Kapsi, assembled his people and ascended Mount Abirus.[5] The Assyrian king pursued him, defeated him, carried off his booty, and destroyed his cities, but he does not seem to have deposed him as he later received a tribute of one hundred horses.[6] Upash was the successor, maybe the son, of Bâtânu who had submitted to Tiglath-pileser during his first campaign in 744 and had been treated favorably. Thus, the rulers of Bît-Kapsi remained vassals of the Assyrian king until the region was annexed to Assyria.[7]

After having destroyed the cities, Tiglath-pileser proceeded to rebuild them, placing in their midst the weapon of the god Assur and settling people from foreign lands there. As usual, he "placed [...eunuchs as provincial governor]s over them."[8] Two countries quoted in this passage had been turned into Assyrian provinces in 744: Parsua and Bît-Hamban.[9] Since they seem to have rebelled again in 737, they were once more turned into Assyrian provinces.

The Assyrian king wanted to leave several testimonies of his Median campaign of 737: an inscribed arrow and several stelae. The arrow inscription states: "At that time (744), [I made a pointed iron] arrow, inscribed [the mig]hty deeds of (the god) Aššur, my lord, on it, (and) I set (it) up at the spring of the city Bīt-Ištar."[10] The stelae erected in Iran were enumerated by the Assyrian king: "I erected my royal image in the land of Tikrakki, in the cities Bīt-Ištar (and) Ṣibur, in the land of Ariarma—*the land of roosters*—(and) at [Mount S]ilḫazu."[11] The identification proposed for the city of Bît-Ishtar is modern Ravânsar, 57 km northwest of

---

3. RINAP 1:51, 16.9–11; 52, 17.1–2; 120–21, 47.31–32.38.

4. RINAP 1:102, 41.9′–10′ (restoration); 120, 47.32 (unclear relation with this mount).

5. RINAP 1:49, 15.9; 72, 28.7; *PNA* 3.2:1390.

6. RINAP 1:86, 35.ii.32′.

7. RINAP 1:97, 39.17–20; 102, 41.4′–6′; *PNA* 1.2:277.

8. RINAP 1:53, 17.8.

9. RINAP 1:52, 17.5–7; 84, 35.i.5′–10′; Radner, "Provinz. C. Assyrien," 57, no. 41 and 45.

10. RINAP 1:49, 15.8–9; 72, 28.6.

11. RINAP 1:53, 17.8; 86, 35.ii.27′–29′; 121, 47.37–38; Bonacossi, "Stele e statue reali assire," 112 and fig. B, 114 and fig. C, 142–53.

8. THE THIRD PHASE OF THE CAMPAIGNS (737–735)   119

Kermanshah.[12] The rest of these toponyms have not yet been identified, and the stelae have not been discovered. The so-called Iran stela, on the other hand, consists of three fragments, two of them now in the Israel Museum and the third one in a private collection. According to Tadmor and Yamada, the fragments possibly originated from Luristan or from the region of Kermanshah in western Iran.[13] The first and largest fragment was said to have been discovered in 1972 in the Luristan region.[14] The second fragment was said to have been discovered in 1973 near Kermanshah.[15] The stela was probably found nearby the Great Khorassan road, which formed the frontier between the valley of Kermanshah and Luristan. If the location of the stela is one of the five places mentioned in the inscriptions, it could be Bît-Ishtar.[16] Another stela was erected at Shikrakki or Tikrakka, both forms being used in the inscriptions, located on the edge of a salt desert, near Mount Bikni and Mount Rûa.[17] It has been suggested that Mount Bikni was Mount Karkas, that Mount Rûa was close to the modern town of Kashan, and that the salt desert was in the Dash-i Kavir.[18] Tikrakka was identified by Roman Ghirshman with modern Tapeh Sialk.[19] The erection of a stela at Tikrakka by Tiglath-Pileser is confirmed by a bas-relief in Sargon II's palace in Khorsabad, which shows the Assyrian siege of the Median fortress of Tikrakka.[20] A

---

12. Radner, "Assyrian View of the Medes," 37–64; Karen Radner and Stefan Kroll, "Ein Bronzedolch des Simbar-Šipak von Babylon (1025–1008): Überlegungen zu Waffenweihungen im Vorderen Orient," *ZA* 96 (2006): 220–21.
13. RINAP 1:80–81; Mirjo Salvini, "Some Historic-Geographical Problems Concerning Assyria and Urartu," in *Neo-Assyrian Geography*, ed. Mario Liverani (Rome: Università di Roma "La sapienza," 1995), 44, fig. 1.
14. Louis D. Levine, *Two Neo-Assyrian Stelae from Iran* (Toronto: Royal Ontario Museum, Art and Archeology Editorial Board, 1972), 11–24.
15. Pablo Herrero, "Un fragment de stèle Néo-Assyrienne provenant d'Iran," *DFI* 3 (1973): 105–13.
16. Alibaigi, "Location of the Second Stele," 47–50.
17. RINAP 1:53, 17.8; 120, 47.32.
18. Sajjad Alibaigi and Iraj Rezael, "Bikni, Bīt-ṭābti, and Uqnū: Searching for Appropriate Identifications for Toponyms and Terms Mentioned in Neo-Assyrian Texts," *JNES* 77 (2018): 15–30.
19. Roman Ghirshman, *Iran: From the Earliest Times to the Islamic Conquest* (Harmondsworth: Penguin Books, 1954), 77; Louis D. Levine, *Geographical Studies in the Neo-Assyrian Zagros* (Toronto: Royal Ontario Museum, 1974), 106–17.
20. Fuchs, *Die Inschriften Sargons II. aus Khorsabad*, 105, Ann. 99a–100; Alibaigi, "Location of the Second Stele," 50 and fig. 3.

stela bearing the image of an Assyrian king is represented on the left side of the scene, in front of two cavalrymen attacking the fortress.

The cities and countries that were not integrated into the new provinces of Parsua and Bît-Hamban became vassal states of Assyria. Tiglath-pileser allowed them to remain autonomous and to keep the same rulers, unless they were hostile to Assyria. The cities had to make allegiance to the Assyrian king and to pay the "tribute" (*mandattu*): "[I received] the payme[nt of the Medes, the people of the land of Ellipi, and the city rulers of all the mountain regions, as far as Mount Bikni: ..., horse]s, mules, Bactrian [camels, oxen, and sheep and goats, without number."[21] The tribute is more detailed in a passage of the Iran stela, somewhat damaged, with the names of the rulers, cities, and countries (twenty), and the number of horses given by each of them (between thirty-two and three hundred).[22] A specific mention concerns the "yearly" (*šattišam*) tribute paid by Iranzu of Mannea and Taltâ of Ellipi.[23]

While Tiglath-pileser himself conducted the two Median campaigns in 744 and 737, he also delegated some expeditions to his officials, as noted in the following: "I sent a eunuch of mine, Aššur-da"inanni, [ag]ainst the migh[ty] Medes in the east. He took 5,000 horses, people, oxen, and sheep and goats, without number."[24] This expedition is mentioned twice in summary inscriptions after the mention of the two Median campaigns, but it is impossible to know exactly when it was launched. Ashur-da"inanni, eponym in 733, was governor of Zamua.[25] This eastern province, created in 842 by Shalmaneser III,[26] was located in the region of Sulaymaniyah and was the closest province to the territory of the Medes. The governor had sufficient troops at his disposal for this expedition. The aim of the campaign was apparently to collect a great quantity of booty, especially horses for the army, but also to bring back prisoners, possibly to integrate them into the Assyrian army. The Assyrian king organized the collaboration between the royal army and the governor's provincial troops.

---

21. RINAP 1:53, 17.9–10; Reade, "Iran in the Neo-Assyrian Period Geography," 31–42.
22. RINAP 1:86, 35.ii.30′–44′.
23. RINAP 1:87, 35.iii.24–30.
24. RINAP 1:103, 41.13′–15′; 121, 47.42; *PNA* 1.1:177.
25. SAAS 2:59.
26. Radner, "Provinz. C. Assyrien," 51–52, no. 22.

8. THE THIRD PHASE OF THE CAMPAIGNS (737–735)   121

8.2. The Campaign to the Urartian Border

The account of the tenth *palû* (736) is broken off in the annals of Tiglath-pileser. It is only mentioned in two fragments from Nimrud and a summary inscription.[27] The Eponym List for year 736 mentions: "To the foot of Mount Nal."[28] All we know from these fragmentary inscriptions is that this campaign took place around Mount Nal, that the Assyrian king conquered several rebellious cities and destroyed, devastated, and burned them, that he organized deportations, and that he added the conquered cities to the nearby province of Ulluba and to that of the treasurer. Some cities in this area had possibly already been annexed to the same province in 738.[29] There is a contradiction concerning the city of Sardauriana, which was added to the province of Ulluba. It is stated a few lines further on that Sardauriana was added to the province of the treasurer; this is probably a scribe's error.[30]

Some of the conquered cities were fortresses of Urartu. A few of them can be identified. First, where was Mount Nal? It should most likely be identified with the mountain ridge south of Ulluba, along the Lesser Habur, present-day Chiyâ Bêhêr.[31] The city of Lusia is mentioned in a passage as being a fortress of Urartu integrated into the province of the treasurer, and in another passage it is listed as "the lead land" integrated into the province of Nairi.[32] There were probably two different cities called Lusia, the first one close to Mount Nal and the second one located in the Upper Tigris area.[33] Other cities were fortresses of Urartu, such as Tapsia and Suba.[34] A letter, probably sent to Tiglath-pileser by a governor or a high official whose name is lost,[35] was linked to this area. The beginning of the letter could refer to a line of fortresses situated facing Urartu and belonging to

---

27. RINAP 1:88–89, 36.8′–10′; 130, 49.9′–13′; 98, 39.30–36.
28. SAAS 2:59.
29. Yamada, "Ulluba and Its Surroundings," 25.
30. RINAP 1:130, 49.9′–13′.
31. John Nicholas Postgate, "The Inscription of Tiglath-pileser III at Mila Mergi," *Sumer* 29 (1973): 57; RGTC 7/2-2, 445–46.
32. RINAP 1:36, 10.7′; 130, 49.12′, 18′; 88, 36.8′; 98, 39.27; RGTC 7/2-1, 377.
33. Yamada, "Ulluba and Its Surroundings," 21 and n. 25.
34. RINAP 1:98, 40.27; 130, 49.12′ (Tapsia); 130, 49.12′ (Suba); RGTC 7/2-2, 536–37, 588.
35. SAA 19:71, 69. For the different proposals, see bibliography in Yamada, "Ulluba and Its Surroundings," 31–32.

several Assyrian provinces in the region. KUR.*bi-rat* (for plural *birāte*) would mean "the land of fortresses," but KUR is probably a scribal error for URU.[36] In any case, the sender of the letter probably had the mission to supervise the situation along the Urartian border. This letter was most likely written just after the conquest of Ulluba and its surroundings, either in 739 or 736. The aim of Tiglath-pileser was probably to consolidate the Assyrian northern frontline facing Urartu, focusing on the creation of new provinces and on the enlargement of the northern and northwestern ones created by Shalmaneser III. Tiglath-pileser's strategy was not new but borrowed from his ancestor and developed further.[37]

8.3. The Campaign into the Heart of Urartu

The account of the campaign of 735, one of Tiglath-pileser's most daring, is broken off in the annals. The date is known from the Eponym List.[38] Part of the report of these events is presented in a fragment of slab decorating the palace of Nimrud.[39] A damaged passage relating the beginning of the campaign is engraved on a fragment of statue found in the Ninurta temple of Nimrud.[40] A summary of the campaign is given in three so-called summary inscriptions.[41] This summary continues, without interruption, with the long flight of Sarduri (Seduri), king of Urartu, after his defeat in 743. Since Tiglath-pileser was not able to capture Sarduri, he compensated for this failure by conducting the campaign of 735 into the heart of Urartu.[42] We can also observe that, in these later inscriptions, it is Sarduri, and not Mati'-ilu of Arpad, who is represented as the instigator of the Syrian-Urartian coalition. Mati'-ilu had lost interest because Arpad had been taken and turned into an Assyrian province, while Sarduri of Urartu had become the archenemy of Assyria. The summary account of this campaign can be reconstructed as follows: Sarduri was besieged in Turushpa (in Turkish Tushpa), his capital; he was defeated in front of his city gate; Tiglath-pileser

---

36. SAA 19:71, note to no. 69.5.
37. Yamada, "Ulluba and Its Surroundings," 33–36.
38. SAAS 2:59.
39. RINAP 1:54–57, 18 and 19.
40. RINAP 1:89, 36.11′–13′.
41. RINAP 1:98, 39.23–25; 103, 41.21′–26′; 129, 49.3′–5′.
42. Hayim Tadmor, "Assyria at the Gates of Tushpa," in *Treasures on Camels' Humps*, ed. Mordechai Cogan and Dan'el Kahn (Jerusalem: Magnes, 2008), 269–73.

8. THE THIRD PHASE OF THE CAMPAIGNS (737–735)

erected his stela in front of the gate; Tiglath-pileser marched triumphantly across Urartu, with nobody resisting him.[43] Finally, a letter addressed to the king of Assyria gives precious information on the events that occurred in the month preceding the departure of the expedition; the letter urged the king to reattempt the capture of Turushpa, which had failed.[44]

Before undertaking a military campaign against Urartu, Tiglath-pileser used diplomacy: first discussing before making war. The reverse of the tablet of the letter mentions "messengers from Urartu and messengers who came along with them."[45] The Urartian messengers received bread and water for themselves and fodder for their horses. Then they returned to Urartu. The diplomatic negotiations between the king of Assyria and Urartu failed, so Tiglath-pileser decided to launch a campaign. The name of the sender of the letter has not survived; he was probably an official: "This month, the king, my lord, will go up to Urartu. Aššur (and) Šamaš have delivered Ṭurušpâ into the hands of the king, my lord. May the king, my lord, direct his campaign toward Urartu and may he conquer Ṭurušpâ." The sender of the letter wished his master success in his campaign to Urartu and in conquering Turushpa, which would make the king's name famous for eternity.

Before his departure, Tiglath-pileser consulted oracles, as was usual before waging a war. He received two positive oracles, one from Assur, his main god, and one from Shamash, the lord of liver omens. Since this campaign was not mentioned in Sarduri's annals, Salvini had doubts about its reality in spite of the fact that it was mentioned in the Eponym List for 735.[46] He objected that the crossing of the Euphrates is not mentioned, but the beginning of the account is broken off. Salvini also argued that Tiglath-pileser did not met any opponent, which is wrong because Tiglath-pileser fought with several cities and countries before reaching Turushpa.

---

43. Tadmor, "Assyria at the Gates of Tushpa," 271, proposed an additional element ("the wide land of Urartu is devastated"), but the devastation of Urartu occurred before the arrival of Tiglath-pileser at Turushpa. PNA 3.1:1099 (Sarduri); 2.2:745 (Mati'-ilu).
44. Karen Radner, "Assyrians and Urartians," in *The Oxford Handbook of Ancient Anatolia, 10,000–323 B.C.E.*, ed. Sharon R. Steadman and Gregory McMahon (Oxford: Oxford University Press, 2011), 740.
45. SAA 19:77–78, 76.r.1–5; Tadmor, "Assyria at the Gates of Tushpa," 272–73.
46. Salvini, *Geschichte und Kultur der Urartäer*, 73–76; Salvini, "Some Historic-Geographical Problems Concerning Assyria and Urartu," 53; Salvini, "Assyrie-Urartu," 55–58; CTU 5.

The precise date of Tiglath-pileser's departure can be deduced from a damaged passage on a fragment of statue, which could possibly be restored as follows: "[I crossed the] Arşania [River] when [*it was in flood* ... *I made my troops jump across* the ...]a [river] as if it was a ditch [....]"[47] If this river was in flood, it would mean that the crossing of the Assyrian troops occurred in spring, after the snow had melted, and they would have had to wait for the high mountain passes to be free of snow to be able to reach Urartu.

What was the actual distance from Nimrud to Turushpa, and how long did the journey take? It is about 250 km as the crow flies. Since the Assyrian army on campaign covered an average distance of 25 to 30 km per day,[48] theoretically the army would have needed about ten days. However, the real time taken to cover the distance was much longer because the troops did not advance as the crow flies but had to travel along winding roads in a highly mountainous area, and they needed to make halts when necessary. Moreover, on their way they encountered several hostile cities that they had to capture and organize. Hence, they needed much more than ten days, possibly arriving at Turushpa at the beginning of summer.

After the gap regarding the beginning of the campaign, the names of some twenty captured cities are mentioned, with several other names broken off. Some names are mentioned in other inscriptions, such as Harabisinna, Tasa, Ulurush River, Elizanshu, Danziun, Luqia, and Ura.[49] A few identifications have been proposed for some toponyms.[50] In one inscription, the city of Ura was located in the land of Musurni and in another in the land of Bâzu.[51] The cities that were defeated are listed in three groups, which probably represented three successive stages of the campaign. First, Tiglath-pileser "captured (and) defeated the cities [...],

---

47. RINAP 1:89, 36.11′–13′ and note: "The proposed restorations are conjectural."
48. Joannès, *Dictionnaire de la civilisation mésopotamienne*, 154–55.
49. RINAP 1:55–56, 18–19. See index 200–205. Tarsa, connected with Ullurush, should not be confused with the city mentioned in the letters of Sha-Ashur-dubbu, governor of Tushhan: SAA 5:31.11; 34.r.10–16; Karlheinz Kessler, "Šubria, Urartu and Aššur: Topographical Questions around the Tigris Sources," in Liverani, *Neo-Assyrian Geography*, 60, 63; RGTC 7/2-2, 590–91 (Tasa), 627; Parpola and Porter, *Helsinki Atlas of the Near East*, 3.19 (Ulurush); RGTC 7/2-1, 168–69 (Elizanshu); 135 (Danziun); 631–32 (Ura); 7/2-2, 376 (Luqia).
50. Other toponyms, such as Harabisinna, for example, are not listed in RGTC.
51. RINAP 1:56, 18.7; 130, 49.20′; RGTC 7/2-2, 437–38 (Musurni).

8. THE THIRD PHASE OF THE CAMPAIGNS (737-735) 125

Ḫista, Ḫarabisinna, Barbaz, (and) Tasa, as far as the Uluruš River."⁵² He enumerated the people deported (8,650) and the booty carried off: (...) horses, 300 mules, 660 asses, 1,350 oxen, and 19,000 sheep. As usual, these cities were destroyed, devastated, and burned and then rebuilt and repopulated by foreign people conquered elsewhere. The weapon of Assur was set up, and the area, located north of the Murad-Su, was added to the province of Nairi. The second group of cities captured and defeated included Daiqansha, Sakka, Ippa, Elizanshu, Luqadansha, Quda, Elugia, Dania, Danziun, Ulaya, Luqia, Abrania, and Eusa.⁵³ Nine hundred people were deported, and 150 oxen and 1,000 sheep, horses, mules, and asses was carried off. These cities were destroyed, devastated, and burned, but their integration into an Assyrian province is not mentioned. This second group is much less important than the first group, possibly because this area is located high in the mountains, as the Assyrian army moved northward. A third stage is the action against the ruler(s) of Ura, whose name(s) have not survived: "their sons, their daughters, [their] fam[ily, ...] I cut off [their hands] and I [released] (them) in their (own) land.... I captured (and) defeated him [...."⁵⁴ This damaged passage also mentioned booty (horses and mules), capture, destruction, devastation, and burning of the cities in this area. In fact, Tiglath-pileser continued the military operations of the preceding campaign of 736 by totally pacifying the southern region of Urartu, en route from Assyria to the capital Turushpa. He encountered no further resistance on his way to the Urartian capital.

Turushpa was located on the southeastern shore of the Lake of Van. It corresponded to the site of Van Kalesi with the fortress built on top of the rocky escarpment overlooking the lake and the city below. Turushpa became the capital of Urartu under the reign of Sarduri I (832-825), who was defeated by Shalmaneser III of Assyria.⁵⁵ The Turushpa fortress was 1,050 m long and between 50 and 125 m wide, occupying an area of about 4 hectares. The city below had a surface area of about 30 hectares. The fortress included the so-called castle of Sarduri and mausoleums dug in the rock. The city was protected by cyclopean-type stone walls approximately

---

52. RINAP 1:55, 18.1.1; Kessler, "Šubria, Urartu and Aššur," 63; RGTC 7/2-1, 234 (Ḫista).
53. RINAP 1:55, 18.4-5; RGTC 7/2-1, 5, 131-32, 134, 169-70, 173, 248, 375-76, 625; 7/2-2, 496, 518.
54. RINAP 1:57, 19.1-7.
55. RIMA 3:69, A.0.102.14.144-145; RGTC 7/2-1, 93 (Barbaz).

3 m wide.⁵⁶ The fortified city of Turushpa with its high fortress probably gave the impression of being impregnable.

When he arrived, Tiglath-pileser first "confined him [Sarduri] to the city Ṭurušpâ, his city."⁵⁷ Then Tiglath-pileser is said to have "inflicted a great defeat upon him before his city gates." This would mean that Tiglath-pileser confronted some Urartian troops, without their king, outside the city. The king's third action was the following: "I erected my royal image in front of the city Ṭurušpâ." Tiglath-pileser carried out these three actions before deciding to retreat. This decision contradicted all Assyrian ideological norms: Tiglath-pileser had not taken Turushpa and had not captured Sarduri, who remained on the throne of Urartu. In other words, this campaign was a failure for the Assyrian king, the only one of his reign, a major failure because Sarduri was his archenemy. Therefore, the Assyrian scribe found a literary solution to this ideological problem. First, the unsubmissive enemy was enclosed and could not leave his city. A similar topos was used later, in Sennacherib's inscriptions, for Hezekiah of Judah, who was enclosed in Jerusalem "like a bird in a cage."⁵⁸ Then there was a battle with some of the king's troops, who were defeated before the city gate, that is, before Sarduri's very eyes. Finally, the Assyrian king humiliated the Urartian king by erecting his own stela in front of the city. The stela was not discovered, most likely because it was destroyed just after the Assyrian army's departure.⁵⁹

Now why did Tiglath-pileser not besiege Turushpa? It was probably because of his realistic analysis of the situation. The position and the fortifications of the city made it very difficult to capture. A siege would have necessitated several months, if not several years, until the pressures of hunger and thirst brought victory. The Assyrian king would have remembered the siege of Arpad, which had lasted three years. Moreover, it may

---

56. Oktay Belli, *Van, capitale de l'Urartu (Anatolie orientale)* (Istanbul: Net, 1986); Mirjo Salvini, "Tušpa, die Hauptstadt von Urartu," in *Staat im 1. Jahrtausend v. Chr.*, ed. Volkert Haas, Xenia Heft 17 (Konstanz: Universitätsverlag Konstanz, 1986), 31–58; Alireza Hejebri-Nobari, *L'architecture militaire urartéenne* (Lille: A.N.R.T., 1998); Béatrice André-Salvini and Mirjo Salvini, "Architecture et programme dynastique: Les monuments de la capitale de l'Urartu, sur le rocher de Van," in *Les espaces syro-mésopotamiens: Volume d'Hommage offert à Jean-Claude Margueron*, Subartu 17 (Turnhout: Brépols, 2006), 261–79.

57. RINAP 1:98, 39.23–24; 103, 41.21′–22′; 129, 49.3′.

58. Elayi, *Sennacherib*, 76.

59. Morandi Bonacossi, "Stele e statue reali assire," 142.

8. THE THIRD PHASE OF THE CAMPAIGNS (737–735)

not have been possible to surround the city completely on its abrupt side overlooking the lake where it could receive supplies. The Assyrian siege technique was of a high standard, but Tiglath-pileser had probably not transported siege machines all the way to Turushpa since he was not aware of its quasi-impregnable character and since it would have been difficult to cross the high mountains with such machines. A final problem was the winter conditions, which, at an altitude of 1640 m, were too harsh for the Assyrians who were familiar with a hot climate. Even though it was still summer when they reached Turushpa, autumn was fast approaching, and it was already getting cold. It was high time for the army to go back to Assyria.

However, the army's retreat in the wake of a failure was still presented in a positive manner: "For a distance of seventy leagues, I proudly marched through the extensive land of Urarṭu, from above to below, and I had no opponent (therein)."[60] This passage gives the impression that Tiglath-pileser had conquered the whole kingdom of Urartu, that it was totally pacified, and that he visited his possessions. In reality, he was probably describing the way back to Assyria because he went "from above [Turu-shpa] to below [Nimrud]" (*ul-tu e-liš a-di šap-liš*).[61] The absence of resistance on his way back can be explained by the fact that he took the same route along which he had devastated all the cities on the outward journey. The distance given was "seventy leagues," that is, approximately 756 km, since the *bēru* ("double hour"), an Akkadian unit of distance based on the unit of time, was about 10.8 km.[62] The variations in the measurement of the *bēru* could be explained on the basis of various marching speeds. This distance is substantially greater than the 250 km as the crow flies from Nimrud to Turushpa. Either it expressed the real distance of the total itinerary, or it was an exaggerated figure in order to show that he had crossed the whole kingdom of Urartu, or it was a scribe's error.

Although he presented his failure as a victory in order to save appearances, Tiglath-pileser understood that he was unable to conquer the pow-

---

60. RINAP 1:98, 39.24–25; 103, 41.25′–26′; 129, 49.5′.

61. The interpretation of Tadmor "from one end to the other" is not exact because the Assyrian king did not go through the whole Urartian territory; Turushpa was in its center.

62. *CAD* 2:210, s.v. "bēru," A2; Jeremy Black, Andrew George, and John Nicholas Postgate, *A Concise Dictionary of Akkadian*, SANTAG 5 (Wiesbaden: Harrassowitz, 2000), s.v. "berū(m) III."

erful kingdom of Urartu. He averted the threat for some years by settling a protection zone of Assyrian provinces administered by high officials and buffer states between Assyria and Urartu. Sarduri of Urartu probably also understood that Assyria was a threat for him and that it would be better to keep the status quo. However, Sarduri II died in 733, and his successor, Rusâ I (730–714), continued to threaten Assyria. In 714, Sargon II would undertake his eighth campaign against Urartu, which put an end to Assyro-Urartian confrontation in the northeast of the empire, even though Urartu remained a powerful empire that Assyria would have to keep a watchful eye on.[63]

---

63. Elayi, *Sargon II*, 229–31.

9
THE FOURTH PHASE OF THE CAMPAIGNS (734–732)

After having consolidated the Assyrian Empire on its northern border, in 734 Tiglath-pileser resumed his conquest of the West, which had been interrupted between 738 and 735. He had conquered North Syria and the northern Mediterranean seacoast. Now, he logically decided to progress southwards, along both the coastal area and in the hinterland. Over a period of three years, from 734 to 732, he confronted Phoenician and Philistine cities; the kingdoms of Israel, Judah, and Damascus; and the Arabs. His most important actions from the Assyrian point of view were mentioned in the Eponym List: "to Philistia" in year 734 and "to Damascus" in years 733 and 732.[1] These events have been preserved in the annals, in some long and short summary inscriptions, on a fragmentary stela from Assur, on a relief in the palace at Nimrud, and in several letters.[2] Biblical documents also present the impact of the 734–732 campaigns on the kingdom of Israel[3] and on the kingdom of Judah from the Judahite point of view.[4] As the events of the 734–732 campaign are imbricated and without precise chronology, I shall analyze them by geographical groups, following, where possible, a chronological order.

---

1. SAAS 2:59.
2. RINAP 1:58–60, 20–21; 105–7, 42; 111–12, 44; 115, 46; 122, 47.1'–6'; 123, 47.r.16'; 127–28, 48.14'–27'; 131–33, 49.1–26; 134, 50.1–5; 143, 54.8–14; 145–46, 56. Henry William Frederick Saggs, *The Nimrud Letters, 1952*, CTN 5 (London: British School of Archaeology in Iraq, 2001), 150–66, ND 2064, 2417, 2430, 2686, 2715, 2716, 2766, 2767; SAA 19:177–78, 178; 179–80, 181; 31–32, 24; 30, 23; 28–29, 22; 36–37, 30; 42–44, 37; 180, 182; Peter Dubovský, "Tiglath-pileser III's Campaigns in 734–732 B.C.: Historical Background of Isa 7; 2 Kgs 15–16 and 2 Chr 27–28," *Bib* 87 (2006): 153–54.
3. 2 Kgs 15:29–31; 16:5, 8.
4. 2 Kgs 15:32–16, 20; Isa 7:1–25; 2 Chr 27:1–28:27.

9.1. The Campaigns against the Phoenician Cities

In his previous campaign of 738, Tiglath-pileser had created the province of Simirra, which included the north Syria seacoast, except for the island of Arwad. The southern border of this province spread to the north of Kashpûna, and the city was only annexed in 734: "... *I exercised authority*] from the city of Kašpūna, which is on the shore of the sea, [as far as ... (and) I placed] (it) under the authority of a eunuch of mine, the provincial governor of the city of Si[mirra]."[5] The location of Kashpûna has been much debated. This toponym was first misread Rashpuna, which led to false identifications.[6] The etymology of Kashpûna (*Kaspon) also has not helped. The name is possibly the same as *kašpu*, "silver," which has led some scholars to argue that Kashpûna was a port of silver trade.[7] However, the evidence for this is inconclusive. Before examining the different hypotheses proposed for the location of this city, its characteristics as indicated in the Assyrian inscriptions need to be listed: Kashpûna was on the shore of the "Lower Sea" (*tam-tim e-li-ti*), probably by opposition with the "Upper Sea" on the north Syrian coast.[8] It was located on the southern border of the province of Simirra, in the vicinity of Simirra and Arqâ.[9] It was a fortified city, housing a garrison as we learn from a Nimrud letter. In a letter, the king ordered that the city's fortification be rebuilt, that the surrounding rubbish at the side be torn down, that the great gate in the inner wall be repaired, and that good quality water be supplied from Immiu (Immiha).[10] Kashpûna was in the vicinity of Mount Saue "which abuts Mount Lebanon."[11] Mount Saue has been identified with Mount Terbol, possibly rightly so because it is not parallel with but perpendicular to the

---

5. RINAP 1:126, 48.7′–9′.

6. Rost, *Die Keilschrifttexte Tiglat-Pilesers III*, pl. XXV; RGTC 7/1, 138–39 (with bibliography).

7. Lipiński, *Dictionnaire de la civilisation phénicienne et punique*, 243; Claudio Saporetti, "Testimonianze neo-assire relative all Fenicia da Tiglat-Pileser III ad Assurbanipal," in *Studi storici sulla Fenicia: L'VIII e il VII secolo a.C.*, ed. Massimo Botto, Quaderni de orientalistica pisana I (Pisa: Università degli studi di Pisa, 1990), 136, n. 54.

8. RINAP 1:105, 42.5′ and note: Tadmor corrected without reason *tam-tim e-liti*, "Upper Sea."

9. RINAP 1:115, 46.22–23.

10. Saggs, *Nimrud Letters, 1952*, ND 2715.r.30′–45′; ND 2686.20′; SAA 19:30, 23.28–29.

11. RINAP 1:42, 13.5–6; 74, 30.1–2; RGTC 7/1, 114–15.

9. THE FOURTH PHASE OF THE CAMPAIGNS (734–732) 131

Lebanon range.[12] Traditionally, however, scholars identified Kashpûna with Kûsbâ because of the similarity of the two toponyms and because Immiu, the city supplying its water, was identified with Amiun.[13] However, Kashpûna was on the coast, while Kûsbâ is more than 12 km inland. Other hypotheses of the location do not seem likely, such as the northern border of the kingdom of Damascus, again because Kashpûna was on the coast.[14] The hypothesis of Minat el-Kassab on the Syrian-Turkish border also has to be rejected because Kashpûna was on the southern border of Simirra; Tabbet al-Hammam should be rejected for the same reason.[15] Other authors have proposed to situate Kashpûna at Al-Mina, the harbor of the Lebanese city of Tripoli.[16] This location would fit, but up to now no material evidence has been found to date Al-Mina's natural moorages before the Persian period.[17] The last and most plausible proposal in the present state of documentation is Kastina (et-Taale) at the mouth of the Nahr el-Bared, on its southern bank.[18] This tell suffered severe damage due

---

12. Éric Gubel, "Desperately Seeking Kašpuna… Notes on the Historical Topography of the 'Akkar plain-III," *Akkadica* 139 (2018): 115. Or it was identified with the Jebel Ansariyeh: Nadav Na'aman, "Damascus, Hatarikka and Simirra in Tiglath-pileser III's Summary Inscriptions," *NABU* (2001): 2, 26–26, no. 24.

13. Na'aman, "Looking for KTK," 230–31; Manfred Weippert, "Zur Syrienpolitik Tiglatpilesers. III," in *Mesopotamien und Seine Nachbarn Politische und Kulturelle Wechselbeziehungen im Alten Vorderasien vom 4. bis 1. Jahrtausend v. Chr.*, ed. Hans-Jörg Nissen (Berlin: Reimer, 1982), 405–6 and n. 21; Nadav Na'aman, *Ancient Israel and Its Neighbors: Interaction and Counteraction* (Winona Lake, IN: Eisenbrauns, 2005), 58, 219–21; Lipiński, *Dictionnaire de la civilisation phénicienne et punique*, 243; Jean Sapin, "Essai sur les structures géographiques de la toponymie araméenne dans la trouée de Homs (Liban-Syrie) et sur leur signification historique," *Trans* 2 (1990): 80–81; RGTC 7/7/1, 138 (Kashpûna); 114–15 (Immu); Bagg, *Die Assyrer und das Westland*, 78–79, 126, 161.

14. Tadmor, Inscriptions of Tiglath-pileser III, 138, hypothesis rejected by Galil, "New Look at the Inscriptions of Tiglath-pileser III," 511.

15. Lipiński, *Aramaeans*, 288–89; Robert R. Stieglitz, "The City of Amurru," *JNES* 50 (1991): 48.

16. Kessler, "Die Anzahl der assyrischen Provinzien," 60–61; RGTC 7/7/1, 138.

17. Nicolas Carayon, "Les ports phéniciens du Liban, milieux naturels, organisation spatiale et infrastructures," *AHL* 36–37 (2012–2013): 8–10.

18. Gubel, "Desperately Seeking Kašpuna," 109–26. On the Nahr el-Bared, see Gubel, "Ibirta et le 'Nahr el-Bared': Notes de toponymie historique akkariote I," *Syria* 86 (2009): 221–32; Gubel, "'By the Rivers of Amurru': Notes de topographie historique du Akkar-II," in *Tiro, Cartagine, Lixus: Nuove acquisizioni, Atti del Convegno Internazionale in onore di Maria Giulia Amadasi Guzzo, Roma, 24–25 novembre 2008,*

to the construction of the Iraqi Petroleum pipeline and the Tripoli-Tartus highway; moreover, it was plundered by treasure hunters who unearthed several gold bowls and fragments.[19] This tell was probably the fortified harbor of Ullaza in the Amarna Age. It was possibly destroyed during the Sea Peoples' passage, and it (or part of it) was called Kashpûna in the Iron Age, when its walls had to be rebuilt. Finally, in the Hellenistic period it became Orthosia, a name preserved to this day in the surrounding fields, which are called Ard Arthousi.[20]

If Kashpûna was located at the mouth of the Nahr el-Bared, Tiglath-pileser, before annexing it, had logically decided to crush the revolt of the king of Arwad, Mattanba'al II, who had put up resistance to him and had not paid the tribute in 738, when he conquered the northern shoreline of Syria. Tiglath-pileser could not accept this opposition. The only text where this event is described is damaged, mainly at the beginning.[21] The names of the rebellious city and of its king are broken off, but the context seems to indicate Arwad and Mattanba'al II.[22] The king of Assyria probably first attacked one of his cities, located "on dry land" (*ina na-ba-li*), maybe Amrit (Marathus). He slaughtered the inhabitants of this city and devastated it as well as another one "[...in] the midst of the sea" ([...*ina*] *qabal tamtim*).[23] The king probably meant the island of Arwad, which he may have boasted as having conquered in the broken passage.

---

ed. Gilda Bartoloni, Paolo Matthiae, Lorenzo Nigro and Licia Romano (Rome: Università degli studi La Sapienza, 2010), 123–24.

19. André Parrot, "Acquisitions et inédits du Musée du Louvre," *Syria* 41 (1964): 240–50; Oscar W. Muscarella, *The Lie Became Great: The Forgery of Ancient Near Eastern Cultures* (Groningen: Styx, 2000), 198–200.

20. René Dussaud, *Topographie historique de la Syrie antique et médiévale* (Paris: Presses de l'IFPO, 1927), 77–80; Stefan Wild, *Libanesische Ortsnamen: Typologie und Deutung*, 2nd ed. (Beirut: Orient-Institut, 2008), 343.

21. RINAP 1:126, 48.1'–9'.

22. Alt, "Tiglathpileser III," 151–57; H. Jacob Katzenstein, *The History of Tyre* (Jerusalem: Schocken Institute for Jewish Research, 1973), 215–16; Oded, "Phoenician Cities and the Assyrian Empire," 46; Eph'al, *Ancient Arabs*, 30; Tadmor, *Inscriptions of Tiglath-pileser III*, 282; Elayi and Elayi, *Arwad*, 95–98. For other interpretations, see Vogt, "Die Texte Tiglath-Pilesers III," 349–50; Dubovský, "Tiglath-pileser III's Campaigns," 159 (Arwad or Tyre); Na'aman, "Tiglath-pileser III's Campaigns against Tyre and Israel," 56–57; Shigeo Yamada, in RINAP 1:125–26 (Tyre).

23. RINAP 1:126, 48.1'–4'; Elayi, *History of Phoenicia*, 148–49. Tadmor's restoration is more likely than Na'aman's restoration ("Tiglath-pileser III's Campaigns against Tyre and Israel," 59).

9. THE FOURTH PHASE OF THE CAMPAIGNS (734–732)

It is impossible to think that Tiglath-pileser assembled a war fleet capable of defeating the powerful Aradian fleet. Moreover, he would have boasted of having won a naval victory if it had occurred. What happened exactly then? When Mattanba'al heard that Tiglath-pileser had conquered a city of his continental territory, he was afraid and decided to make allegiance in order to have his life spared. "He put on a sackcloth" as a token of mourning or repentance, which was a custom followed by the Phoenicians as well as by the Assyrians. He offered the Assyrian king a rich tribute: among other items, ivory, ebony inlaid with precious stones, gold, fine oil, all types of aromatics, and Egyptian horses. After the king of Arwad's submission, the whole coastline, from Kashpûna to Arwad, was placed under the authority of the governor of Simirra. Thus, Mattanba'al lost his continental territory, but by submitting to Tiglath-pileser he succeeded in keeping his island independent. The island alone was not self-sufficient for its supplies of food, water, and timber. The king of Arwad depended on his continental territory, which was now integrated into the Assyrian province of Simirra; that is, he relied on good relations with the Assyrian governor. Otherwise, he remained free on his island and could continue his trading activities as he wanted. This event probably occurred in 734, at the beginning of the new Assyrian campaigns in the West. Mattanba'al retained his throne and again paid the tribute in around 732, together with King Hiram II of Tyre and King Shipitba'al of Byblos.[24]

The next passage of the same text, also damaged, described a battle against a certain city, whose name is broken off: "[…] inside his palace […]. I accepted (their plea) [to *forgi*]ve their rebellion and I s[pared] their land […]."[25] Tiglath-pileser filled the plain with warriors who had been killed and collected booty such as oxen, sheep, and goats. Then he accepted the enemy's plea, forgave them for their rebellion, and spared (or destroyed?) their land. One clause remains unexplained: "inside his palace," because the singular is used instead of the plural in the rest of the text. Several hypotheses have been proposed: Tyre, Dor, Israel, Damascus, or some Phoenician or Philistine city.[26] The phrase could refer to Tyre as this passage follows a logical geographical order: after the submission of Arwad and before the conquest of Gaza.

---

24. RINAP 1:123, 47.r.10'.
25. RINAP 1:126, 48.10'–14'.
26. Na'aman, "Tiglath-pileser III's Campaigns against Tyre and Israel," 56–57 (with bibliography).

It is not certain that the suppression of the revolt of Tyre occurred in the same year as that of the revolt of Arwad. It probably occurred in the next stage of these western campaigns, more southwards. Since the Assyrian army depended heavily on its chariotry and cavalry, the decision to attack the south coastal region first could be explained by the fact that the flat terrain would allow the troops to advance rapidly.[27] Alternatively, before attacking Rahiânu, king of Damascus, Tiglath-pileser may have wanted to cut him off from his coastal allies, following the strategy already used against Arpad in 742, and to crush the revolts of Gaza and Tyre on the way. According to the Eponym List, the struggle against the Philistine cities took place in 734, so it is possible that the problem of Tyre was solved in its stride.

King Hiram II of Tyre, who reigned in around 739–730, paid tribute to Assyria in 738, after Ittobaʻal who had paid tribute in around 739.[28] At that time, the king of Tyre governed the double kingdom of Tyre and Sidon, which was created in the ninth century and probably disappeared at around the end of the eighth century.[29] Hiram joined the anti-Assyrian coalition led by Rahiânu of Damascus, together with Peqah of Israel: "Hi]ram of the land of Tyre, who conspired with Raḫiānu ... (against me)."[30] Compared to this northern alliance, the southern area could have reacted differently: the Philistine cities of Ashkelon and Gaza, as well as the queen of the Arabs may have revolted independently because it is not written that they joined the coalition; as for Ahaz of Judah, he called for help from the Assyrian king.[31] However, the good relations between the kings of Tyre and Israel seem to be interrupted, in particular the alliance between Hiram and Peqah.[32] Hiram was severely punished for his participation in the anti-Assyrian coalition: "I captured (and) plun[dered the city] of Maḫalab, his fortified city, together with (other) large cities (of his)."[33] Mahalab is identified with Khirbet el-Mahallib, 6 km northeast of Tyre. Hiram went before the king of Assyria, who was probably not far from Tyre, and kissed his feet as a sign of submission. He paid tribute, among

---

27. Dubovský, "Tiglath-pileser III's Campaigns," 162.
28. RINAP 1:46, 14.11; 70, 27.3; 77, 32.2; 87, 35.iii.6.
29. Elayi, *History of Phoenicia*, 131–33.
30. RINAP 1:131, 49.r.5–6; 106, 42.15′–19′.
31. RINAP 1:61, 21.12′–16′ (Ashkelon); 105, 42.8′–10′ (Gaza); 19′–22′ (Samsi).
32. Amos 1:9–10.
33. RINAP 1:131, 49.r.5–6.

which were twenty talents of gold, multicolored garments, linen garments, eunuchs, male and female singers, and Egyptian horses.[34] Tiglath-pileser's acceptance of Hiram's allegiance can be understood by the fact that Tyre was located on an island and had a powerful fleet. It would have been difficult, as for Arwad, to try to capture this island and also a mistake because harming this rich and powerful maritime power would have entailed a financial loss to the Assyrian Empire. Tiglath-pileser also realized that the partial domination of Tyre was better than its conversion into an Assyrian province because it served as a buffer-state between Assyria and Egypt and could eventually be used as a base for operations against Egypt.

In two long summary inscriptions after Hiram's submission and tribute, possibly dated in 734, the receipt of tribute from his successor Mattan (Metenna) is mentioned in around 730–729: "I sent a eunuch of mine, the chief eunuch, to the city Tyre. I received from Metenna of the city Tyre 150 talents of gold (and) 2,000 talents of silver [...."[35] Although one of the two texts mentioned only 50 talents of gold, this tribute was much higher than the one paid by Hiram in 734 (only 20 talents and no silver).[36] Why did Tiglath-pileser send his chief eunuch, commander-in-chief, to Tyre? The king was occupied in Babylonia, but we do not know whether the chief eunuch had to crush a new revolt, control the accession of the new king, or whether his mission was simply to receive the tribute. Anyway, the fact that the tribute was much higher than before meant that there was a serious problem with Tyre. Tadmor has proposed that the tribute was the audience gift of the new king because he read the sign *ta*-[, restored as *tāmartašu* ("gift, contribution, tribute"). However, this heavy tribute could have been punishment for usurpation as was the case for Hoshea of Samaria and Hullî of Tabal.

9.2. The Campaign against the Philistine Cities

The campaign against the Philistine cities was the major campaign in 734, since it was mentioned in the Eponym List. However, if the revolt of Gaza was suppressed in 734, the revolt of Ashkelon was suppressed later, in 733 or 732, because King Mitinti of Ashkelon became afraid when he saw the

---

34. RINAP 1:131, 49.r.7–8.
35. RINAP 1:123, 47.r.16'; 133, 49.r.26; *PNA* 2.2:750 (Metenna).
36. RINAP 1:131, 49.r.6.

defeat of Rahiânu.[37] Hanunu, king of Gaza, had revolted against Assyria, possibly joining the anti-Assyrian coalition led by Rahiânu of Damascus. However, he did not expect Tiglath-pileser or want to confront him: "he became frightened by my powerful weapons and escaped to Egypt."[38] Tiglath-pileser conquered Gaza and carried off gold, 800 talents of silver, and people, together with Hanunu's possessions, his wife, his sons, his daughters, as well as his property and his gods. The following passage contains an unexplained contradiction: "[I fashioned] (a statue bearing) image(s) of the gods, my lords, and my royal image out of gold, [erected (it)] in the palace [of the city of Gaza], (and) I reckoned (it) [am]ong the gods of their land."[39] While Tiglath-pileser carried off the gods of Gaza to Assyria, he erected in Gaza a statue bearing the images of the Assyrian gods among the local gods. Then, probably on the order of Tiglath-pileser, Hanunu came back from Egypt and was reinstalled on his throne after having paid a tribute of gold, silver, multicolored garments, linen garments, and large horses. Hanunu paid tribute on another occasion, probably later.[40] The Assyrian king considered one of Hanunu's harbors as an "Assyrian emporium" (É.ka-a-ri KUR aš-šur.KI),[41] that is, a commercial site and a tribute collecting center. It was probably located at the site of Tell er-Ruqeish, 7 km southwest of Gaza.[42]

After conquering Gaza, Tiglath-pileser flaunted himself along the border of Egypt (Wadi el-Arish) in order to deter the pharaoh from intervening. He appointed the Arab Idibi'ilu as the "gatekeeper facing Egypt."[43]

---

37. RINAP 1:61, 21.14; Nadav Na'aman, "Two Notes on the History of Ashkelon and Ekron in the Late Eighth-Seventh Centuries B.C.E.," *TA* 25 (1998): 222.
38. RINAP 1:105–6, 42.8'; 127, 48.14'; 132, 49.r.13.
39. RINAP 1:106, 42.10'–11'; 127, 48.16'; 132, 49.r.13–14.
40. RINAP 1:123, 47.r.12'.
41. RINAP 1:106, 42.14'.
42. E. D. Oren et al., "A Phoenician Emporium on the Border of Egypt" [Hebrew], *Qad* 75/76 (1986): 83–91; Oren, "Ruqeish," *NEAEHL* 4:1293–94; Alon Shavit, "Settlement Patterns of Philistine City-States," in *Bene Israel: Studies in the Archaeology of Israel and the Levant during the Bronze and Iron Ages in Honour of Israel Finkelstein*, ed. Alexander Fantalkin and Assaf Yasur-Landau, CHANE 31 (Leiden: Brill, 2008), 153. For other propositions of identifications, see Ronny Reich, "The Identification of the 'Sealed kāru of Egypt,'" *IEJ* 34 (1984): 33 n. 7 (with bibliography); André Lemaire, "Populations et territoires de la Palestine à l'époque perse," *Trans* 3 (1990): 46; Anson F. Rainey, "Herodotus' Description of the East Mediterranean Coast," *BASOR* 321 (2001): 60.
43. RINAP 1:63, 22.13'; 107, 42.34'; 112, 44.16'; 122, 47.r.6'.

9. THE FOURTH PHASE OF THE CAMPAIGNS (734–732) 137

Na'aman has proposed to restore another damaged passage as follows: "[Siru]att[i the Me'unite and] Idibi'ilu I appointed as su[pervis]ors (*qe-pu-ti*) over [the entrance? of Egy]pt."⁴⁴ Siruatti, like Idibi'ilu, was an Arab, and his territory was "below Egypt,"⁴⁵ probably designating the location of his tribe. However, Egypt was beset by such dissensions between rival powers that it was unable to oppose Assyrian expansion. Pharaoh Osorkon IV, for example, was helpless before the rise of the city of Sais and its leader Tefnakht. Based on an albeit damaged passage where the name is broken off, it is possible that Osorkon made allegiance to the king of Assyria subsequent to the submission of Hanunu of Gaza and the appointment of Siruatti as supervisor over the border of Egypt.⁴⁶ However, this could be propaganda, false information, or another ruler, not the pharaoh. At any rate, Assyrian interest in Gaza was primarily economic: the acquisition of taxes and tribute, the exploitation of local economic structures, and the control of lucrative caravan trade routes.⁴⁷ It was also strategic: creating a buffer zone between Assyria and Egypt and securing the southern border.

The suppression of the Ashkelon revolt occurred in 733 or 732. This phase of the campaign can possibly be reconstructed in this way: Tiglath-pileser captured Galilee, then moved southwest and captured Gezer, and finally settled the problem of Ashkelon.⁴⁸ Mitinti of Ashkelon had neglected his "loyalty oath" (*Adê*) and had revolted against Assyria, possibly joining the coalition of Rahiânu of Damascus.⁴⁹ When Mitinti saw the defeat of Rahiânu, he would have been stricken with panic, had a lapse of judgment or a state of insanity, and died.⁵⁰ Rûkibtu, Mitinti's son or usurper, then sat on the throne and was confirmed in his function. In order to justify Tiglath-pileser's recognition of Rûkibtu as a legitimate king of Ashkelon, the scribe insisted

---

44. Nadav Na'aman, "Siruatti the Me'unite in a Second Inscription of Tiglath-pileser III," *NABU* (1998): 7, 6; RINAP 1:112–13, 44.15′–16′.
45. RINAP 1:127, 48.22′; *PNA* 3.1:1152 (Siruatti); 2.1:505 (Idibiilu). According to 2 Chr 26:7–8, the Meunites paid tribute to Uzziah of Judah.
46. RINAP 1:127, 48.20′–21′; 132, 49.r.23–25.
47. J. T. Walton, "Assyrian Interest in the West: Philistia and Judah," *ErIs* 33 (2018): 175*–82*.
48. Carl S. Ehrlich, *The Philistines in Transition: A History from ca. 1000–730 BCE* (Leiden: Brill, 1996), 99; Dubovský, "Tiglath-pileser III's Campaigns," 161.
49. RINAP 1:61, 21.12′; *PNA* 2.2:757–58 (Mitinti). According to Na'aman ("Two Notes," 70), he had joined the anti-Assyrian coalition.
50. RINAP 1:61, 21.15′; 63, 22.9′; *PNA* 3.1:1053–54 (Rahiânu); Na'aman, "Two Notes," 69.

on the disloyalty of the previous king of Ashkelon and on his ignominious death. Conversely, the new king meandered, seeking to be recognized as an Assyrian vassal, and paid a heavy tribute of 500 talents of silver.[51] Ashkelon, like Gaza, was kept as a vassal state, a buffer state between Assyria and Egypt.

Ashdod is not mentioned in the royal inscriptions like other Philistine cities, but it could figure in a broken passage. In an administrative letter sent by the crown prince Shalmaneser (V), probably not earlier than 734, Ashdod is mentioned as a tributary city of the Assyrian king.[52] Ashdod is possibly also mentioned in a fragmentary letter sent by Qurdi-ashur-lâmur to Tiglath-pileser.[53] The Ashdodite king implored Qurdi-ashur-lâmur to forward his appeal to the Assyrian king. He reminded him that the cities of Qadarua, Lidu, and Hadidu were included as part of the loyalty oath (*adê*) that had been concluded with Assyria and in which the extent of Assyria's territorial control over them was confirmed. The three cities seem to be in the geographical proximity of Ashdod: Qadarua could be Gedera (Tel Qatra), Lidu could be Lydda/Lod, and Hadidu Hadid.[54] This letter informs us of how Assyria's relations with Ashdod developed: Assyria was counting on Ashdod's loyalty, and, in return, Ashdod expected support from Assyria. The letter also informs us that, in the southern Levant, submission to Assyria involved a loyalty oath as early as in the reign of Tiglath-pileser. However, prophets such as Hosea and Isaiah of Jerusalem saw Israel's covenant relationship with Yahweh as incompatible with submission to Assyria through a loyalty oath.[55]

9.3. The Campaign against Israel and Judah

The anti-Assyrian coalition led by Rahiânu of Damascus is traditionally called the Syro-Ephraimite war by biblical specialists, "Syro-" designat-

---

51. As restored by Na'aman: RINAP 1:63, 22.11'; 122, 47.11'.
52. SAA 19:10–11, 8; Shawn Zelig Aster, "An Assyrian Loyalty-Oath Imposed on Ashdod in the Reign of Tiglath-pileser III?," *Orientalia* 82.3 (2018): 277–78.
53. SAA 19:35, 28 (Ashdod is partly restored); Aster, "Assyrian Loyalty-Oath," 278–80.
54. Aster, "Assyrian Loyalty-Oath," 281–87.
55. C. L. Crouch, *Israel and the Assyrians: Deuteronomy, the Succession Treaty of Esarhaddon, and the Nature of Subversion*, ANEM 8 (Atlanta: SBL Press, 2014); Peter Machinist, "Ah Assyria… (Isaiah 10:5ff). Isaiah's Assyrian Polemic Revisited," in *Not Only History: Proceedings of the Conference in Honor of Mario Liverani Held in Sapienza-Università di Roma, 20–21 April 2009*, ed. Gilda Bartoloni and Maria Giovanna Biga (Winona Lake, IN: Eisenbrauns, 2016), 183–218.

9. THE FOURTH PHASE OF THE CAMPAIGNS (734–732) 139

ing the kingdom of Damascus and "Ephraim" the name of one of the twelve tribes.[56] These events are documented in Assyrian inscriptions and biblical sources, which present some discrepancies that need to be examined carefully.[57] The members of the coalition led by Rahiânu that were recorded as tribute bearers in 738 were Menahem of Samaria and Hiram II of Tyre. Other members of the coalition were possibly Hanunu of Gaza, Mitinti of Ashkelon, and Samsi queen of the Arabs.[58] The history of the kingdom of Israel after the death of Jeroboam II in 743 was a troubled period, with internal unrest, uproars of factions, and foreign threats.[59] The last half of the eighth century is also a difficult period for determining precise dates.[60] Zechariah succeeded Jeroboam but was assassinated six months later in Gilead by Shallum, who reigned for only one month, being assassinated in his turn.[61] Then Menahem seized the throne and reigned until 738 when he sent tribute to the Assyrian king. Apparently Menahem had the support of the ancient capital of Tirzah but encountered resistance in the area of Tipsah (Khirbet Tipsah?), possibly not from the year of his seizure of the throne but from his fourth or fifth year.[62] The recognition of Menahem as the vassal of Tiglath-pileser should have strengthened his position: "When Assyria's King Tiglath-pileser marched against the land, Menahem gave Tiglath-pileser one thousand silver kikkars in order to become his ally and to strengthen his hold on the kingdom" (2 Kgs 15:19). Nevertheless, 738 was his last regnal year and his son and successor Peqahiah reigned less than two years (738–737) before being assassinated by Peqah, a usurper: "Peqah, son of Remaliah, his lieutenant, formed a conspiracy against him and, with the help of fifty Gileadites, attacked him in the citadel of the royal house … killed him and reigned in his stead" (2 Kgs 15:25). Having usurped

---

56. Siddall, "Tiglath-pileser III's Aid to Ahaz," *ANES* 46 (2009): 93–106.
57. Joachim Begrich, "Der syrisch-ephraimitische Krieg und seine weltpolitische Zusammenhänge," *ZDMG* 83 (1927): 213–37; Bustenay Oded, "The Historical Background of the Syro-Ephraimite War Reconsidered," *CBQ* 34 (1972): 153–65; Stuart A. Irvine, *Isaiah, Ahaz, and the Syro-Ephraimite Crisis*, SBLDS 123 (Atlanta: Scholars Press, 1990); Dubovský, "Tiglath-pileser III's Campaigns," 153–70.
58. RINAP 1:46, 14.10–11; *PNA* 3.1:1085.
59. Crouch, *Israel and the Assyrians*; Edward Lipiński, *A History of the Kingdom of Israel*, OLA 275 (Leuven: Peeters, 2018), 111–16 (with bibliography).
60. William H. Shea, "Menahem and Tiglath-Pileser III," *JNES* 37 (1978): 43–49.
61. 2 Kgs 15:8–13.
62. Lipiński, *History of the Kingdom of Israel*, 112.

the throne in 737, Peqah joined the anti-Assyrian coalition formed by Rahiânu of Damascus. In Tiglath-pileser's inscriptions, Menahem was regarded as the king of Samaria, while Peqah was considered the king of Bît-Humria, "House of Omri," probably because Peqah presented himself as a successor of the Omride dynasty. At that time, the kingdom of Israel extended into the valleys of Jordan and Israel, part of the coastal plain, Galilee, and part of Transjordan. It was limited northward by the Phoenician cities, eastward by the kingdoms of Damascus, Ammon, and Moab, and southwards by the Philistine cities and the kingdom of Judah.

Ahaz (ca. 742–726) succeeded his father Jotham (ca. 749–743) on the throne of Judah, after Jotham had been deposed by the pro-Assyrian factions. The kingdom of Judah was a smaller kingdom than that of Israel; it was located to the south, and its capital was Jerusalem, with the Philistine cities located westwards, the kingdom of Moab eastwards, and the kingdom of Edom southwards.[63] The anti-Assyrian coalition considered it natural that Judah join it, but Judah, assessing the realities of the situation, did not. There is a debate as to whether the reason for the attack on Judah by the Syro-Ephraimite coalition was an anti-Assyrian movement or the continuation of an existing territorial conflict in Transjordan.[64]

Rahiânu of Damascus and Peqah of Israel did not accept Ahaz's refusal to join the anti-Assyrian coalition because they were unwilling to have a neutral power in their rear when they confronted the Assyrians. Therefore, they decided to depose Ahaz and to replace him by the son of Tabeel, who was supposed to be favorable to an anti-Assyrian policy: "Let us go up against Judah and terrify it and conquer it for ourselves and make the son of Tabeel king in it" (Isa 7:6 NRSVue). The biblical accounts of Kings and Chronicles differ in the way they describe

---

63. H. Spieckermann, *Juda unter Assur in der Sargonidenzeit* (Göttingen: Vandenhoeck & Ruprecht, 1982).

64. Begrich, "Der syrisch-ephraimitische Krieg und seine weltpolitische Zusammenhänge," 213–37; Oded, "Historical Background," 153–65; Benedikt Otzen, "Israel under the Assyrians," in *Power and Propaganda: A Symposium on Ancient Empires*, ed. Mogens Trolle Larsen (Copenhagen: Akademish Forlag, 1979), 255–61; John Bright, *A History of Israel*, 3rd ed. (London: SCM, 1981); Irvine, *Isaiah, Ahaz, and the Syro-Ephraimite Crisis*; Nadav Na'aman, "Forced Participation in Alliances in the Course of the Assyrian Campaigns to the West," in Cogan and Eph'al, *Ah, Assyria*, 92; Joseph Blenkinsopp, *Isaiah 1–39: A New Translation with Introduction and Commentary*, AB 19 (New York: Doubleday, 2000), 154.

the Syro-Ephraimite campaign against Judah and in the intentions and results of this punitive campaign.[65] There are four main discrepancies between Kings and Chronicles.[66] The first discrepancy concerns the identity of the enemy attacking Judah: in Kings, the enemy was Damascus and Israel, while in Chronicles, the enemy attack came first from Damascus and Israel, then from the Edomites and the Philistines. The second discrepancy concerns the extent of the attack on Judah: according to Kings and Isaiah, the allies could not defeat Judah; in Chronicles, 120,000 Judahites were killed; 200,000 were captured; and a large amount of booty was brought to Samaria. The third discrepancy is related to the result of Tiglath-pileser's intervention: according to Kings, Tiglath-pileser helped Ahaz by defeating the Syro-Ephraimite coalition; according to Chronicles, Tiglath-pileser's intervention did not help Ahaz. The fourth discrepancy concerns the conclusion of the war: in Kings, the Assyrian intervention ended the war; in Chronicles, Judah was severely defeated, but the prophet Oded intervened in order to save the Judean captives taken to Samaria.

Several scholars have attempted to solve these inconsistencies. Some scholars have suggested textual corruptions.[67] Others have pointed to differing religious and ideological attitudes of the authors of Kings and Chronicles. For Stuart A. Irvine, additional information has been included in Chronicles in order to emphasize the divine punishment for Ahaz's idolatrous practices.[68] According to Gary N. Knoppers, the Chronicler intended to portray the kings who despoiled the royal treasure as morally deficient.[69] For other scholars, the condemnation of Ahaz and idealization of good Judean kings in Chronicles were intended to

---

65. Dubovský, "Tiglath-pileser III's Campaigns," 156–57 (with bibliography).
66. 2 Kgs 16:5–9; 2 Chr 28:5–21. Most of Isa 7:1–2 agrees with Kings.
67. Mordechai Cogan and Hayim Tadmor, *II Kings: A New Translation with Introduction and Commentary*, AB 11 (New York: Doubleday, 1988), 184–87; Tadmor and Cogan, "Ahaz and Tiglath-Pileser in the Book of Kings," 496–99; John Raymond Bartlett, *Edom and the Edomites*, JSOTSup 77 (Sheffield: Sheffield Academic, 1989), 127; John Lindsay, "Edomite Westward Expansion: The Biblical Evidence," *ANES* 36 (1999): 76–79.
68. Irvine, *Isaiah, Ahaz, and the Syro-Ephraimite Crisis*, 91–93.
69. Gary N. Knoppers, "Treasures Won and Lost: Royal (Mis)appropriations in Kings and Chronicles," in *The Chronicler as Author: Studies in Text and Texture*, ed. M. Patrick Graham and Steven L. McKenzie, JSOTSup 263 (Sheffield: Sheffield Academic, 1999), 200–201.

create a moral contrast.[70] Anson F. Rainey and R. Steven Notley focused on the historical information provided by each of the biblical accounts and concluded that they referred to different Assyrian campaigns in 734 and 732.[71] According to others, what first appears to be contradictory between Kings and Chronicles can, in fact, be understood as the Chronicler's supplementary information, coming from the "Chronicles of the Kings of Judah" and the "Chronicles of the Kings of Israel," that was available and could be consulted.[72]

Siddall considered that the author of Kings was only concerned with Ahaz's foreign relations with Israel and Damascus, while the Chronicler related both the Syro-Ephraimite attack and the attack of the Edomites and Philistines.[73] Therefore, in Kings, Tiglath-pileser's aid is viewed as a significant force in Ahaz's defense of Judah; in Chronicles, the Assyrian king's aid failed because it did not return the Edomites and Philistines under Judean control but turned them into Assyrian vassals. All things considered, this hypothesis is interesting, and there are also some positive considerations in the other hypotheses. In the end, the main source remains the Assyrian inscriptions, even though they present some deficiencies and elements of propaganda. However, it is impossible to completely rule out the discrepancies between the two biblical accounts, for example, the fact that Ahaz was defeated or not by his enemy or that the Assyrian intervention was beneficial or negative for him.

In both accounts, Ahaz of Judah, seeing his kingdom attacked, opted for a diplomatic solution: he invited Tiglath-pileser to save him and sent messengers to him saying: "I am your servant and your son. Go up for saving me from the king of Aram and the king of Israel, who rise up

---

70. Peter R. Ackroyd, *The Chronicler in His Age*, JSOTSup 101 (Sheffield: Sheffield Academic, 1999), 116–20; Isaac Kalimi, *The Reshaping of Ancient Israelite History in Chronicles* (Winona Lake, IN: Eisenbrauns, 2005), 332–34.

71. Anson F. Rainey and R. Steven Notley, *The Sacred Bridge: Carter's Atlas of Biblical World* (Jerusalem: Carter, 2006), 228–32.

72. 1 Kgs 14:29; 15:7 (kings of Judah); 1 Kgs 14:15–31 (kings of Judah); Noel K. Weeks, *The Sufficiency of Scripture* (Edinburgh: Banner of Truth Trust, 1988), 57–62; Anson F. Rainey, *The Chronicler as Historian*, ed. M. Patrick Graham, Kenneth G. Hoglund, and Steven L. MacKenzie, JSOTSup 238 (Sheffield: Sheffield Academic, 1999), 30–72, 65–66.

73. Jacob M. Myers, *II Chronicles: Introduction, Translation and Notes*, AB 13 (New York: Doubleday, 1965), 163; Siddall, "Tiglath-pileser III's Aid to Ahaz," 93–106.

9. THE FOURTH PHASE OF THE CAMPAIGNS (734-732)

against me."[74] In order to convince the Assyrian king, Ahaz accompanied his request with a large tribute, probably paid in 734: gold and silver from the house of the Lord and treasuries from the royal palace. In the Assyrian sources, the name of the king of Judah involved in this incident was Jehoahaz (*Jāu-ḫazi*), which was probably the full name for Ahaz.[75] However, the Assyrian inscriptions do not mention any invitation coming from Ahaz. In the biblical accounts, Ahaz's invitation was highly criticized by Isaiah, because he preferred to make a request to Tiglath-pileser rather than to Yahweh (Isa 7:10–12). Yet as can be deduced from both the Assyrian inscriptions and Kings, Ahaz made the right choice; he saved his country from destruction and assured himself the throne of Jerusalem until the end of his life.

If this event really did occur, Ahaz's request was a good pretext for the king of Assyria to intervene in the Levant, but even without this pretext, Tiglath-pileser would have made his campaign of 734–732 because the conquest of the West had been programmed into his military strategy. Tiglath-pileser intervened rapidly and marched on Damascus in 733. The devastation of Israel probably took place after the operation in Transjordan. After Damascus, the Assyrian king turned southward into northern Transjordan and captured Gilead and the territory down to Abel-Shittim, "which are the border of the land of Bît-Humria."[76] A relief from Tiglath-pileser's palace in Nimrud represents the capture of a fortified city, with the following epigraph: "the city Astaratu."[77] This city is thought to be biblical Ashtaroth in Gilead, identified with Tell Astara in northern Transjordan. Its capture, not mentioned in the inscriptions but represented in a relief, probably took place in 733, during the conquest of Transjordan Astaratu was located in the new province of Qarnîna (Qarnê).[78]

A similar relief represents the capture of another city, accompanied by the following epigraph: "the city Gazru."[79] Gazru is apparently the biblical Gezer (Abu Shusheh), located at the border of the Shephelah, 16 km from

---

74. 2 Kgs 16:7; 2 Chr 28:16 (with "kings" instead of "king").
75. RINAP 1:122–23, 47.r.11'; Tadmor, *Inscriptions of Tiglath-pileser III*, 277; Manfred Weippert, *Historisches Textbuch zum Alten Testament* (Göttingen: Vandenhoeck & Ruprecht, 2010), 376, n. 77; *PNA* 2.1; Marc Z. Brettler, "Ahaz," *ABD* 1:106.
76. RINAP 1:105, 42.6'.
77. RINAP 1:144–46, 56.
78. Radner, "Provinz. C. Assyrien," 61–62, 56; RINAP 1:85, 35.ii.7'.
79. RINAP 1:146, 57.

the sea, midway between Jerusalem and Tel Aviv. Tadmor dated Gezer's capture to the end of the wars in Syria-Palestine, in 732–731; however, in the latest edition of Tadmor and Yamada, the date proposed is without question 733. As Gezer is located at a considerable distance from northern Transjordan, it is more likely that it was captured in 734, during the campaign against the Philistine cities.[80]

In 732, Tiglath-pileser moved through Israel and Galilee. The population of Galilee was deported and much booty was taken off to Assyria. Some cities can be identified in two damaged passages: Da]barâ, located near Mount Tabor; possibly Sa[mhuna on the northwestern margins of the Jezreel valley; Marom, identified with Tell Qarnei Hittin in Lower Galilee; Hinatuna (Hannathon); Yatbite (Yotbah); and Aruma (Rumah), located near the Beth-Netophah valley.[81] The same event is related in the Bible: "In the days of Peqah, king of Israel, Tiglath-pileser, king of Assyria, came and seized Iyyôn, Abel Beth-Maakah, Janoah, Qedesh, Hazor, Gilead, and Galilee, even all the land of Nephtali, and deported them to Assyria" (2 Kgs 15:29). Iyyôn has been identified with modern-day Merjayûn in Lebanon, and Abel-Maakah was possibly Tel Dan.[82] Janoah is often identified with modern-day Yânûh in Lebanon.[83] Qedesh should be identified with Tell Qadis, to the northwest of Lake Hula.[84] Besides the deportations from those cities, biblical sources also mention the deportations of the Reubenites, the Gadites, the half-tribe of Manasseh, and of Beerah, the chieftain of the Reubenites (1 Chr 5:6, 26).

The passages concerning the attack on Israel are damaged, but the inscription can be read that Tiglath-pileser took sixteen of its districts, devastated its territory, carried off livestock, and isolated its capital Samaria.[85] Tiglath-pileser boasted of having conquered the kingdom of

---

80. Mordechai Cogan, "When Was Gezer Captured by Tiglath-pileser III?," *IEJ* 65 (2015): 96–99.

81. RINAP 1:61, 21.1′–11′; 62–63, 22.1′–8′; 2 Kgs 15:29; Na'aman, *Ancient Israel and Its Neighbors*, 202–3; RGTC 7/7-1, 107–8 (Hinatuna), 27 (Aruma).

82. Lipiński, *History of the Kingdom of Israel*, 114.

83. Félix-Marie Abel, *Géographie de la Palestine II* (Paris: Gabalda, 1938), 354; Stefan Wild, *Libanesische Ortsnamen*, Beiruter Texte und Studien 9 (Beirut: Orient-Institut, 1973), 269–70. This identification is questioned by Lipiński, *History of the Kingdom of Israel*, 114.

84. Lipiński, *History of the Kingdom of Israel*, 114.

85. RINAP 1:61, 21.3′; 62, 22.3′; 112, 44.17′–18′.

9. THE FOURTH PHASE OF THE CAMPAIGNS (734–732) 145

Israel in its entirety and to have annexed it together with its belongings.[86] However, the Assyrian king annexed only part of the kingdom, since there were still kings on the throne afterwards. The Assyrian inscriptions are not very clear concerning the fate of King Peqah of Israel: either he was overthrown by his subjects, killed by his subjects, or killed by the Assyrians.[87] According to the biblical sources, Peqah was killed by Hoshea, a captain in Peqah's army and the head of the pro-Assyrian party in Samaria (2 Kgs 15:30). Tiglath-pileser rewarded Hoshea by making him king over Israel, which had been reduced to smaller dimensions: "I placed Hoshea [as king o]ver them. I received from them ten talents of gold, …talents of silver, [together with] their [proper]ty, and [I brou]ght them [to Assyria]."[88] The tribute was brought by Hoshea or by his envoys to the Assyrian king who was in Sarrabânu, a great city of the Bît-Shilâni in Chaldea, that is, during his campaign of 731 (see below).[89] Thus, the beginning of Hoshea's reign had a pro-Assyrian orientation, which was one of the reasons why Samaria was spared by Tiglath-pileser.[90]

As for Judah, Tiglath-pileser had saved King Ahaz by invading the kingdoms of Damascus and Israel; he continued to treat Ahaz as a vassal, and Ahaz continued his reign for more than ten years. The only information in the Assyrian inscriptions related to the kingdoms of Ammon, Moab, and Edom concerns the tribute paid to Tiglath-pileser in 738 or 734 by the following kings: Sanîpu of Bît-Ammon, Salâmânu of Moab, and Qaush-malaka of Edom.[91] Additional information is provided by the Bible: Salâmânu of Moab attacked the city of Beth-Arbel, possibly Irbid in Gilead.[92] According to Chronicles, the Edomites "came and inflicted a defeat on Judah and took captives" (2 Chr 28:17). Rahiânu of Damascus "drove out the Judahites from Elath, and the Edomites came to Elath and settled there, as is still the case" (2 Kgs 16:6). It is not totally certain that these events concerning the Moabites and Edomites were related to and contemporaneous with the Syro-Ephraimite War. Anyhow, the local

---

86. RINAP 1:131, 49.r.9.
87. RINAP 1:112, 44.18' (restored); 106, 42.17'.
88. RINAP 1:106, 42.17'–19'.
89. RINAP 1:132, 49.r.11. The reading of the city name is based on the collation of P.Hulin.
90. 2 Kgs 17:3; Tadmor, *Inscriptions of Tiglath-pileser III*, 281.
91. RINAP 1:122–23, 47.10'–11'; *PNA* 3.1:1069, 1090.
92. Hos 10:14; Lipiński, *History of the Kingdom of Israel*, 115–16.

events of Israel and Judah did not interest the Assyrians who made no report about them. Tiglath-pileser's intention was to extend his empire to the west and to organize the new territories by creating new Assyrian provinces and vassal states in the south ruled by loyal kings and serving as buffer states between Assyria and Egypt.

9.4. The Campaign against Damascus

Damascus, an independent and rich kingdom, was called *Ša-imērišu* or *Bīt-Ḫaza'ili* in Akkadian, originating from the name of its king, Hazael, who reigned from the mid-ninth century to 803 (?).[93] It was also called Aram (2 Kgs 8:28–29) to indicate that it was under Aramean control. It was probably in the tenth century that Damascus became the capital of the most important Aramean state in the Levant. In 853, Adad-Idri (Bar-Hadad II), king of Damascus, played a leading role in the anti-Assyrian coalition that confronted Shalmaneser III at the battle of Qarqar. In 849 and 848, Adad-Idri led more actions against the Assyrians, before the final crushing of the coalition in 845.[94] His successor Hazael, probably a usurper, maintained the same anti-Assyrian policy. In 803, Hazael died, and Adad-nârârî III attacked and conquered Damascus. In ca. 800, Bar-Hadad led a new coalition of sixteen Syrian and eastern Anatolian rulers against Zakkur of Hamath, supported by the Assyrians. In 773, Shalmaneser IV sent an army conducted by Shamshî-ilu against Hadyan (Hadiânu) II of Damascus, who was forced to pay a heavy tribute to avoid destruction. After a short-lived subjection to King Jeroboam II of Israel,[95] Damascus became independent under its last king, Rahiânu, who reigned from the mid-eighth century until 732, paid tribute in 738, and led another anti-Assyrian coalition in 733. According to the Eponym List, the campaigns against Damascus in 733 and 732 were major ones.

In 733, after the neutralization of Rahiânu's allies, the Phoenician and Philistine cities, during the previous year, Tiglath-pileser attacked Damas-

---

93. RINAP 1:46, 14.10; 105, 42.7'; Lemaire, "Hazaël de Damas, roi d'Aram," 91–108; Bryce, *World of the Neo-Hittite Kingdoms*, 175–78. On Damascus, see Pitard, *Ancient Damascus*, 114–44; Giovanni Battista Lanfranchi, "An Empire Names Its Periphery: The Assyrian Toponym for Damascus," in Battista Lanfranchi et al., *Leggo!*, 399–434.
94. RIMA 3:23, 37–38, 39.
95. RINAP 1:38, 11.4'; 46, 14.10; 70, 27.3; 76, 31.9; 77, 32.1.

9. THE FOURTH PHASE OF THE CAMPAIGNS (734–732)   147

cus. A damaged text reported a battle between Rahiânu and the king of Assyria, who defeated Rahiânu and who "with the blood of his warriors dyed the river … red like a flower."[96] Tiglath-pileser intended to demean his enemy by describing his cowardly nature: "In order to save his life, he fled alone and entered the gate of his city [like] a mongoose."[97] The choice of Rahiânu to take refuge in the city probably corresponded to a strategic measure, as he relied upon the impossibility of the city being conquered by means of a siege. Then Tiglath-pileser behaved as was customary for an Assyrian king after a battle: he impaled the foremost men alive while forcing the people of Damascus to watch. His purpose was to terrify the people so that they surrendered. Since they did not surrender, Tiglath-pileser was obliged to blockade the city: "For forty-five days I set up my camp [aro] und his city and confined him (there) like a bird in a cage."[98] This blockade of the city was not based on the use of machines or technical devices but on intentional actions that cause hunger and thirst in order to force the enemy to surrender. The verb *esēru*, "to enclose, to confine,"[99] also appears in the inscriptions of Shalmaneser III and Adad-nârârî III reporting their military actions against Damascus. The Assyrian scribes could not reduce the blockade of Damascus to an unsuccessful capture due to the massive defensive walls, but they emphasized the operation of enclosing the king of Damascus "like a bird in a cage" as a military strategy, also used by Sennacherib for Hezekiah of Judah in Jerusalem.[100] In order to make the

---

96. RINAP 1:59, 20.1′–7′.
97. RINAP 1:59, 20.8′–9′.
98. RINAP 1:59, 20.10′–11′. On the simile with animals, see D. Marcus, "Animal Similes in Assyrian Royal Inscriptions," *Orientalia* 46 (1977): 86–106; Lucio Milano, "Il nemico bestiale: Su alcune considerazioni animalesche nella letteratura sumero-accadica," in *Animali tra zoologia, mito e letteratura nella cultura classica e orientale*, ed. E. Cingano, A. Ghersetti, and Lucio Milano (Padova: S.a.r.g.o.n., 2005), 47–67; Stefan Zawadski, "Depicting Hostile Rulers in the Neo-Assyrian Royal Inscriptions," in *Studies on Ancient Near Eastern Worlds and Beyond, Dedicated to Giovanni Battista Lanfranchi on the Occasion of His Sixty-Fifth Birthday on June 23, 2014*, ed. Salvatore Gaspa et al. (Münster: Ugarit-Verlag, 2014), 767–78.
99. *CAD* 4:334–35; Walter R. Mayer, *Politik und Kriegskunst der Assyrer* (Münster: Ugarit-Verlag, 1995), 310.
100. David Nadali, "Sieges and Similes of Sieges in the Royal Annals: The Conquest of Damascus by Tiglath-pileser III," *KASKAL* 6 (2009): 145; Walter R. Mayer, "Sennacherib's Campaign of 701 BCE: The Assyrian View," in *'Like a Bird in a Cage': The Invasion of Sennacherib in 701 BCE*, ed. Lester L. Grabbe (London: Sheffield Academic, 2003), 168–200.

blockade efficient, Tiglath-pileser destroyed the environs of Damascus: "I cut down his plantations…, (and) orchards, which were without number; I did not leave a single one (unspoiled)."[101] The rich orchards around the city were probably situated at the famous oasis of the Gutah surrounding Damascus. The felling of trees can be read as an indirect indication that the siege did not succeed or was not completed.[102] According to the same text, the devastation of the orchards was followed by the capture of Rahiânu's ancestral city, his birthplace.[103] Tiglath-pileser then destroyed 591 cities in sixteen districts of Damascus, quoting only three of them: Kurussâ, Samâya, and Metuna, which indicates that the figures given were vastly exaggerated. He carried off 2,100 captives (800 + 750 + 550). The campaign of 733 was first directed against Damascus, then against Transjordan and the Arabian queen Samsi.[104]

The campaign of 732 probably started with the conquest of Galilee and part of Israel and ended with the conquest of Damascus. The only surviving record of this conquest and of the death of Rahiânu is a biblical statement: "The Assyrian king listened to him [Ahaz], went against Damascus, and captured it. He deported the inhabitants to Quir and put Rahiânu to death" (2 Kgs 16:9). In 1852–1854 Rawlinson discovered a fragment of a colossal slab that he did not transport back to England.[105] He made no copy of the inscription, and the slab was lost. It would have been the only inscription relating the death of Rahiânu. However, the conquest of Damascus in 732 is attested by the Eponym List and by several royal inscriptions mentioning the annexation of this kingdom being turned into an Assyrian province: "[I annexed] to Assyria the extensive [land of Bīt]-Ḫaza'ili in its entirety, from Mount [Lebanon as far as the cities of Gilead (and) Abil-šitti, which are on the bor]der of the land of Bīt-Ḫumria, (and) [I placed a eunuch of mine as governor over them]."[106] Gilead was located east of the city of Jericho. Abil-shitti was the biblical Abel-shittim or Shit-

---

101. RINAP 1:59, 20.11′–12′.
102. Nadali, "Sieges and Similes of Sieges," 141–42; Bryce, *World of the Neo-Hittite Kingdoms*, 273–74.
103. RINAP 1:59, 20.13′–14′: the city …]ḫādara, otherwise unknown. RGTC 7/1, 149 (Karussâ), 206 (Samâya), 175 (Metuna).
104. Dubovský, "Tiglath-pileser III's Campaigns," 160–61.
105. George Smith, "The Annals of Tiglath-Pileser II [sic]," ZÄS 7 (1869): 14; RINAP 1:57, 20.
106. RINAP 1:131, 49.r.3–4; 134, 50.r.3–4; Radner, "Provinz. C. Assyrien," 58; RGTC 7/1, 49 (Bit-Hazaili).

9. THE FOURTH PHASE OF THE CAMPAIGNS (734-732)   149

tim. It is clear that the Assyrians considered these two cities as part of the annexed territory of Damascus.[107] After the capture of Damascus, Tiglath-pileser was temporarily established in the city where he received the homage of vassals such as Ahaz of Judah (2 Kgs 16:10).

9.5. The Campaign against the Arabs

Massive Assyrian expansion under Tiglath-pileser brought Assyrian troops into direct contact with the Arabs. In 733, the Assyrian king defeated Samsi, "queen of the country of the Arabs" (*šarrat māt aribi*) and then in 733 or 732 subjected the Arab tribes. Five years earlier, in 738, another queen of the Arabs, Zabibe, paid tribute to the Assyrian king, probably in the hope of preventing the Assyrians from intervening in the overland trade controlled by the Arabs.[108] Therefore, there was a preexisting political relationship that was most likely sealed with Zabibe, seemingly Samsi's predecessor, during the first Assyrian western campaign.[109] There may be additional evidence in a damaged letter from Nimrud reporting on the capture of a group of Arabs by the commander-in-chief.[110] The social structures of the kingdom suggest that women enjoyed a high degree of independence, that they could even occupy the throne and were possibly priestesses.[111] Zabibe and Samsi were followed by four other queens of the Arabs during the period from the reign of Tiglath-pileser to that of Ashurbanipal: Iatie, Te'elhunu, Tabua, and Adia. However, there were also some kings of the Arabs such as Hazael, Karib-il, and Yautha'. Zabibe and Samsi ruled a kingdom that was probably a

---

107. Na'aman, "Damascus, Hatarikka and Simirra," 25–26, nos. 20, 24.
108. RINAP 1:48, 15.2; 70, 27.6; 77, 32.8; 87, 35.iii.19.
109. Ryan Byrne, "Early Assyrian Contacts with Arabs and the Impact on Levantine Vassal Tribute," *BASOR* 331 (2003): 18; Elayi, *Sargon II*, 195.
110. Saggs, *Nimrud Letters, 1952*, 175–77; SAA 19:3 (ND 2644); Byrne, "Early Assyrian Contacts," 18.
111. Joannès, *Dictionnaire de la civilisation mésopotamienne*, 61–63; Mohammed Maraqten, "Der Afqal/Apkallu im arabischen Bereich: Eine epigraphische Untersuchungen," in *Assyriologica et Semitica: Festschrift für Joachim Oelsner anlässlich seines 65. Geburtstages am 18. Februar 1997*, ed. Joachim Marzahn and Hans Neumann, AOAT 252 (Münster: Ugarit-Verlag, 2000), 263–83; Alessandra Avanzini, "Remarques sur le 'matriarchat' en Arabie du sud," in *L'Arabie antique de Karib'îl à Mahomet*, ed. Christian Robin (Aix-en-Provence: Édisud, 1991–1993), 157–61; Frahm, *Companion to Assyria*, 300–301.

kind of tribal confederation called "the country of Arabia." It was a tribal protostate, which was located in and around the Wâdî Sirhân in northern Arabia, maybe centered on the oasis of Duma. Aribi (Arabia) and Qidri (Qedar) were probably unified at that time and ruled by one queen or king. Later on, around 680, Te'elhunu was "queen of the Arabs" and Hazael "king of Qedar."[112] This would mean that the two kingdoms were separated and ruled by a queen and a king, respectively.

Samsi, queen of the Arabs, was probably allied with the coalition headed by her neighbor Rahiânu of Damascus and thus "had transgressed her oath (sworn by) the god Šamaš" (*ša ma-mit ᵈšá-maš te-ti-qu-ma*).[113] She was defeated in 733 by Tiglath-pileser at Mount Saquri in the north of Jordan.[114] He took away 1,000 prisoners; 30,000 camels; 20,000 oxen; 5,000 pouches of all types of aromatics; thrones of Samsi's gods; weapons and staffs of her goddesses; and her property. Samsi fled in order to save her life: she "set out] like a female onager [to the de]sert, a place (where one is always) thirsty."[115] Tiglath-pileser boasted to have carried off the rest of her people and possessions and to have burnt the tents of her camp. The presentation of the looting in two passages possibly means that it occurred in two different places: her mobile camp and a sedentary settlement. Samsi is said to have been startled by Tiglath-pileser's mighty weapons, and she submitted, bringing to him camels, she-camels, and their young. Camels represented an important part of the booty in Arabia, which is why the word for "camel" (*a-na-qa-a-te*) with the first attestation of the North Arabic definite article *han-*(*nāqat*) is an Arabic loan in Akkadian.[116] Samsi was reinstalled on her throne, but she was placed under Assyrian control: "I pl]aced [a representative [*qe-e-pu*] (of mine) over her and [...] <10,000> soldi[ers...]. I made [...] bow [down at] my [feet]."[117] Tiglath-pileser's main goal was to consolidate his control over southern Syria.

---

112. Eph'al, *Ancient Arabs*, 82; Ernst Axel Knauf, *Ismael Untersuchungen zur Geschichte Palästinas und Nordarabiens im 1. Jahrtausend v. Chr.*, ADPV 7 (Wiesbaden: Harrassowitz, 1985), 45.

113. RINAP 1:59, 20.18'.

114. RGTC 7/1, 213.

115. RINAP 1:106, 42.22'–23'; 132, 49.19–20.

116. RINAP 1:107, 43.25'; Jaakko Hämen-Anttila, "The Camels of Tiglath-pileser III and the Arabic Definite Article," in *Of God(s), Trees, Kings, and Scholars: Neo-Assyrian and Related Studies in Honour of Simo Parpola*, ed. Mikko Luukko, Saana Svärd and Raija Mattila (Helsinki: Societas Orientalis Fennica, 2009), 99–101.

117. RINAP 1:107, 42.26'–27'; 111, 44.6'–7'; 122, 47.r.2'; 132, 50.r.22.

9. THE FOURTH PHASE OF THE CAMPAIGNS (734–732) 151

Tiglath-pileser realized that he did not have the means to eliminate Samsi's tribal protostate, so he allowed the queen to keep her throne but under the control of an Assyrian political agent. It is possible that the 10,000 soldiers represented a regiment provided to this agent; however, the number of soldiers is excessive for such a minor mission, and it was probably misread or exaggerated by the scribe.

After the submission of Samsi, queen of the Arabs, a number of other Arab tribes brought "their gifts" (*šùl-ma-ni-šú-nu*)—gold, silver, camels, she-camels, and all types of aromatics—to the king of Assyria, who had temporarily established his seat in Damascus, and kissed his feet.[118] These tribes were on the border of the western lands and according to a usual formula, were unknown to his predecessors. They were enumerated as follows: "the people of the cities [Maša (Massa) (and) Tema (Tayma), the (tribe) Sab]a, the people of the cities Haya[ppa, Badanu, (and) Hat]te, and the (tribes) I[dibi'ilu."[119] These Arab tribes were politically less well-organized than Samsi's protostate. Their territories stretched from the Syro-Arabian desert to northern Sinai. Not all their names are identified, but Tayma is in the north and Saba in the south of the Arabian peninsula. The Massa are mentioned in the Bible as "sons of Ishmael."[120] Hayappa is also mentioned in Sargon II's inscriptions.[121] The tribal name Idibi'ilu is similar to that of Ishmael's son Adbeel in the Bible and to the Arab Idibi'ilu appointed by the king of Assyria as gatekeeper facing Egypt.[122] Tiglath-pileser III inaugurated a new policy consisting of using people from vassal tribes to safeguard the borders of the Assyrian Empire.

As a result of the submission of Samsi and the Arab tribes in 733 and possibly in the beginning of 732, the coalition led by Rahiânu lost control over the desert. The global result of Tiglath-pileser's military strategy was quite impressive. He had defeated all the allies of Rahiânu, separated both epicenters of the coalition, Samaria and Damascus, from each other, and deprived Rahiânu of his sources of supply by devastating his orchards and gardens. Only then did Tiglath-pileser venture to bring his victory

---

118. RINAP 1:111, 44.15′.
119. RINAP 1:111, 44.8′–10′; see also 1:107, 43.27′-28′; 122, 47.r.3′; *PNA* 2.1:505 (Idibi'ilu).
120. Gen 25:12, 15.
121. *ARAB* 2.17, 118; Fuchs, *Die Inschriften Sargons II. aus Khorsabad*, 34, Zyl 20; 110, Ann 121; Gadd, "Inscribed Prisms of Sargon II," 173–201, nos. 119–120, l. 18.
122. Gen 25:13; RINAP 1:107, 42.34′; 112, 44.16′.

to a successful conclusion in 732. This strategy, one that he had already employed in his victory of 740 over the Syrian-Urartian coalition, became one of the favorite military tactics of his successors as well.

The reorganization of the Levant illustrates another aspect of Tiglath-pileser's strategy. He used the policy of massive deportation in order to prevent possible future rebellions. The largest groups of deportees were mainly taken from Damascus, Israel, and Samsi's people. The recorded number of deportees in his inscriptions is 16,620.[123] In tributes and gifts, the Assyrian king received more than 80 talents of gold and 2,800 talents of silver. Moreover, he seized the property of Hiram of Tyre, Hanunu of Gaza, Samsi of the Arabs, and at least 14,320 people.[124] The administrative reorganization of the Levant strengthened Assyrian control. The province of Damascus was created, including Transjordan, from Gilead to Abel-Shittim. The kingdom of Israel was turned into a smaller district called Bît-Humria in the Assyrian inscriptions: it was limited to Samaria and its vicinity west of the Jordan and south of Jezreel. The kings of both Israel and Judah became Assyrian vassals. The city of Gezer became an Assyrian administrative center.[125] Tyre, Ashkelon, and Gaza, where Tiglath-pileser had established an Assyrian emporium, became Assyrian vassals. Tiglath-pileser left behind him not only ruined cities but also monuments in recollection of his power and sovereignty. Tax collectors were another reminder of the Assyrian presence. Finally, Assyrian officials visited the vassal cities and reported on the situation in the annexed territories.[126]

---

123. Dubovský, "Tiglath-pileser III's Campaigns," 164–65, 169–70.
124. Dubovský, "Tiglath-pileser III's Campaigns," 165, 169–70.
125. Ronny Reich and Baruch Brandl, "Gezer under Assyrian Rule," PEQ 117 (1985): 41–54.
126. For example, Saggs, Nimrud Letters, 1952, ND 2417, 2662, 2686, 2773, and 2716; SAA 19:179–80, 181; 35, 28; 30, 23; 35–36, 29; 36–37, 30.

10

THE FIFTH PHASE OF THE CAMPAIGNS (731–727)

10.1. The Campaign against the Aramean and Chaldean Tribes

The fifth and final phase of Tiglath-pileser's campaigns (731–727) represents a continuation of the first campaign of 745 into northern and eastern Babylonia and against the Aramean tribes near Dûr-Kurigalzu and east of the Tigris. Tiglath-pileser had wisely postponed the conquest of Babylon for some fifteen years because he understood that he was not ready to successfully achieve it. In 731 (his fifteenth *palû*), the situation was different in many respects. First, Tiglath-pileser had extended and organized the Assyrian Empire eastward, northward, and westward: it was now time to conquer and organize the south. Second, Tiglath-pileser's army had become much more powerful, and the king himself had, by now, amassed enough experience to succeed in this conquest.

Moreover, the difficulties encountered by the Babylonian dynasty made an intervention much easier. Indeed, in 732, King Nabû-nâdin-zêri, Nabû-nâsir's son, was killed by rebels and replaced by Nabû-shuma-ukîn (II), the leading officer of the rebellion.[1] After only one month and two (?) days of reign, Nabû-shuma-ukîn was deposed and replaced by Nabû-Mukîn-zêri (whose name is usually abbreviated to Mukîn-zêri), leader of the Bît-Amukkâni, who reigned over Babylon from 732/731 to 729. While Mukîn-zêri usurped the throne of Babylon, Tiglath-pileser was committed to the siege of Damascus. However, Tiglath-pileser reacted quickly, returning to Assyria in order to make the appropriate diplomatic and military preparations for the next three years. Tiglath-pileser's objective was to keep the various factions divided and establish diplomatic relations separately with the various social and political groups representing the

---

1. Grayson, *Assyrian and Babylonian Chronicles*, 72, Chronicle 1.12–18.

heterogeneous Babylonian reality. In this way, the Assyrian army did not have to face a united defensive front but separate confrontations, and it could gain control of the region more easily. Before conquering Babylon, Tiglath-pileser's logical strategy consisted in first defeating the Chaldean tribes. Then, if he could drive out the Chaldean leader from the throne of Babylon, the Babylonians would be grateful toward him.

Did the Assyrian king confront Aramean tribes during his campaigns of 731 and 729? The three related texts are damaged or confused. Tadmor has dated two fragments of the annals belonging to the same slab from 731.[2] The first one mentioned the defeat of the city of Atu[...], the tribes Qabe and Bû[du], and Labbanat, the Arameans' fortress. The second reported the crossing of a river, probably the Tigris, on rafts and the subjugation of the Aramean and Chaldean chieftains. The third text is a long summary inscription where the accounts of the campaigns of 745, 731, and 729 in Babylonia are reported together, without precise dating.[3] There is also a letter related to the Aramaic tribes of Li'tarnu and Hagarânu, mentioning problems regarding grain rationing.[4] Therefore, it is possible that the Assyrian king had to confront some Aramean tribes again. If so, it was a limited operation, and his main action was directed against the Chaldean tribes because one of their leaders had taken the throne of Babylon.

Who were the Chaldeans? In contrast to the Arameans, the Chaldeans are not documented in written sources before 878 BCE.[5] While the Aramean leaders were usually called *nasikāni*, the Chaldean leaders were called *ra'sāni*.[6] However, the Aramean and Chaldean leaders were sometimes both called *malki*.[7] Chaldean place names were characterized by the noun *bīt*, "house," followed by the West Semitic personal name of an eponymous ancestor figure (e.g., Bît-Amukkâni).

---

2. RINAP 1:64–65, 23.1–7; 24.1–5. Previous authors had placed these texts at the beginning of the annals in 745: George Smith, *Assyrian Discoveries: An Account of Explorations and Discoveries in the Site of Nineveh, during 1873 and 1874* (New York: Scribner, 1875); Rost, *Die Keilschrifttexte Tiglat-Pilesers III*.

3. RINAP 1:118–19, 47.5–28.

4. SAA 19:128.

5. Brinkman, *Political History of Post-Kassite Babylonia*, 265–67, 281–85 (with bibliography).

6. Brinkman, *Political History of Post-Kassite Babylonia*, 265, 273–75; Israel Eph'al, "'Arabs' in Babylonia in the Eighth century B.C.," *JAOS* 94 (1974): 108–10.

7. RINAP 1:124, 124.24'.

10. THE FIFTH PHASE OF THE CAMPAIGNS (731–727) 155

The social, economic, and political structure was centered upon the tribal unit of which all subjects were "sons" (*mār*). Each tribal unit or confederation was directed by a chieftain called *ra'su*. The chieftains mutually recognized their status within a territorial-political complex ideally uniting all the Chaldean confederations, as is shown by a Nimrud letter describing the young Merodach-baladan as "one of the chieftains of the land of Chaldea" (*ina libbi re'asāni ša māt Kaldi*).[8] The social and political structure of the Chaldean tribes was based on kinship ties. They had a basically sedentary way of life in their southern Euphrates enclaves, based on agriculture (including date-palm), stock raising (horse and cattle breeding), and intraregional trade.[9] It would seem they had alternated intensive agricultural exploitation along the rivers with periods of transhumance in steppe areas. The strategic position of the territories of the Chaldean tribes from the region of Borsippa (modern Birs Nimrud) to the region of Ur and the marshlands, that is, along the westernmost and southern axes of the Mesopotamian plain, had crucial implications for trade. The Chaldean chieftains offered all sorts of goods as a tribute to Tiglath-pileser, for example, Merodach-baladan of Bît-Yakîn offered: "natural, unrefined gold in great quantity, jewelry made of gold, a gold necklace, pearls, beams of ebony, *ellūtu*-wood, *ašqulālu*-plants, *amilānu*-plants, multi-colored garments, all types of aromatics, oxen, and sheep and goats."[10] Such goods proved that the Chaldean tribes had full control of the trade routes in the Babylonian region, a vast commercial network reaching Mesopotamia from the Levant, northern Arabia, and Egypt by land.[11] A new southern Mesopotamian axis, using the recently introduced exploitation of the camel as a pack animal, competed with the northern axis, dominated by the Assyrians. Based on this new trade axis, the power of Chaldean tribes was increased by commercial benefits, the support of Aramean and Arabian tribes, and the military cooperation offered by the Elamite state, which generated economic advantages.[12]

---

8. Saggs, *Nimrud Letters, 1952*, 25–26:5'–6'; SAA 19:87.5'–6'.
9. Brinkman, *Prelude to Empire*, 8–11; Steven William Cole, *The Early Neo-Babylonian Governor's Archive from Nippur* (Chicago: The Oriental Institute of the University of Chicago, 1996), 18–22.
10. RINAP 1:120, 47.28.
11. Fales, "Moving around Babylon," 96–97.
12. John A. Brinkman, "Elamite Aid to Merodach-Baladan," *JNES* 24 (1965): 161–66.

During the reign of Tiglath-pileser, there were three main Chaldean tribes. From north to south, the first tribe occupied the territory of the Bît-Dakkûri, extending from Borsippa to Marad (modern Diwaniyah): the second occupied the territory of the Bît-Amukkâni, between Nippur and Uruk approximately; the third occupied the territory of Bît-Yakîn, in the south of the alluvial plain, including marshlands. Other, less important tribes occupied the territories of the Bît-shilâni/silâni to the east of the Bît-Dakkûri and of the Bît-Sha'alli/Sa'alli near the Persian/Arabian Gulf. Tiglath-pileser adopted various attitudes toward these different tribes: his main target was the Bît-Amukkâni to which Mukîn-zêri, king of Babylon, belonged; he defeated the two tribes of the Bît-Shilâni and Bît-Sha'alli; he did not attack the Bît-Dakkûri and Bît-Yakîn, which paid tribute to him.

A general presentation of Tiglath-pileser's operations against Chaldea is proposed in the following passage: "I ensnared Chaldea in its entirety as with a bird-snare," and against three Chaldean tribes: "Like *tells* after the Deluge, I destroyed the lands of the Bīt-Šilāni, Bīt-Amukkāni, and Bīt-Ša'alli in their entirety, (and) turned (them) into mounds of ruins."[13] The specific conquest of each tribe is also described. The most violent one described is against the Bît-Shilâni.[14] First Tiglath-pileser defeated its leader, Nabû-ushabshi, in the outskirts of the tribe's capital, Sarrabânu. The Assyrian king then impaled Nabû-ushabshi before the gate of his city, forcing the people of his land watch. Tiglath-pileser captured Sarrabânu by means of earthworks and battering rams. He carried off Nabû-ushabshi's wife, his sons, his daughters, his gods, his possessions, and the treasures of his palace, and he deported 55,000 people. Tiglath-pileser also captured the cities of Tarbasu and Yahallu and the cities in their environs and carried off 30,000 people. The second tribe that Tiglath-pileser attacked was the Bît-Sha'alli because its leader Zaqiru had "neglected the loyalty oath (sworn by) the great gods and [conspir]ed with [his enemies]."[15] Tiglath-pileser personally captured Bît-Sha'alli and his nobles. He placed them in iron fetters and took them to Assyria. Tiglath-pileser captured the royal city of Dûr-Balihâya by means of artificial mounds and siege machines and demolished it. He also conquered the city of Amlilatu. He carried off Zaqiru's wife, his sons, his daughters, his gods, and 40,500 people. Then the Assyrian king swept over the land

---

13. RINAP 1:119–20, 47.15, 24–25.
14. RINAP 1:97, 39.8–11; 119, 47.15–18; 136, 51.11–13.
15. RINAP 1:119, 47.19–23; 136, 51.12–15.

10. THE FIFTH PHASE OF THE CAMPAIGNS (731–727)

of the Bît-Sha'alli in its entirety, devastated its settlements, and annexed it to Assyria. In a summary inscription, Tiglath-pileser gives the total number of deported people belonging to the two tribes of the Bît-Shilâni and Bît-Sha'alli: 155,000 people[16] instead of 125,500 (55,000 + 30,000 + 40,500). However, the difference could come from the people deported from the city of Amlilatu whose number is not indicated.[17]

Tiglath-pileser's action against his main target, the Bît-Amukkâni, is described in detail.[18] He confined Mukîn-zêri in Shapîya (Sapê), his royal city, after having inflicted a heavy defeat upon him before his city gates. Then he devastated the outskirts of the city: "I cut down the orchards (and) *musukkannu*-trees that were near his (city) wall; I did not leave a single one (standing). I killed date-palms throughout his land by ripping off their … fruit and filling the meadows (with them)."[19] Tiglath-pileser said that he destroyed Mukîn-zêri's cities, except for Shapîya. Then he received the tributes of the other Chaldean leaders: Balâssu of the Bît-Dakkûri and Marduk-apla-iddina (Merodach-baladan of the Bible) of Bît-Yakîn, leaders who had never presented themselves to any of Tiglath-pileser's ancestors. This last leader offered the Assyrian king a large quantity of gold, jewelry, precious woods, plants, aromatics, garments, and cattle.[20]

Several Nimrud letters sent by the governors and rulers are related to the second campaign in Babylonia. In Letter 82, Ashur-shallimanni, governor of Arrapha, informed Tiglath-pileser about the military movements of the Elamites near Dêr around 731.[21] In Letter 87, the governor informed the king about Mukîn-zêri's attempt to forge an alliance with Balâssu, leader of the Bît-Dakkûri, through their kingship ties (he was probably a son of Balâssu's sister).[22] However, this attempt was intercepted by the Assyrians, putting Balâssu in a difficult position, as Zaqiru of the Bît-Sha'alli wrote to Merodach-baladan.[23] Some letters inform us about the leaders who supported the Assyrians: Merodach-baladan of Bît-Yakîn, Balâssu of the Bît-Dakkûri, and probably Nâdinu, ruler of

---

16. RINAP 1:136, 55.14.
17. RINAP 1:119, 47.22.
18. RINAP 1:97, 39.11; 119–20, 47.23–25; 136, 51.16.
19. RINAP 1:119, 47.23–24.
20. RINAP 1:120, 47.26–28.
21. SAA 19:xxix, xliii, 82.
22. SAA 19:xxix, 87.
23. SAA 19:xxix–xxx, 90–92, 87.

Larak, who, together with Ashipâ, used boats and waterskin rafts for transporting barley to the cities in northern Babylonia.[24] Ashipâ's title and rank are not specified in the Nimrud letters, but he may be the same person who later served as governor of Tushhan.[25] Shamash-bunaya, Assyrian prefect in northern Babylonia, wrote that he had been to Marad, an important city in the Bît-Dakkûri, to monitor the people recruited from tribes allied with the Assyrians.[26] In Letter 122, Merodach-baladan confirmed his loyalty to the Assyrian king.[27] This phase of the campaign, intended to isolate Mukîn-zêri, led to a strengthening of the Assyrian position along the Tigris, probably as far as Larak. In response to the Assyrian attempt to isolate him, Mukîn-zêri tried to extend his alliances in the Middle-Lower Euphrates.[28]

The next phase, around 730, was directed against the city of Babylon itself. Tiglath-pileser succeeded in forcing Mukîn-zêri to take refuge in his fortified capital city, Shapîya. Then the Assyrian diplomatic mission aimed to encourage the inhabitants of Babylon to transfer their support to the Assyrian king. Letter 98 concerns this mission: Shamash-bunaya and Nabû-nammir, two Assyrians, were sent to talk to the Babylonians, but Zasinnu (or Sasinnu), one of Mukîn-zêri's men, obstructed them in their task.[29] The Assyrian diplomatic mission met with other failures but finally attained its objective.[30] In fact, only a few temple oblates followed Mukîn-zêri in a raid on Dilbat, while most of the inhabitants of Babylon remained in their city.[31] The officials delegated by Tiglath-pileser to suppress Mukîn-zêri's rebellion dealt with it totally on their own, reporting their actions to the king and expecting him to arrive for his triumphal entry into Babylon to celebrate his victory. The brief mention of a white donkey for the king was probably related to the preparation of his entrance into the city riding the donkey.[32] The final phase was around 723, with the

---

24. SAA 19:xxx, 110, 111.
25. SAA 19: xl, 113–14, 115–17.
26. SAA 19:xxx, 101.
27. SAA 19:xxx, 122.
28. SAA 19:xxx, 126: a man from Hindanu, in the service of Mukîn-zêri, was captured by the Assyrians.
29. SAA 19:xxx, 98; Mikko Luukko, "How Could the Assyrian King Enter Babylon Conciliatory?," *NABU* (2007): 85–86, no. 71.
30. SAA 19:xxx, 129.
31. SAA 19:xxx, 125.
32. SAA 19:98.r.7; May, review of SAA 19, 480.

siege of Shapîya resulting in the death of Mukîn-zêri.[33] Shamash-bunaya probably maintained an important post in the succeeding period, such as that of prefect exercising military power. However, for the military control of the region, Tiglath-pileser did not solely employ Assyrians, but also local, (quasi) independent tribal leaders, flanked by Assyrian soldiers. This may have been the case for Balâssu and Nâdinu.[34]

The chronology of the period 731-729 is not totally clear because there are some discrepancies between the different sources. The annals related to this period are much damaged: a fragmentary slab discovered at Nimrud seems to be concerned with the subjugation of Aramean and Chaldean chieftains, then with the religious preparation by the Babylonian priests for Tiglath-pileser's ascent to the throne of Babylon.[35] However, these successive events are not dated. The Eponym List, which is the second source, gives quite a surprising chronology.[36] In 731, it indicates "to Shapîya," the royal city of Mukîn-zêri in the Bît-Amukkâni, but Mukîn-zêri cannot have been defeated then as he was king of Babylon, probably, until 729. In 730, the list mentions "in the land." In 729 and 728, it twice mentions: "the king took the hands of Bêl," which means that Tiglath-pileser ascended to the throne: this repetition is clearly a scribe's mistake. The third source, the Babylonian Chronicles, gives a different account. It indicates that Mukîn-zêri removed Nabû-shuma-ukîn II from the throne and ruled Babylonia for three years. The Assyrian campaign is then described: "The third year of (Nabu)-Mukîn-zêri, when Tiglath-pileser had gone down to Akkad, he ravaged the Bit-Amukkanu and captured (Nabu)-Mukîn-zêri."[37] In this chronicle, the campaign apparently occurred in 729, because in 728 Tiglath-pileser replaced Mukîn-zêri on the throne, and in 727 (his second year of reign over Babylon), Mukîn-zêri died. The capture of Mukîn-zêri is not mentioned in the Assyrian inscriptions, which is hard to understand since Tiglath-pileser would have certainly boasted of it, as he did for the two other defeated leaders: Nabû-ushabshi of the Bît-Silâni and Zaqiru of the Bît-Sha'alli.[38] The letters are not dated, but their contents enable us to distinguish different phases: around 731, around 730, and around 729.

---

33. SAA 19:xxx, 84, 80.
34. SAA 19:xxxi, 4.
35. RINAP 1:64-65, 24.
36. SAAS 2:59.
37. Grayson, *Assyrian and Babylonian Chronicles*, 72, Chronicle 1.I.18-25.
38. RINAP 1:136, 51.12.

How is it possible to reconstruct the sequence of events from these somewhat contradictory sources? After the conquest of Damascus in 732, Tiglath-pileser began preparing his conquest of Babylon, that is, starting with the subjugation of the Chaldean and Aramean tribes. If the mention of a campaign to Shapîya in 731 in the Eponyms List is exact, it is possible that there was a first attack attempt or a reconnaissance mission directed by the Assyrian king or by one of his officers to the capital city of Mukîn-zêri. This first phase of the campaign started with diplomatic missions in order to forge independent alliances with the leaders of the tribes and to recruit people from the tribes into the Assyrian army. In 730, it is possible that the king stayed in Assyria preparing this important campaign against Babylonia by directing missions and operations in Babylonia. Tiglath-pileser probably then succeeded in forcing Mukîn-zêri to take refuge in Shapîya and sent envoys to convince the inhabitants of Babylon to rally to him. Mukîn-zêri probably fled to Shapîya because he would be secure there and could organize the defense of his city. He could not rely on the Babylonians, at least not on most of them, because they did not accept Chaldean domination. Since the legitimate dynasty had been devastated by successive coups d'état, the Babylonians were too weak to fight against the Assyrians who probably appeared as the lesser of two evils. Anyway, the subjugation of the tribes was probably effective in 729 as reported in the Babylonian Chronicles. The Eponym List mentioned a campaign against the city of "Hi[...]" at the beginning of 728: this city was possibly Hilimmu on the border of Elam, annexed to Assyria with other neighboring centers in order to impede involvement and the risk of becoming powerful allies of the Chaldean rebels.[39] Tiglath-pileser besieged Shapîya, but we have no mention that he succeeded in seizing it, as he said he had captured the royal cities of Nabû-ushabshi and Zaqiru, the two other main Chaldean leaders. The deportations that the king carried out in the Bît-Amukkâni were numerous and were still remembered in the Aramaic Assur Ostracon a century later.[40] Several Nimrud letters mentioned deportations from Yasubu, Puqudu, Ulluba, Arameans from the Lower Tigris and from Borsippa, and Babylonians.[41]

---

39. SAAS 2:59; RINAP 1:136, 51.17.
40. RINAP 1:97.39.11; *KAI* 282–83, 233.15.
41. SAA 19:xxxvii–xxxviii, table III, 22, 56, 81, 87, 93, 102, 127, 141.

10.2. The Conquest of Babylon

The conquest of Babylon was not described in the royal inscriptions as a usual type of city conquest. However, Babylon was then a strong fortified city. If there had been a siege followed by the capture of the city, no doubt this memorable feat would have been described in detail and amplified. But the conquest of Babylon was mentioned quite briefly and discreetly, probably because it occurred without a glorious fight. How can the sequence of events be reconstructed from the different sources? According to the Babylonian Chronicles, Tiglath-pileser, after having captured Mukîn-zêri, king of Babylon, automatically ascended the throne.[42] Letter 99, dated around 729 and possibly sent by Shamash-bunaya, was related to the passing of Babylon into Assyrian hands.[43] The fragmentary slab discovered at Nimrud, already mentioned, records that, after the subjugation of the tribes, priestly collegiums of major Babylonian temples (Esagil, Ezida, Emeslam) brought before Tiglath-pileser the sacrificial remnants of the gods Bêl (Marduk), Nabû, and Nergal.[44] It was in the temple of Nabû that the new king received his scepter.[45] However, the candidate for kingship had to seize the hands of Marduk in Esagil, the temple in Babylon, in order to become king of Babylon. The offer of the sacrificial remnants to Tiglath-pileser was the initial step by which the priests gave him sovereignty over Babylonia. It means that the priests were favorable to the ascent of the Assyrian king to the throne of Babylon and powerful enough to allow it.

Tiglath-pileser behaved as a pious king toward the Babylonian gods in different Babylonian cities: "In Sippar, Nippur, Babylon, Borsippa, Cutha, Kish, Dilbat, and Uruk, cult centers without rival, I offered pure sacrifices to the deities Bêl, Zarpanîtu, Nabû, Tashmêtu, Nergal (and) Las, the great gods, my lords, and they loved my priestly services."[46] It is not quite clear when Tiglath-pileser offered these sacrifices, but it was probably slightly before or slightly after he became king of Babylonia. It was most likely while or after he was campaigning against the Chaldean tribes. Babylon is mentioned among the cities because this passage was

---

42. Grayson, *Assyrian and Babylonian Chronicles*, 72, Chronicle 1.I.21–22.
43. SAA 19:xxiv, 104, 99.
44. RINAP 1:65, 24.5–7.
45. Joannès, *Dictionnaire de la civilisation mésopotamienne*, 552, 727–28.
46. RINAP 1:118, 47.11–12; 136, 51.9–10.

not presented in chronological order but was a summary of all the sacrifices Tiglath-pileser performed in different Babylonian temples at different moments. This pious attitude of the Assyrian king was probably part of his strategy to facilitate his conquest of Babylon by gaining the priests' good will.

The previous Assyrian diplomatic mission had also prepared all the inhabitants of Babylon for the king's arrival. Thus, Tiglath-pileser's entrance into Babylon, carefully prepared in advance, was almost a formality: "I enter[ed] Babylon (and) offered [pure sacrifices be]fore the god Marduk, my lord."[47] Tiglath-pileser behaved as a pious Babylonian king, whose main god was Marduk. From this time onward, Tiglath-pileser's title in his royal inscriptions was: "king of Assyria, king of Babylon, king of Sumer and Akkad (that is to say Babylonia)."[48] He became king of Babylon under the name of Pulû, the etymology of which remains uncertain, probably in order to spare the susceptibility of the Babylonians by giving them the illusion that they had a specific king.[49] Tiglath-pileser did not place an Assyrian governor in Babylon because his intention was to give the region an appearance of autonomy. Thus the expedient of the double throne was created. Tiglath-pileser expressed briefly but clearly the conquest of Babylon: "I exercised authority over the extensive land of Karduniaš (Babylonia) to its full extent and exercised kingship over it," and its new organization: "(and) I firmly established tribute (and) payment on the chieftains of Chaldea."[50]

Immediately after the war, logistics and communication between Assyria and Babylonia, a highly populated and important center, were of extreme importance, both for supplies and for military and intelligence purposes. This activity was under the control of several officials who may not all have been Assyrian governors, but they were all powerful men who already held important roles in the administration of Babylon, such as Ashur-shallimanni, Ashipâ, Nabû-nammir, and Shamash-bunaya.[51]

---

47. RINAP 1:100, 40.15.
48. RINAP 1:100, 40.1–2; 116, 47.1–2; 135, 51.1–2; 138, 53.1–2; Filipe Soares, "The Titles 'King of Sumer and Akkad' and 'King of Karduniaš,' and the Assyro-Babylonian Relationship during the Sargonid Period," *Rosetta* 19 (2017): 20–35.
49. Joannès, *Dictionnaire de la civilisation mésopotamienne*, 119, 850, 899 (possibly an hypochoristic built on *aplu*); PNA 3.1:999–1000 ("corner-stone").
50. RINAP 1:118, 47.12–13; 136, 51.11; 97, 39.14; 102, 41.3′–4′.
51. SAA 19:xxx–xxxi.

10. THE FIFTH PHASE OF THE CAMPAIGNS (731-727) 163

According to Letters 99 and 95,[52] Shamash-bunaya must have been the Assyrian prefect of Babylonia whose function was to assist in and much more likely to control and direct the activities of a council of the Babylonians, in charge of the administration of the region. The text of Letter 99 is written in Neo-Babylonian and includes a salutation typical of southern Mesopotamia: "we would gladly die for our lord!" (*ana dinān bēlini nillik*).[53]

The inauguration of the double kingship, Assyro-Babylonian, was unprecedented in the history of the Assyrian kingship.[54] However, this double kingship had already existed in the tenth, ninth and eighth centuries in the western kingdoms. David (around 1010-970) and, after him, Solomon (around 970-931) were kings of both Israel and Judah. Ittoba'al I (around 888-856) and his successors, possibly until the end of the eighth century, were kings of both Tyre and Sidon.[55] Lulî was king of Tyre and Sidon in the late eighth century, though Sennacherib put an end to this Phoenician double kingdom during his third campaign in 701.[56]

---

52. SAA 19:xxxii, 99; SAA 17:95.
53. SAA 19:xxxii, 99.
54. Garelli and Lemaire, *Les empires mésopotamiens*, *Israël*, 113.
55. Elayi, *History of Phoenicia*, 131-33.
56. Elayi, *Sennacherib*, 53-59.

11
THE KING IS DEAD! LONG LIVE THE KING!

11.1. The Mysterious End of Tiglath-pileser's Reign

The end of Tiglath-pileser's reign is mysterious because of the lack of sources on the event. The Babylonian Chronicle reported the king's death laconically as usual: "The second year: Tiglath-pileser died in the month of Tebet. For <eighteen> years Tiglath-pileser (III) ruled Akkad and Assyria. For two of these years he ruled in Akkad. On the twenty-fifth day of the month Tebet Shalmaneser (V) ascended the throne in Assyria <and Akkad>."[1] The cause of Tiglath-pileser's death is not indicated; this was the case for some other kings as well, such as Shalmaneser V, although the cause of death was reported for other kings such as Nabû-nâsir, who "became ill," and Sennacherib, who "was killed in a rebellion."[2] Therefore, it is impossible to interpret why the cause of Tiglath-pileser's death is not specified. The Eponym List, quite damaged for year 727, gives: "to [ ]; [Shalman]eser [sat on the throne]."[3] This informs us that there was a campaign in a city whose name falls in the missing text. This was the last known event before Tiglath-pileser's death. We do not know where this campaign took place nor who conducted it. As a mere hypothesis to be confirmed, Tiglath-pileser may have conducted this campaign and may have been killed there. Since he died in the month of Tebêtu (January), this campaign occurred in winter, which would be somewhat surprising because military campaigns were not usually conducted in this season.

---

1. Grayson, *Assyrian and Babylonian Chronicles*, 72–73, Chronicle 1.I.24–28; Fabrice de Backer, "Le roi est mort. Vive le roi: Une base de réflexion pour le rituel funéraire royal néo-assyrien," *Res Antiquae* 17 (2020): 43–74.
2. Grayson, *Assyrian and Babylonian Chronicles*, 73, Chronicle 1.I.29; 71.11; 81.34–36.
3. SAAS 2:59.

However, it could have started in autumn and continued through until the beginning of winter. If the campaign had failed and the king had died, one could imagine that his successor would have undertaken the same campaign again at the beginning of his reign. Unfortunately, the annals of Shalmaneser V are not preserved, if they ever existed.[4] Therefore, Tiglath-pileser's death remains a mystery.

11.2. Anticipating the Succession

It was logical for a king who was an excellent strategist and administrator to think about the future of the empire he was building, that is, about his own succession. Moreover, Tiglath-pileser would have wanted his successor to rise to power smoothly and not have to encounter the same difficulties as he did when ascending the throne. Tiglath-pileser had always been attentive to ensuring the stability of the government when he was campaigning, which was frequently, almost yearly. The initiative of anticipating his succession was systematically reproduced by his successors, the so-called Sargonids. Shalmaneser V inherited the dual kingship of Assyria and Babylonia without any trouble, as he was nominated as crown prince during his father's reign.

Shalmaneser's nomination as crown prince is confirmed by a few letters written by him in the epistolary corpus called the "Nimrud letters." These letters were first published by Henry William Frederick Saggs in the 1950s and reedited and studied in 2012 by Mikko Luukko.[5] They were addressed to King Tiglath-pileser by Ulûlâyu. Shalmaneser had a throne name: S/Šalmānu-ašarēd, which meant "the god Salmânu is foremost."[6] Ulûlâyu was probably his birth name, as attested in various sources. It meant "one who (was born) in the month Ulûlu (Elûlu, September)."[7] The name is spelt ITI.KIN-*a-a* in the letters that Ulûlâyu sent as crown prince

---
4. RINAP 1:171–88.
5. Saggs, *Nimrud Letters, 1952*; SAA 19:l–lii, 8–11, 158.
6. *PNA* 3.1:1071; Claudio Saporetti, *Onomastica Medio-Assira*, StPohl SM 6.1 (Rome: Biblical Institute Press, 1970), 387; Karen Radner, "Der Gott Salmānu ('Šulmānu') und seine Beziehung zur Stadt Dūr-Katlimmu," *WdO* 29 (1998): 34–35; Hartmut Kühne, *Die Zitadelle von Dūr-Katlimmu in mittel- und neuassyrischer Zeil* (Wiesbaden: Harrassowitz, 2021).
7. *PNA* 3.2:1375–78; Brinkman, *Political History of Post-Kassite Babylonia*, 62 n. 320 and 243 n. 1560; Karen Radner, "Salmanassar V. in den Nimrud Letters," *AfO* 50 (2003–2004): 96–97.

to his father, the king. This name is also mentioned in the Babylonian King List A (*ú-lu-la-a-a*), in the Aramaic Assur Ostracon (*'lly*), and in the Ptolemaic canon in a Greek form ('Ιλουλαίου).[8]

Ulûlâyu's letters were first assigned to the reign of Sargon II; then Ulûlâyu was convincingly identified with Shalmaneser V when he was crown prince.[9] It is uncertain whether letter ND 2719,[10] whose sender's name is broken off, can be assigned to Ulûlâyu. It is related to the king of Que and the sending of ten horsemen from the house of the queen. Radner assigned it to Ulûlâyu because it contains a typical formula employed by this crown prince.[11] Moreover, she considers that the mention of the king of Que can be explained by the relations between Assyria and Que, when Urikki (Urik) was the last king of Que, vassal of Tiglath-pileser,[12] before the Assyrian conquest. This explanation fits with the fact that the conquest of Que occurred under Sargon's reign, probably in 715.[13] Luukko attributes this letter, less convincingly, to the crown prince Sennacherib, writing to Sargon: according to Luukko, the introductory formulas of Ulûlâyu and Sennacherib as crown princes are slightly different.[14] This view was supported by Keiko Yamada and Shigeo Yamada.[15] Even though the attribution of this letter to Ulûlâyu remains a hypothesis, four other letters bear the name of the sender Ulûlâyu: ND 2372, ND 2762, ND 2792, and ND 2409. All these letters open with the following introductory formula: "To the king, my lord: your servant Ulûlâyu. The best of health to the king, my lord: Assyria is well, the temples are well, all the king's forts are well. The king, my lord, can be glad indeed." Letter ND 2372 contains only the introductory formula, with no message.[16] According to Simo Parpola, it was a "routine report," in other words, a report that all was well in the

---

8. Grayson, "Königslisten und Chroniken," 93, iv.9; 101; *KAI* 283, 233.15.
9. Saggs, *Nimrud Letters, 1952*, 195, 205; SAA 19:11–13, 9–10; Radner, "Salmanassar V. in den Nimrud Letters," 95–105, following Brinkman's earlier suggestion: *Political History of Post-Kassite Babylonia*, 244 n. 1564; Tadmor, *Inscriptions of Tiglath-pileser III*, 153.
10. SAA 19:160, 158.
11. Radner, "Salmanassar V. in den Nimrud Letters," 101–2.
12. Elayi, *Sargon II*, 90–98.
13. RINAP 1:38, 11.8'; 122, 47.7'.
14. SAA 19:160, 158.
15. Yamada and Yamada, "Shalmaneser V and His Era, Revisited," 396.
16. SAA 19:13, 11.

administrative realm of the crown prince, whose name was not specified because it was known by the addressee.[17]

Letter ND 2762 related to western emissaries is more complex, all the more so because the facts, supposedly known but which we ignore, are not developed.[18] Ulûlâyu complained that emissaries of Kummuhu, Carchemish, Marqasa, Sam'al, Ashdod, and Moab had gone through Til Barsip (URU.*tur-bi-si-ba*) and Gûzâna (URU.*gu-za-na*) without his permission. Til Barsip on the Euphrates was the capital city of the Aramean kingdom of Bît-Adini and later of the province of the commander-in-chief, also known as Kâr-Shalmaneser. Gûzâna was the capital of the Assyrian province of the same name, biblical Gozan, modern Tell Halaf on the Syrian-Turkish border.[19] Ulûlâyu explains that he wrote to an official, whose name is broken, that the emissaries were allowed to cross the river, probably the Euphrates at Til Barsip, but that they were not to proceed further. Ulûlâyu sent a message to detain the emmisaries in the town of Kubana[she] where they were then staying. Kubanashe was located in the province of Gûzâna and may be identified with Tall Hanâfiz, ca. 15 km east of Tell Halaf.[20] Ulûlâyu mentions another emissary of Kummuhu, who apparently met the crown prince and was on his way home. Ulûlâyu was waiting for the next message from Kummuhu in order to forward it to the king. Ulûlâyu wrote to King Tiglath-pileser III in order to tell him the news from Kummuhu transmitted by emissaries.

The subject of Letter ND 2792 is the transportation of a product called *kup(p)û*, whose meaning has been variously interpreted either as "reed, canebrake" or "snow, ice."[21] Ulûlâyu reported in this letter that he himself went to supervise the "crushing" (*ih-[t]aš-lu*) and collecting of "36 bales (?) of *kup(p)û*" (36 *ma-qar-ra-a-ti ša ku-pe-e*) by the river.[22] Then he entrusted the *ša-qurbūti* officer Ubru-Nergal to deliver the bales to the king. If the product mentioned in this letter meant "canebrake," it should be understood as building material. For Luukko, this interpretation is more likely

---

17. SAA 1:xviii–xix.
18. SAA 19: 10–11, 8.
19. Radner, "Provinz. C. Assyrien," 51, no. 20.
20. Kessler, *Untersuchungen zur historischen Topographie Nordmesopotamiens*, 220.
21. Reed, canebrake: *CAD* 8:555–56; *AHw*, 509; SAA 19:lxvi, 233; snow, ice: *CAD* 8:551; *AHw*, 509.
22. SAA 19:10–13, 8 and 11.

from a lexical viewpoint, because the word for "ice" is *qarḫu* and because the bale unit of volume could be used both for straw and reed but not for straw and ice.[23] However, the interpretation as "snow, ice" fits better with the mountainous context of the provinces concerned in the letter, and its preciousness would explain the involvement of the crown prince.[24] Admittedly, the meaning of the word *maqarratu/maqarrutu* continues to present a difficulty since it is almost exclusively used for straw and rarely for reed.[25] Therefore, it could mean "package," applicable to ice or frozen snow.[26] This could be packed and used as a cooling material.

Letter ND 2409 covers the transportation of the same product by waterskin raft. Ulûlâyu had sent "90 bales (?) of *kup(p)û*" (90 *m[a-qar]-ru-tú ša ku-up-[p]e-e*) to the king: twenty had been transferred from the province of the commander-in-chief, forty from the province of the chief cupbearer.[27] These provinces were located close to or in the mountains in the west and north of the Assyrian homeland.[28] Ice was used for cooling wine and foods since the Old Babylonian period: it was transported from Tur Abdin to the palaces of Mari, Terqa, and Saggaratum.[29] This was an ancestor of our modern refrigerators. This letter gives the date of delivery as the third day of Ayyâru (May) but not the year.

Where was Ulûlâyu at the time of this correspondence? His area of activity seems to have been the region of Til Barsip and Gûzâna based on the toponyms mentioned in his letters. He was probably in charge of western lands such as north Syria. However, the opening formula of these letters, reporting the peace of Assyria, temples, and king's forts was probably not a mere formula. It probably implies that Ulûlâyu's major area of responsibility was in central Assyria because such a formula was absent from the contempo-

23. SAA 19:li, lxvi–lxvii, 233–237.
24. See also letter ND 2409; Yamada and Yamada, "Shalmaneser V and His Era, Revisited," 399.
25. SAA 19:57, 52.14'; SAA 1:184–85, 236.r. 2.
26. Radner, "Salmanassar V. in den Nimrud Letters," 101–2, interpretation followed by Heather D. Baker, "Salmanassar V," *RlA* 11 (2008): 586; Yamada and Yamada, "Shalmaneser V and His Era, Revisited," 399 and n. 43.
27. SAA 19:12, 10.r.3–4.
28. Radner, "Salmanassar V. in den Nimrud Letters," 99, 102–3; Radner, "Provinz. C. Assyrien," 48–49.
29. Francis Joannès, "L'eau et la glace," in *Florilegium marianum II: Recueil d'études à la mémoire de Maurice Birot*, ed. Dominique Charpin and Jean-Marie Durand (Paris: SEPOA, 1994), 140–50.

rary local governor's letters but did appear in letters from provincial governors of Assur and Nimrud in the reign of Sargon II.[30] Ulûlâyu probably sent these letters from within or close to the Assyrian heartland, when he was in Nimrud or in its vicinity and the king was away on a military expedition, that is, almost every year. Ulûlâyu acted as the king's deputy, taking responsibility for all matters related to government. It cannot be excluded that the crown prince departed on some missions by order of the king, while the latter stayed in Nimrud. For example, Ulûlâyu's supervision of the ice transportation on the bank of the Tigris might have been one of these missions.[31]

Other mentions of Shalmaneser as crown prince are uncertain. In a Babylonian letter to the king, Tiglath-pileser and Shalmaneser are mentioned in a broken context, not dated.[32] In an inscription of Tiglath-pileser, Shalmaneser is also mentioned in a damaged passage in connection with a campaign in north Syria.[33] This text is earlier than the Syrian campaigns of 734–732, probably before 738. The last five lines read: "I annexed [to Assyria ... as far as (?)] the Upper [Sea] of the setting sun. [...] I settled [all the people of ... in] peaceful [dwellings]. I presented [... Shal]maneser (SILIM]-ma-nu-MAŠ)." The context apparently narrated the establishment of the provinces of Arpad, Unqi, and Simirra by the eighth *palû* (738) of Tiglath-pileser, and the last five lines probably form part of the same context. This is either a reference to Shalmaneser or to the city of Kâr-Shalmaneser. Wolfram von Soden considers the word as the placename Kâr-Shalmaneser (Til Barsip).[34] He is followed by Keiko Yamada and Shigeo Yamada, who consider that the end of the text describes the presentation and distribution of booty or tribute at Kâr-Shalmaneser, the basis of Tiglath-pileser's western expansion.[35] The early date of the text may explain the unique reference to Kâr-Shalmaneser, before the creation of the Assyrian provincial system in Syria. Contrary to this interpretation, Tadmor prefers to see a reference to Shalmaneser because it fits better with the expression "peaceful dwellings" (*šubat nēḫtu*) in the preceding line.[36]

---

30. Yamada and Yamada, "Shalmaneser V and His Era, Revisited," 399–400.
31. Yamada and Yamada, "Shalmaneser V and His Era, Revisited," 400 and n. 45.
32. CT 54 66 b.e.25'; *PNA* 3.1:1077 (with bibliography).
33. RINAP 1:115, 46.25–29.
34. *AHw*, 1498a, 4.a.
35. Yamada and Yamada, "Shalmaneser V and His Era, Revisited," 402.
36. Tadmor and Yamada, *Inscriptions of Tiglath-pileser III King of Assyria*, 115, 47.28–29.

According to Tadmor, Tiglath-pileser involved his son in western affairs, which can be explained in this connection. This would imply that Ulûlâyu officially assumed his royal name "Shalmaneser" before 738 and that he was present in the west, controlling the administration there. Shalmaneser possibly received his new name on the occasion of his official designation as royal successor but started to use it actively only after he had become king.[37] Even if Shalmaneser was in central Assyria when he sent his letters to the king, he could have departed on some missions elsewhere in the empire. Therefore, if Shalmaneser is referred to in the above text, it would mean that he was designated crown prince early in his father's reign, before 738. It would not be surprising that this initiative was taken by Tiglath-pileser early on. Grayson ascribes to Tiglath-pileser the innovation of putting the crown prince in charge of the empire's administration while the reigning king was on campaign, a practice that would become common among his successors.[38]

Shalmaneser's image as crown prince is represented in some palace reliefs. Distinctive iconographic features allow us to identify a crown prince, such as the diadem with two ribbons (*pitūtu*) and a pendant behind.[39] Based on these criteria, Shalmaneser as crown prince appears on six fragmentary slab reliefs from Tiglath-pileser's palace in Nimrud.[40] The king is recognizable because, besides his diadem with two ribbons, he is wearing a tall, conical cap, flat at the top and surmounted by a small pointed tip. It is difficult to determine the location and period represented by these scenes, due to the fragmentary state of the reliefs and to the absence of epigraphs. If it is the crown prince who is represented on plate

---

37. Eckart Frahm, "Observations on the Name and Age of Sargon II and on Some Patterns of Assyrian Royal Onomastics," *NABU* (2005): 49 n. 17; David Kertai, "The Iconography of the Late Assyrian Crown Prince," in *From the Four Corners of the Earth: Studies in Iconography and Cultures of the Ancient Near East in Honour of F. A. M. Wiggermann*, ed. David Kertai and Olivier Nieuwenhuyse (Münster: Ugarit-Verlag, 2017), 111–34.

38. Grayson, "Assyria: Tiglath-pileser III to Sargon II," 83.

39. Julian E. Reade, "Two Slabs from Sennacherib's Palace," *Iraq* 29 (1967): 45–48; Reade, "Neo-Assyrian Court and Army," 93; Reade, "Kronprinz. B. Archäologisch," *RlA* 6 (1980): 249–50.

40. Barnett and Falkner, *Sculptures*, pls VIII, LIX, LXXX, LXXXIV/LXXXV, LXXXVI, XCV/XCVI; Tadmor, *Inscriptions of Tiglath-pileser III*, 249–56, fig. 12. The identification is uncertain for pls VIII, LXXX, and LXXXV: see Yamada and Yamada, "Shalmaneser V and His Era, Revisited," 402–3 nn. 54–55.

VIII, the scene would concern the Babylonian campaign of the first *palû* (745).⁴¹ The question is whether Tiglath-pileser had designated the crown prince at such an early date in his reign. The scene represented in plate XCVI could be related to the events of the sixth *palû* (740, against Arpad), eighth *palû* (738, against Patin), or of the twelfth *palû* (734, against Gaza).⁴² Therefore, it is difficult to know exactly when Tiglath-pileser decided to name Shalmaneser as crown prince, maybe not too early, but certainly in the first half of his reign, because this innovation constituted an important stage in his building of the Assyrian Empire.

---

41. Barnett and Falkner, *Sculptures*, pl. VIII.
42. Tadmor, *Inscriptions of Tiglath-pileser III*, 240–57; Christoph Uehlinger, "Hanun von Gaza und seine Gottheiten auf Orthostatenreliefs Tiglatpilesers III.," in *Kein Land für sich allein: Studien zum Kulturkontakt in Kanaan, Israel/Palästina und Ebirnâri für Manfred Weippert zum 65. Geburstag*, ed. Ulrich Hübner and Ernst Axel Knauf, OBO 186 (Göttingen: Vandenhoeck & Ruprecht, 2002), 92–125.

12
BUILDING ACTIVITIES

12.1. Tiglath-pileser's Limited Interest in Building Activities

The building activities of Tiglath-pileser, compared to his military and administrative activities and to the constructions of his successors, were limited. For example, even though Sargon II was primarily a warrior king, he was also a great builder king, conceiving of all his magnificent works and his new capital of Khorsabad as prestigious achievements.[1] Almost half of Sennacherib's inscriptions were devoted to building and innovating activities.[2] Conversely, building activities occupy a small place in Tiglath-pileser's inscriptions. The building of his palace in Nimrud is described in a fragment of a colossal slab from this palace, with only four lines being preserved.[3] The date of this text is unknown, but Tadmor tentatively placed it at the end of the annals. The only complete description can be found in the long summary inscription on a large fragment of a clay tablet discovered at Nimrud, which comprises nineteen lines.[4] The fragmentary four lines of text 25 correspond to the beginning of text 47. In this text, the description of the palace is placed at the end of the summary inscription; therefore, it was probably also placed at the end of the annals. In the summary inscription, which presents some undetermined lacunae, it represents nineteen lines out of the surviving eighty lines, that is, less than one quarter of the whole text, which is little. It seems Tiglath-pileser was much less interested in his building activities, even his palace, than in his military and administrative activities. As an Assyrian king, he was obliged to

---

1. Elayi, *Sargon II*, 22–23, 201–10.
2. Elayi, *Sennacherib*, 173–90.
3. RINAP 1:67, 25.1'–4'.
4. RINAP 1:123–24, 47.r.16'–36'.

realize a minimum of building projects. But he did not want to sacrifice his energy for building the Assyrian Empire to build only palaces and temples.

12.2. The Building of the Palace in Nimrud

It was important for an Assyrian king to choose his capital and to build his own palace, more magnificent than those of the previous kings. Tiglath-pileser had decided to keep the same capital as his predecessors (e.g., Ashurnasirpal II and Shalmaneser III): Nimrud (Kalhu). Several palaces, more or less preserved, were discovered at Nimrud: the North-West Palace, the Central Palace, the South-West Palace, the Governor's Palace, and the Burnt Palace.[5] The so-called Central Palace was the palace of Tiglath-pileser; it was discovered in November 1845 by Layard. It was almost completely destroyed, but several sculpted slabs were discovered in its ruins.[6] Other slabs belonging to the Central Palace were discovered in the South-West Palace, the palace constructed by Esarhaddon in the southwest corner of the citadel mound. Layard provided the following explanation: "the sculptured faces of the slabs were turned, it will be remembered, toward the walls of unbaked brick. It appeared, therefore, that the central building had been destroyed, to supply materials for the construction of the more southern edifice."[7] The Central Palace was built by Adad-nârârî III (810–783), successively occupied by Shalmaneser IV, Ashur-Dân III, and Ashur-nârârî V, and then reworked by Tiglath-pileser, but it remained unfinished.[8]

Tiglath-pileser was the first Assyrian king since Ashurnasirpal II to decorate his palace with sculpted and inscribed orthostats, which had the political function of celebrating the feats of the king.[9] Tiglath-pileser

---

5. Mallowan, *Nimrud and Its Remains*.

6. Barnett and Falkner, *Sculptures*, 34–46.

7. Austen Henry Layard, *Nineveh and Its Remains* (London: Spottiswoodes & Shaw, 1849), 1:19–20, 41; 2:27. He mistakenly assumed that the site of Nimrud was Nineveh.

8. Layard, *Nineveh and Its Remains*, 1:24; Tadmor, *Inscriptions of Tiglath-pileser III*, 10–12.

9. Bachelot, "La fonction politique des reliefs néo-assyriens," 109–28; Natalie Naomi May, "Triumph as an Aspect of the Neo-Assyrian Decorative Programm," in *Organization, Representation, and Symbols of Power in the Ancient Near East*, ed. Gernot Wilhelm, RAI 54 (Winona Lake, IN: Eisenbrauns, 2012), 461–88; Melanie Gross and David Kertai, "Becoming Empire: Neo-Assyrian Palaces and the Creation

followed Ashurnasirpal's tradition of decorative reliefs and accompanying texts, but he also deviated from it concerning their arrangement and location. The king had versions of his annals written across several series of sculpted orthostats and had nonannalistic texts inscribed on the threshold and pavement slabs of his palace. The reliefs are occasionally accompanied by an epigraph. Except for the epigraphs, there is no direct relation between the inscriptions and the actions depicted in the registers of the slab, above and below. New subjects were introduced: carrying away the statues of the gods, scribes counting the spoils, the king sitting on his throne, the king receiving his vizier or prisoners, the interior of a military camp, pitching the royal tent, and the sea with islands and boats.[10] These reliefs were part of royal propaganda.

Besides the remains of this palace and the representations of the reliefs, the royal inscriptions provide the king's own point of view as regards his building. He was able to build his palace because he had been endowed by the god Ea with an exceptional intelligence: "the keen understanding (and) broad knowledge that the sage of the gods, the prince, the god Nudimmud (Ea), granted to me."[11] This excessive pride became further exacerbated with his successors Sargon II and Sennacherib.[12] Tiglath-pileser goes on to say that he built a cedar palace for his lordly residence and "a bīt-ḫilāni, a replica of a palace of the land of the Ḫatti."[13] This was possibly incorporated into the palace, as was probably the case for the palace of Sennacherib. In the next albeit damaged passage of the inscription, Tiglath-pileser provides further details on how he reworked the previous palace. He describes how he expanded the dimensions of the site of the palace: "sixty large cubits in width," that is, 18 m, one cubit being around 30 cm. The length is missing because of a lacuna. Tiglath-pileser explained that he obtained dimensions larger than the former palace of his predecessors by reclaiming land from the Tigris and filling in it. He

---

of Courtly Culture," *Journal of Ancient History* 7 (2019): 1–31; Gross, *At the Heart of an Empire: The Royal Household in the Neo-Assyrian Period*, OLA 292 (Leuven: Peeters, 2020).

10. Barnett and Falkner, *Sculptures*, 34–36; Postgate and Reade, "Kalḫu," 304–15.
11. RINAP 1:123, 47.r.17'.
12. ARAB 2.105; Fuchs, *Die Inschriften Sargons II. aus Khorsabad*, 56–59, 301, R, 13–28; RINAP 3.2:243, 166.10–12; 247.
13. RINAP 1:123, 47.r.18'; RINAP 3.1:225, 34.64; David Kertai, "Embellishing the Interior Spaces of Assyria's Royal Palaces: The Bēt Ḫilani Reconsidered," *Iraq* 79 (2017): 85–104.

piled up heavy limestone blocks to a depth of 20 large cubits, that is, 6 m, and constructed terraces on them. In this way, he prevented flooding and secured the foundations of his palace. Tiglath-pileser was conscious of his skill in realizing this building project but honestly recognized that he was helped by experts in that field: "I cleverly made plans with (the help of) all of the skilled craftsmen."[14] If this damaged passage can be correctly understood, the height of the rooms of the palace was "one half *nindanu* (and) two-thirds of a cubit," that is, about 3.33 m.[15] Then Tiglath-pileser enumerated the various precious materials used in the building of his so-called cedar palace: "ivory, ebony, boxwood, *musukkannu*-wood, c[eda]r, *šur*[*mēnu*]-wood, [*burāšu*-juniper and] juniper."[16] These materials came from the tributes sent by the kings of Hatti and from Aramean and Chaldean rulers. Tiglath-pileser explained how he obtained their submission: "with the power of my heroism."[17]

Tiglath-pileser gives the height of the palace with precision: "(to a height of) five and one half *nindanu* (and) four cubits from the depth of the water to (their) copings, I designed their structure and I made their workmanship more resp[len]dent than the palaces of (foreign) lands."[18] Therefore, from the ground level to its summit, the palace had a height of about 35 m. It was roofed with long beams of sweet-smelling cedar, imported from Mount Amanus, Mount Lebanon, and Mount Ammanâna, probably the Anti-Lebanon range.[19] The locks were decorated with appropriate splendid embellishments and the gates were made of stones fashioned by the stone cutter's craft. The double doors of cedar and *šurmēnu*-wood were decorated with bands of shiny silver (*zaḫalû*) and *ešmarû*-silver. These doors "bestow (great) pleasure on those who enter them (and) whose fragrance wafts into the heart."[20] The sculptures at the palace entrances were stylishly executed: lions, *šēdu*, and winged bulls (*lamassu*); they were splendidly clothed, and the threshold at their feet was covered with lumi-

---

14. RINAP 1:123, 47.r.20'.
15. Joannès, *Dictionnaire de la civilisation mésopotamienne*, 665.
16. RINAP 1:123–24, 47.r.23'–24'.
17. RINAP 1:124, 47.r.24'.
18. RINAP 1:124, 47.r.25'.
19. Mordechai Cogan, "… From the Peak of Amanah," *IEJ* 34 (1984): 255–59; Josette Elayi, "L'exploitation des cèdres du Mont Liban par les rois assyriens et néo-babyloniens," *JESHO* 31 (1988): 14–41.
20. RINAP 1:124, 47.r.28'–29'.

nous slabs of gypsum and alabaster. Around the palace's supporting wall were placed stone images, guardians of the great gods and terrifying creatures of the *apsû* (fish-men). The finishing touch was put in the palace halls, which were decorated with shining knobbed pegs of gold, silver, and bronze. Tiglath-pileser finally describes his royal abode, seemingly proud of its realization: "I set up therein a glittering chamber inlaid with precious stones."[21] He ends the description of his palace by giving names, in the traditional way, with imperialistic pride, to the palatial halls: "of joy which bear abundance, which bless the king, (and) which make their builder long-[liv]ed," and to the gates: "of justice, which give correct judgment for the rulers of the four quarters of the world, which offer the yield of the mountains and the seas, (and) which admit the produce of mankind before the king their lord."[22] This only complete builder account from Nimrud to have survived gives information on Tiglath-pileser's point of view: he did what he had to do as a builder king; he appreciated this building achievement but less enthusiastically than when he reported his victories.

When was his palace built? The only information we have is that it was almost completed in 729 because text 47, eight-six lines of a long summary inscription, was composed in or shortly after Tiglath-pileser's seventeenth *palû* (729) for his palace of Nimrud.[23] The inscriptions written between the carved registers of the slabs seem to belong to the annals of the king, giving the events of his reign year by year. Each room probably contained the entire text of the annals, written in columns having the same number of lines.[24] Except for the separate epigraphs, there was probably no direct relationship between the inscriptions and the actions depicted in the registers above and below.

In 729, even though the palace was not finished, it is likely that Tiglath-pileser lived in it. At the beginning of his reign, he was probably dwelling in the palace built by Adad-nârârî III and occupied by his predecessor Ashur-nârârî V. When Tiglath-pileser started to rework the palace, he probably lived in another one, possibly in that of Ashurnasirpal II. At any rate, Tiglath-pileser spent little time in Nimrud because he was campaign-

---

21. RINAP 1:124, 47.r.33'.
22. RINAP 1:124–25, 47.r.34'–36'; Shigeo Yamada, "Names of Walls, Gates, and Palatial Structures of Assyrian Royal Cities: Contents, Styles, and Ideology," *Orient* 55 (2020): 87–104.
23. RINAP 1:115–16, 47.
24. Reade, "The Palace of Tiglath-pileser III," 72–73.

ing every year; the only year when he stayed "in the land," as mentioned in the Eponym List, was 730.[25] Since he was more interested in building an empire than building a palace, Tiglath-pileser probably did not start the work at the beginning of his reign, but only after having subdued the kings of Hatti and the Aramean and Chaldean rulers since they provided ivory and precious woods for building the palace.[26]

12.3. Tiglath-pileser's Other Building Activities

Besides his palace at Nimrud, Tiglath-pileser was involved in other building activities, much less numerous than those of his successors. However, some of them are possibly unknown because of the bad state of preservation of his inscriptions. In addition to Nimrud, Tiglath-pileser built other royal residences just as his predecessors had done. For example, Ashurnasirpal II "erected a palace for his royal dwelling" in the city of Alila in the land of Zamua; Shalmaneser III "built a palace for his royal abode" in the northern city of Mûru.[27] Three royal residences were mentioned in the preserved inscriptions of Tiglath-pileser, but there were possibly more. In 745, during his first campaign to Babylonia, Tiglath-pileser built his first royal residence on the way to Elam: "I built a city on the top of a tell called [Ḫumut]. I b[uilt (and) co]mpleted (it) from the foundations to its parapets. [Inside (it), I founded] a palace for my royal residence. I named it Kār-Aššur."[28] There he installed the weapon of the god Assur and settled people from conquered foreign lands. Tiglath-pileser used to place this weapon as a central cultic object in conquered cities that were reorganized as provincial centers: it did not imply the imposition of the cult of Assur, as is sometimes assumed, but it was a political-ideological sign of integration into the empire.[29]

In 739, during his campaign to Ulluba, Tiglath-pileser built a second royal residence in Lesser Habur, north of Dohuk: "I built a city in the

---

25. SAAS 2:59.
26. RINAP 1:123–24, 47.r.23′–24′.
27. *ARAB* 1.154:458, 207:582; RIMA 2:208, 1.ii.84–86; RIMA 3:68, 14.126–131.
28. RINAP 1:26–27, 5.1–3; 29, 6.1–3.
29. Mordechai Cogan, *Imperialism and Religion: Assyria, Judah and Israel in the Eighth and Seventh Centuries B.C.E.* (Missoula, MT: Scholars Press, 1974), 53–55; Cogan, "Restoring the Empire," *IEJ* 67 (2017): 151–67; Steven W. Holloway, *Aššur Is King! Aššur Is King! Religion in the Exercise of Power in the Neo-Assyrian Empire* (Leiden: Brill, 2002), 160–77; Bagg, "Palestine under Assyrian Rule," 126.

12. BUILDING ACTIVITIES 179

land Ulluba (and) I named it Aššur-iqīša. Inside (it), I founded [a palace for] my royal [resid]ence. I set up the weapon of (the god) Aššur, my lord, therein, (and) [settled the] people of (foreign) la[nds conquered by me therein]."[30] Another royal residence was built in or after 733 at Hadattu (Arslan Tash), in the province of Til Barsip. Tiglath-pileser appears to have entrusted this building to Ninurta-ilâya, who is perhaps to be identified with the governor of Nasibîna, who was eponym in 736.[31] In the excavations of 1928, François Thureau-Dangin discovered a pair of inscribed monumental basalt bulls.[32] The inscriptions are badly damaged. They begin with Tiglath-pileser's name and narrate in particular his victory over Aramean tribes in Babylonia and his campaign of 733 against Samsi, queen of the Arabs. This last mention provides a *terminus post quem* in 733. The inscriptions then record a building account at Hadattu, written in the first person, although Ninurta-ilâya conducted the work: "[*At the command of*] the goddess Ištar, I stationed in its gate wild bulls of solid basalt."[33]

What were the functions of such royal residences? The first function was probably to incarnate in a prestigious way the presence of the king in the newly conquered lands. These royal residences were in a manner copies of the royal palace in the capital city of the empire. Yet, we notice that they were built at different moments of the reign (745, 739, 733, or later), and at different places of the empire: in the east (Humut/Kâr-Ashur), in the north (Ashur-iqîsha), and in the northwest (Hadattu/Arslan Tash). They possibly also had a strategic function as they were used as halting-places and as bases for the king to advance further in the conquest of new lands. These royal residences were built in submitted lands, at the frontier of new territories to be conquered. When the Assyrian king was campaigning for more than one year in the same area, he did not necessarily come back to Assyria but might have preferred to stay where he was for convenience. For example, in 738, Tiglath-pileser appears to have remained in

---

30. RINAP 1:121, 47.43–44.
31. SAA 5:44 and 59.
32. François Thureau-Dangin, *Arslan-Tash* (Paris: Geuthner, 1931) (AO 11500, AO 11501); Burkhart J. Engel, *Darstellungen von Dämonen und Tieren in assyrischen Palästen und Tempeln nach den Schriftlichen Quellen* (Mönchengladbach: Hackbarth, 1987), 75–76; Joannès, *Dictionnaire de la civilisation mésopotamienne*, 616.
33. RINAP 1:140, 53.23.

the land of Hatti to personally oversee the organization of provinces in northwest Syria.[34]

Tiglath-pileser presented himself as "the one who restores sanctuaries."[35] He restored the Nabû temple at Nimrud according to a fragment of a clay tablet discovered there.[36] He also restored the temple of the god Assur at Assur as is shown by the inscriptions written on six bricks from this city: "Palace of Tiglath-pileser (III), king of Assyria, son of Adad-nārārī, king of Assyria: (this brick) belongs to the platform of the temple of (the god) Aššur."[37] Ten stamped bricks from Assur bear a similar inscription but referred to the restoration of the temple of the god Adad: "Tiglath-pileser (III), great king, mighty king, king of the world, king of Assyria: (this brick) belongs to the pedestal (under) the bulls of the gateway of the temple of the god Adad."[38] Another brick, smaller and written with several orthographic variants, bears the same text but was very damaged with the first line having been restored: "(Palace of) Tiglath-pileser."[39] We have noted the contradiction between the mentions of the palace and the platform of the temple. The palace was probably where Tiglath-pileser resided when he visited the religious city of Assur. It is not clear why the palace is mentioned on inscribed objects belonging to the temples of the gods Assur or Adad. Several other objects from Assur are inscribed as follows: "Palace of Tiglath-pileser, king of Assyria."[40] One of them is an enameled clay tile discovered in the Old Palace at Assur, which would mean that Tiglath-pileser happened to stay in this palace.[41] There is a debate as to which Tiglath-pileser this was: I, II, or III.[42] Some of these objects may be assigned to Tiglath-pileser III, but their assignment to one of his other two namesakes cannot be excluded. Another fragmentary inscription written on a rectangular stone block from Assur and later reused in the construction of another building can safely be assigned to Tiglath-pileser III

---

34. RINAP 1:41.
35. RINAP 1:114, 46.3.
36. RINAP 1:137–38, 52.
37. RINAP 1:147–48, 58.1–3.
38. RINAP 1:148–49, 59.1–4.
39. RINAP 1:149–50, 60.1–4.
40. RINAP 1:155–59, 1001–1007.
41. RINAP 1:155–56, 1002.1.
42. Friedhelm Pedde and Steven Lundström, *Der Alte Palast in Assur: Architektur und Baugeschichte*, WVDOG 120 (Wiesbaden: Harrassowitz, 2008), 182.

because of the mentions of Sulumal of Melid and Rahiânu of Damascus, contemporaneous kings.[43]

According to his inscriptions, the Assyrian king also used to rebuild cities that he had conquered and destroyed, such as Nikur in the land of Parsua, Bît-Ishtar and Sibur in the land of Ariarma, Hista, Harabisinna, Barbaz, and Tasa in the north.[44] For example, he described this rebuilding of the cities destroyed as a usual procedure: "I rebuilt the cities inside them (those lands), set up the weapon of (the god) Aššur, my lord, therein, (and) brought the people of (foreign) lands conquered by me therein. I placed [...] eunuchs of mine as provincial governors over them."[45] Or he built new cities such as Humut, Ashur-iqîsha.[46] Tiglath-pileser related only one irrigation work: "I dug out the Patti-[Enlil] canal, [which] had lain abandoned for a very long time and [...]. I made an abundance of water gurgle through it."[47] The name of the canal is restored based on the fact that a well-known canal of this name is located near Sippar and Dûr-Kurigalzu.[48] The waterworks were greatly developed by his successors Sargon and Sennacherib.[49]

---

43. RINAP 1:142–43, 54.
44. RINAP 1:26, 5.1; 31, 7.5; 52–53, 17.7–8.
45. RINAP 1:121, 47.36.
46. RINAP 1:26–27, 5.2; 29, 6.1; 114, 46.7; 98, 39.28; 103, 41.30; 121, 47.43.
47. RINAP 1:27, 5.4.
48. RGTC 5, 312; 8, 395.
49. Elayi, *Sargon II*, 202; Elayi, *Sennacherib*, 194–200.

Conclusion
Assessment of Tiglath-pileser's Reign

Tiglath-pileser was commissioned by the gods, mainly Assur, to extend the borders of Assyria and to expand Assyria's vast population.[1] He proudly affirmed that he had performed his mission: "I increased the territory of Assyria by taking hold of (foreign) lands (and) added countless people to its population.... I, Tiglath-pileser, king of Assyria, who personally conquered all the lands from east to west, appointed governors in places where the chariots of the kings, my ancestors, never crossed over... and I exercised authority over the (four) quarters (of the world)."[2] There is no reason to doubt his sincerity. Tiglath-pileser boasted of controlling the whole world, which was true because the maximum expansion of his empire included nearly the whole world as it was known at that time. However, due to the bad state of preservation of his annals, it is difficult to take stock of his conquests. The most relevant inscription for that is the long summary inscription from Nimrud, composed in or shortly after 729 (seventeenth *palû*). The inscription is easy to use because it followed a geographical order: starting from the south and moving anti-clockwise.[3] However, we come up against several difficulties when we try to draw the map of all the conquests of Tiglath-pileser (see fig. 3 on p. 100).

To begin with, the location of many toponyms cannot be identified. One is all but forced to presuppose that all the cities conquered are genuine conquests and not boasts. The creation of new provinces by this Assyrian king is not always clearly indicated in his inscriptions, and even when they are, their borders are unknown. There are also different evolutions of distinct histories attached to each of these provinces during his reign.

---

1. RINAP 1:83, 35.i.32–33; 114, 46.5.
2. RINAP 1:86, 35.ii.15′–24′.
3. RINAP 1:115–25, 47.

Therefore, a map of the provinces of the Assyrian Empire in 727 can be only approximate.

In the south, Tiglath-pileser defeated the Aramaic tribes near Dûr-Kurigalzu and east of the Tigris. He annexed them to Assyria in 731 and appointed a eunuch as governor to rule over them, but it is impossible to locate this new province whose name is not specified. Tiglath-pileser annexed Puqudu and several cities on the border of Elam and placed them under the authority of the provincial governor of Arrapha, also a eunuch. He conquered the Chaldean tribes of the Bît-Dakkûri, Bît-Amukkâni, Bît-Yakîn, and Bît-Shilâni, but he did not mention the creation of a province made up of those tribes. In fact, part of these territories was annexed to Babylonia over which he became king in 728. Sources also make reference to Balâssu, chief of the Bît-Dakkûri, who submitted, offered a rich tribute, and become a vassal of Assyria. The Arab tribes were also subject to the Assyrian king, while Samsi, queen of the Arabs, pledged her allegiance to Assyria, but she was nevertheless placed under the control of an Assyrian representative.

Far to the east, outside of unidentifiable cities, Tiglath-pileser's campaigns in the central Zagros mainly concerned the Bît-Hamban, Namri, Zamua, and Parsua, which Tiglath-pileser annexed to Assyria. He created two new Assyrian provinces over which he placed eunuchs as governors, Bît-Hamban and Parsua, while Zamua was already an Assyrian province, created by Ashurnasirpal II during the first half of the ninth century, and Namri or part of it was integrated into Bît-Hamban. Tiglath-pileser reconstructed the cities that he had destroyed in these provinces and repopulated them with deported populations, relocated from other parts of the empire. At about this time, he might have created the province of the palace herald, which was located northeast of Arbela and which was mentioned for the first time in his inscriptions. Other peoples immediately and unconditionally submitted and offered the Assyrian king rich tributes. These included the Manneans, the Ellipeans, and the Medes. The Mannean king Iranzu traveled to request audience with Tiglath-pileser and kissed his feet as a sign of allegiance in his new city of Dûr-Tiglath-pileser (unidentified).

In the north, the Assyrian king directed his campaigns at Mount Nal and the country of Ulluba, which was under Urartian influence and only 100 km from Nineveh. Tiglath-pileser annexed this region and built a new provincial capital, Ashur-iqîsha, to strengthen local Assyrian control in the face of Urartu, the enemy from the north. He relocated deported populations to the region and installed an eunuch as governor over the province. He also settled deportees in the province of Barhalzi, northwest of Nineveh, which is mentioned in this context for the first time in his inscriptions. He conquered several other localities in the north, notably several Urartian fortresses, and annexed them to the province of the treasurer. This ancient province, created in the ninth century, was located east of Kumme and included the Cizre plain, which was annexed by Tiglath-pileser. He annexed other localities to the province of Nairi, south of the Lake of Van, and still others to the province of the chief cupbearer, which has been difficult for modern historians to locate. Nevertheless, two locations have been proposed: the Iranian Zagros in the east and the Tur Abdin in the Upper Tigris. The latter seems more plausible. Tiglath-pileser also deported people to the province of Tushhan, which is located in these same northern regions, perhaps next to the province of Amidi.

To the northwest and west, Tiglath-pileser mentioned Nasibîna, a province of the Habur area created by Shalmaneser III. He also campaigned against localities on the border of Kummuhu and added them to the province of the commander-in-chief. This province was located on the right bank of the Euphrates, near Samsat. After taking Arpad in 740, Tiglath-pileser transformed it into an Assyrian province. Likewise in 738, he annexed Unqi and transformed it into an Assyrian province. He did the same for the city of Hatarikka where he placed one of his eunuchs as governor. The city of Simirra was similarly transformed into a province. However, the total number of provinces created in north Syria is not clear because the inscriptions mention either two or six provincial governors, all eunuchs. The great kingdom of Aram-Damascus was annexed in 732, a part of it forming the province of Subutu. The Assyrian king also annexed Galilee and Transjordan while the Phoenician cities became vassals of Assyria. The Philistine cities and the Jordanian states of the southeast Levant were considered as buffer states between Assyria and Egypt and enjoyed a relative state of autonomy. Much of Israel's former territory was transformed into the provinces of Dor, Megiddo, and Gilead, and Israel became a puppet kingdom of Assyria. The kingdom of Judah remained autonomous because King Ahaz had allied himself with the Assyrians.

Thus, by means of his energetic and sustained expansionist policy, Tiglath-pileser succeeded in at least doubling the number of Assyrian territories that he had initially inherited in 745, including the provinces and vassal states. However, the control he exercised over the vassal states was relatively tight compared to that of his predecessors, although it fluctuated depending on the degree of compliance with the vassal agreements.

In sum, by 727, Assyria had become an enormous empire. While it was multiethnic and multilingual, it was also unbalanced between the center and the periphery, hence requiring close monitoring and administration. Such a vast empire needed an efficient system of administrative communication. The reforms of Tiglath-pileser were aimed at creating and organizing the empire, but they are not well-known, not due to their lesser importance but because of the lack of evidence. Nevertheless, we do know, for example, that he reformed the army's logistics, strategy, and weaponry. He created trading posts and administrative centers called *kāru* or *bīt-kāri* on the frontiers of the empire, as merely one aspect of the overall Assyrian domination of international trade.[4] Three of them are mentioned in his inscriptions: Kâr-Adad (Aribua?) in north Syria, Kâr-Bêl-mâtâti near Cutha, and Kâr-Shalmaneser (Til Barsip), named by Shalmaneser III.[5] Other *bīt-kāri* were located on the Mediterranean seacoast, such as Siannu, Ellishu, Simirra, Rêshi-sûri, Ahtâ, Sidon, and Gaza.[6]

What kind of empire was the Assyrian Empire, and was it the first world empire? The Assyrian Empire is a modern designation because the Assyrians called their territory "the country of the god Assur." The term *empire* comes from the German *Reich*. It was born in Prussian circles in the nineteenth century to designate the Holy Roman Empire, which was ruled by an emperor appointed by God, a supreme and all-powerful legislator. James Laxer, a Canadian political economy specialist, writes: "We speak of an empire when a nation, tribe or society exercises a long-term domination over one or more nations, tribes or external societies.... The faculty to determine what happens, what the societies under its control produce is what distinguishes an empire from other forms of internal organization."[7] This definition can apply to the Assyrian state since it was sufficiently large and was characterized by permanent hegemonic expansion and a stable state structure. However, these conditions were only met starting in Tiglath-pileser III's reign. The history of the Assyrian Empire therefore stretched from 745 to 610 BCE, that is, for a little less than a

---

4. Yamada, "Neo-Assyrian Trading Posts," 222–27.

5. Shigeo Yamada, "*Kārus* on the Frontiers of the Neo-Assyrian Empire," *Orient* 40 (2005): 58–62, 66–69; Kâr-balâti, Kâr-banapa in Assyrian heartland (?), and Kâr-Nergal in Babylonia near Cutha were probably not created in Tiglath-pileser's reign.

6. RINAP 1:85–86, 35.ii.11′–15′; 105, 42.1′–4′; Yamada, "*Kārus* on the Frontiers of the Neo-Assyrian Empire," 68–69, 75.

7. James Laxer, *Empire* (New York: Groundwood, 2006), 9.

CONCLUSION 187

century and a half, but the entirety of the history of Assyria since its origin prepared for the birth of this empire.[8]

The imperialism of the great states of the Middle East manifested themselves in the third and second millennia BCE, like that of the Hittites, which spread across Turkey and north Syria. Shamshî-Adad I (Samsî-Addu), king of Ekallâtum, (then of Assur), conquered the whole of Upper Mesopotamia and proclaimed himself "king of the world." This title had been previously employed by Ipiq-Adad II and Narâm-Sîn, kings of Eshnunna (Tell Asmar).[9] The forerunner and model of the Assyrian Empire was the united Sumerian-Akkadian kingdom built by Sargon of Agade. But the actions of these kings were still limited to the conquest of regional hegemonies, while the desire for universal domination uniquely characterized the first millennium. It was especially formalized in the inscriptions of the Assyrian king Ashurnasirpal II, but he achieved little more than his predecessors in terms of his contribution to the ascent of Assyria. The true founder of the Assyrian Empire was Tiglath-pileser III. Upon his accession to the throne, he initiated a series of military operations to conquer a vast continental territory, with a maritime opening. He was no longer satisfied with episodic raids to bring back booty but proceeded to set up a genuine imperial-tributary system, stable and efficient, generating a vast source of considerable wealth. It is sometimes said that the first world empire was the Persian Empire or the empire of Alexander. Such a statement can be made only out of ignorance of the Assyrian Empire, which was the first universal empire from antiquity, so large and structured.

Among the different definitions of an empire, according to Herfried Münkler, two decisive parameters characterize a world empire: temporal duration, which is made up of an expansion phase as well as a consolidation phase, and spatial extension. Moreover, it needs to have a civilizing mission.[10] Münkler contrasted civilizing empires to steppe empires, which

---

8. Frederick Mario Fales, *L'impero assiro: Storia e amministrazioni* (Rome: Laterza, 2001); Véronique Grandpierre, *Histoire de la Mésopotamie* (Paris: Gallimard, 2010); Karen Radner, *Ancient Assyria: A Very Short Introduction* (Oxford: Oxford University Press, 2015); Frahm, *A Companion to Assyria*; Mario Liverani, *Assyria: The Imperial Mission* (Winona Lake, IN: Eisenbrauns, 2017); David Nadali, *Gli Assiri: Storia di una civiltà* (Rome: Carocci, 2018).

9. Douglas R. Frayne, *Old Babylonian Period (2003–1595 BC)* (Toronto: University of Toronto Press, 1990), 547, no. 4.

10. Herfried Münkler, *Imperien: Die Logik der Weltherrschaft von Alten Rom bis zu den Vereinigten Staaten* (Berlin: Rowohlt, 2005), 88–89, 132.

concentrate on their military superiority without undertaking infrastructural investments.[11] The Assyrian Empire was neither a steppe empire nor a civilizing empire; it undertook infrastructural investments, and it tried to integrate conquered peoples as Assyrians without having a civilizing mission.

Was the Assyrian Empire created by Tiglath-pileser stable and strong or short-lived and unstable? Tiglath-pileser had started organizing and structuring Assyria as an enormous, multiethnic empire, which was, however, difficult to control and administrate as the experiences of his successors so clearly revealed. After the very short reign of Shalmaneser V about which we know almost nothing, the purpose of the reforms of Sargon II was to centralize and strengthen absolute royal power and to establish the administrative apparatus to rule the Assyrian Empire.[12] It has been said that "Sargon II was the real founder of the empire, contributing decisively to ensuring its power and giving it its final character."[13] In reality, Tiglath-pileser was the founder of the empire, although without the achievements of Sargon, the empire may not have survived. Tiglath-pileser and Sargon successively conquered the enemies of the Assyrians who seized every opportunity to revolt. Finally, the Assyrian Empire bequeathed by Sargon in 705 to his son Sennacherib was more stable and stronger, but it was not easy to rule.[14] Among its failings are probably its excessive and permanent extension, the dissymmetry in its extension (more in the low lands than in the high mountain areas), and the disproportionate exploitation of the peripheral areas.[15] In short, Tiglath-pileser was the founder of the first world empire, an empire that was surely powerful, yet fragile.

---

11. See the critique of Bagg, "Palestine under Assyrian Rule," 119–43.
12. Elayi, *Sargon II*.
13. Garelli and Lemaire, *Les empires mésopotamiens, Israël*, 114.
14. Elayi, *Sennacherib*.
15. Liverani, "Fall of the Assyrian Empire," 384–85.

Selected Bibliography

General Works

Barnett, Richard D., and Margarete Falkner. *The Sculptures of Aššur-naṣir-apli II (883-859 B.C.), Tiglath-pileser III (745-727 B.C.), Esarhaddon (681-669 B.C.) from the Central and South-West Palaces at Nimrud.* London: British Museum, 1962.

Kwasman, Theodore, and Simo Parpola. *Tiglath-pileser III through Esarhaddon.* Part 1 of *Legal Transactions of the Royal Court of Nineveh.* SAA 6. Helsinki: Helsinki University Press, 1991.

Luukko, Mikko. *The Correspondence of Tiglath-pileser III and Sargon II from Calah/Nimrud.* SAA 19. Helsinki: Helsinki University Press, 2012.

Rost, Paul. *Die Keilschrifttexte Tiglat-Pilesers III.* Leipzig: Pfeiffer, 1893.

Tadmor, Hayim. *The Inscriptions of Tiglath-pileser III King of Assyria.* Jerusalem: Israel Academy of Sciences and Humanities, 1994.

Tadmor, Hayim, and Shigeo Yamada. *The Royal Inscriptions of Tiglath-pileser III (744-727 BC) and Shalmaneser V (726-722 BC), Kings of Assyria.* RINAP 1. Winona Lake, IN: Eisenbrauns, 2011.

Chapter 1

Grayson, Albert Kirk. "Assyrian Officials and Power in the Ninth and Eighth Centuries." *SAAB* 7 (1993): 19-52.

Lemaire, André, and Jean-Marie Durand, *Les inscriptions araméennes de Sfiré et l'Assyrie de Shamshi-ilu.* Geneva: Droz, 1984.

Marti, Lionel. "Le banquet d'Aššurnaṣirpal II." *JA* 299 (2011): 505-20.

Porter, Barbara Nevling. "Intimidation and Friendly Persuasion: Re-evaluating the Propaganda of Ashurnasirpal II." *ErIs* 27 (2003): 180-91.

Radner, Karen. "The Assur-Nineveh-Arbela Triangle: Central Assyria in the Neo-Assyrian Period." Pages 321-29 in *Between the Cultures: The*

Central Tigris Region from the Third to the First Millennium. Edited by Peter A. Miglus and Simone Mühl. Heidelberg: Heidelberger Orient-Verlag, 2011.

Yamada, Shigeo. *The Construction of the Assyrian Empire*. Leiden: Brill, 2000.

Chapter 2

Cifola, Barbara. *Analysis of Variants in the Assyrian Royal Titulary from the Origins to Tiglath-pileser III*. Naples: Istituto universitario orientale, 1995.

Dalley, Stephanie. "Yabâ, Atalyā and the Foreign Policy of Late Assyrian Kings." *SAAB* 12 (1998): 83–98.

Elayi, Josette. *Sargon II, King of Assyria*. ABS 22. Atlanta: SBL Press, 2017.

Garelli, Paul. "The Achievement of Tiglath-pileser III: Novelty or Continuity?" Pages 46–51 in *Ah, Assyria... Studies in Assyrian History and Ancient Near Eastern Historiography Presented to Hayim Tadmor*. Edited by Mordechai Cogan and Israel Eph'al. Jerusalem, 1991.

Lewis, Theodore J. "You Have Heard What the Kings of Assyria Have Done: Disarmament Passages vis-à-vis Assyrian Rhetoric of Intimidation." Pages 88–89 in *Isaiah's Vision of Peace in Biblical and Modern International Relations: Swords into Plowshares*. Edited by Raymond Cohen and Raymond Westbrook. CRIR. New York: Palgrave Macmillan, 2008.

May, Natalie Naomi. "Administrative and Other Reforms of Sargon II and Tiglath-pileser III." *SAAB* 21 (2015): 79–116.

Thomas, Felix. "Sargon II., der Sohn Tiglat-pilesers III." Pages 465–70 in *Mesopotamica-Ugaritica-Biblica: Festschrift für Kurt Bergerhof*. Edited by Manfred Dietrich and Oswald Loretz. AOAT 232. Neukirchen-Vluyn: Neukirchener Verlag, 1993.

Yamada, Shigeo. "Inscriptions of Tiglath-pileser III: Chronographic-Literary Styles and the King's Portrait." *Orient* 49 (2014): 31–52.

Chapter 3

Frahm, Eckart. "Revolts in the Neo-Assyrian Period: A Preliminary Discourse Analysis." Pages 76–79 in *Revolt and Resistance in the Ancient Classical World and the Near East*. Edited by John Collins and Joseph Gilbert Manning. Leiden: Brill, 2016.

SELECTED BIBLIOGRAPHY 191

Fuchs, Andreas. "Der Turtān Šamšī-ilu und die große Zeit des assyrischen Großen (830–746)." *WdO* 38 (2008): 61–145.
Lion, Brigitte. "L'andurāru à l'époque médio-babylonienne, d'après les documents de Terqa, Nuzi et Arrapha." Pages 313–28 in *Nuzi at Seventy-Five*. Edited by David I. Owen and Gernot Wilhelm. Bethesda: CDL Press, 1999.
Zawadzki, Stefan. "The Revolt of 746 B.C. and the Coming of Tiglath-pileser III to the Throne." *SAAB* 8 (1994): 53–54.

Chapter 4

Dalley, Stephanie. "Shamshi-ilu, Language and Power in the Western Assyrian Empire." Pages 79–88 in *Essays on Syria in the Iron Age*. Edited by Guy Bunnens. Leuven: Peeters, 2000.
Grayson, Albert Kirk. "The Struggle for Power in Assyria." Pages 233–70 in *Priests and Officials in the Ancient Near East*. Edited by Kazuko Watanabe. Heidelberg, 1997.
Ikeda, Shigeo. "Looking from Til Barsip on the Euphrates: Assyria and the West in Ninth and Eighth Centuries." Pages 281–93 in *Priests and Officials in the Ancient Near East*. Edited by Kazuko Watanabe. Heidelberg, 1997.
Lipiński, Edward. "State Treaties between Katk and Arpad." Pages 256–66 in *Near Eastern Religious Texts Relating to the Old Testament*. Edited by Walter Beyerlin. Philadelphia: Westminster, 1978.
N'Shea, Omar. "Royal Eunuchs and Elite Masculinity in the Neo-Assyrian Empire." *NEA* 79 (2016): 214–21.
Ponchia, Simonetta. *L'Assiria e gli Stati Transeufratici*. Padova: Sargon, 1991.
Postgate, John Nicholas. "The Invisible Hierarchy: Assyrian Military and Civilian Administration in the Eighth and Seventh Centuries BC." Pages 331–60 in *The Land of Assur and the Yoke of Assur: Studies on Assyria 1971–2005*. Oxford: Oxbow, 2007.

Chapter 5

Bagg, Ariel M. "Palestine under Assyrian Rule: A New Look at the Assyrian Imperial Policy in the West." *JAOS* 133 (2013): 119–43.
Dalley, Stephanie. "Foreign Chariotry and Cavalry in the Armies of Tiglath-pileser III and Sargon II." *Iraq* 47 (1985): 31–48.

Dubovský, Peter. "Neo-Assyrian Warfare: Logistics and Weaponry during the Campaigns of Tiglath-pileser III." *Anodos: Studies of the Ancient World* 4–5 (2004–2005): 61–67.
Elayi, Josette. "Terminologie de la Mer Méditerranée dans les Annales assyriennes." *OrAnt* 23 (1984): 75–92.
Kaplan, Jacob. "Recruitment of Foreign Soldiers into the Neo-Assyrian Army during the Reign of Tiglath-pileser III." Pages 135–52 in *Treasures on Camel's Humps, Historical and Literary Studies from the Ancient Near East Presented to Israel Eph'al*. Edited by Mordechai Cogan and Dan'el Kahn. Jerusalem: Magnes, 2008.
Morandi Bonacossi, Daniele. "Stele e statue reali assire: Localizzazione, diffuzione e implicazioni ideologiche." *Mesopotamia* 23 (1988): 106–55.
Tadmor, Hayim. "World Dominion: The Expanding Horizon of the Assyrian Empire." Pages 55–62 in *Landscapes, Territories, Frontiers and Horizons in the Ancient Near East*. Edited by Lucio Milano, Stefano de Martino, Frederick Mario Fales, and Giovanni Battista Lanfranchi. RAI 44. Padova: S.a.r.g.o.n., 1999.
Villard, Pierre. "Quelques aspects du renseignement militaire dans l'empire néo-assyrien." *HIMA* 3 (2016): 87–97.

Chapter 6

Brinkman, John A. "Reflections on the Geography of Babylonia (1000–600 B.C.)." Pages 19–29 in *Neo-Assyrian Geography*. Edited by Mario Liverani. Rome: Universita di Roma "La Sapienza," 1995.
Cole, Steven W. *Nippur IV. The Early Neo-Babylonian Governor's Archive from Nippur*. OIP 114. Chicago: The Oriental Institute of the University of Chicago, 1996.
Eph'al, Israel. "The Bukān Aramaic Inscription: Historical Considerations." *IEJ* 39 (1999): 116–21.
Lanfranchi, Giovanni Battista. "The Assyrian Expansion in the Zagros and the Local Ruling Elites." Pages 79–118 in *Continuity of Empire (?): Assyria, Media, Persia*. Edited by Giovanni Battista Lanfranchi, Michael Roaf, and Robert Rollinger. Padova: S.a.r.g.o.n., 2003.
Lipiński, Edward. *The Aramaeans: Their Ancient History, Culture, Religion*. OLA 100. Leuven: Peeters, 2000.
Luukko, Mikko. "The Governors of Halzi-atbari in the Neo-Assyrian Period." Pages 321–33 in *Studies in Honour of Nicholas Postgate*. Edited

by Yağmur Heffron, Adam Stone, and Martin Worthington. Winona Lake, IN: Eisenbrauns, 2017.

Novák, Mirko. "Assyrians and Aramaeans: Modes of Cohabitation and Acculturation at Guzana (Tell Halaf)." Pages 123–35 in *Assyria to Iberia: Art and Culture in the Iron Age*. Edited by Joan Aruz and Michael Seymour. New York: Metropolitan Museum of Art, 2016.

Postgate, John Nicholas. "The Assyrian Army in Zamua." *Iraq* 62 (2000): 89–108.

Radner, Karen. "An Assyrian View of the Medes." Pages 37–64 in *Continuity of Empire (?): Assyria, Media, Persia*. Edited by Giovanni Battista Lanfranchi, Michael Roaf, and Robert Rollinger. Padova: S.a.r.g.o.n., 2003.

Waetzoldt, Hartmut. "Zu den Strandverschiebungen am Persischen Golf und den Bezeichnungen der Ḫōrs." Pages 159–84 in *Strandverchiebungen und ihrer Bedeutung für Geowissenschaften und Archäologie*. Edited by Jérôme Schäfer and W. Simon. Heidelberg: Vorstand der Vereinigung der Freunde der Studentenschaft der Universität, 1981.

Chapter 7

Astour, Michael C. "The Arena of Tiglath-pileser III's Campaign against Sarduri II (743 B.C.)." *Assur* 2 (1979): 1–23.

Bagg, Ariel M. *Die Assyrer und das Westland: Studien zur historischen Geographie und Herrschaftspraxis in der Levante im 1. Jt.v.u.z.* OLA 216. Louvain: Peeters, 2011.

Bryce, Trevor. *The World of the Neo-Hittite Kingdoms*. Oxford: Oxford University Press, 2012.

Chaaya, Anis. "L'évolution et le changement culturel à Tell 'Arqa après l'invasion de Tiglath-pileser III (Niveaux 10-9)." Pages 213–19 in *Proceedings of the First International Congress on the Archaeology of the Ancient Near East (Rome, May 18th–23rd 1998)*. Edited by Paolo Matthiae et al. Rome: Dipartimento di Scienze Storiche, Archeologiche e Antropologiche dell'Antichità, Univ. degli Studi di Roma "La Sapienza," 2000.

Elayi, Josette. "Les sites phéniciens de Syrie au Fer III/Perse: Bilan et perspectives de recherche." Pages 327–48 in *Essays on Syria in the Iron Age*. Edited by Guy Bunnens. Leuven: Peeters, 2000.

———. *The History of Phoenicia*. Atlanta: Lockwood, 2018.

Elayi, Josette, and Alain G. Elayi. *Arwad, cité phénicienne du nord.* Pendé: Gabalda, 2015.
Hawkins, John David. "The Political Geography of North Syria and South-East Anatolia in the Neo-Assyrian Period." Pages 87–101 in *Neo-Assyrian Geography.* Edited by Mario Liverani. Rome: Universita di Roma "La Sapienza," 1995.
Na'aman, Nadav. "Borders and Districts in Descriptions of the Conquest of the West in Tiglath-pileser III's Inscriptions and in Biblical Historiography." *SAAB* 16 (2007): 42–48.
Yamada, Shigeo. "Ulluba and Its Surroundings: Tiglath-pileser III's Province Organization Facing the Urartian Border." Pages 11–40 in *Neo-Assyrian Sources in Context: Thematic Studies of Texts, History, and Culture.* Edited by Shigeo Yamada. Helsinki: Neo-Assyrian Text Corpus Project, 2018.

Chapter 8

Alibaigi, Sajjad. "The Location of the Second Stele Commemorating Tiglath-pileser III's Campaign to the East in 737 BC." *SAAB* 23 (2017): 47–53.
Elayi, Josette. *Sennacherib, King of Assyria.* ABS 24. Atlanta: SBL Press, 2018.
Reade, Julian E. "Iran in the Neo-Assyrian Period." Pages 31–42 in *Neo-Assyrian Geography.* Edited by Mario Liverani. Rome: Università di Roma "La sapienza," 1995.
Salvini, Mirjo. "Some Historic-Geographical Problems Concerning Assyria and Urartu." Pages 43–53 in *Neo-Assyrian Geography.* Edited by Mario Liverani. Rome: Università di Roma "La sapienza," 1995.
Tadmor, Hayim. "Assyria at the Gates of Tushpa." Pages 266–73 in *Treasures on Camels' Humps.* Edited by Mordechai Cogan and Dan'el Kahn. Jerusalem: Magnes, 2008.

Chapter 9

Aster, Shawn Zelig. "An Assyrian Loyalty-Oath Imposed on Ashdod in the Reign of Tiglath-pileser III?" *Orientalia* 82.3 (2018): 275–80.
Dubovský, Peter. "Tiglath-pileser III's Campaigns in 734–732 B.C.: Historical Background of Isa 7; 2 Kgs 15–16 and 2 Chr 27–28." *Bib* 87 (2006): 153–70.

Galil, Gershon. "A New Look at the Inscriptions of Tiglath-pileser III." *Bib* 81 (2000): 511–30.
Hämen-Anttila, Jaakko. "The Camels of Tiglath-pileser III and the Arabic Definite Article." Pages 99–101 in *Of God(s), Trees, Kings, and Scholars: Neo-Assyrian and Related Studies in Honour of Simo Parpola*. Edited by Mikko Luukko, Saana Svärd, and Raija Mattila. Helsinki, 2009.
Irvine, Stuart A. *Isaiah, Ahaz, and the Syro-Ephraimite Crisis*. SBLDS 123. Atlanta: Scholars Press, 1990.
Mayer, Walter R. "Sennacherib's Campaign of 701 BCE: The Assyrian View." Pages 168–200 in *'Like a Bird in a Cage': The Invasion of Sennacherib in 701 BCE*. Edited by Lester L. Grabbe. London: Sheffield, 2003.
Na'aman, Nadav. *Ancient Israel and Its Neighbors: Interaction and Counteraction*. Winona Lake, IN: Eisenbrauns, 2015.
Oded, Bustenay. "Phoenician Cities and the Assyrian Empire in the Time of Tiglath-pileser III." *ZDPV* 90 (1974): 38–49.
Saporetti, Claudio. "Testimonianze neo-assire relative all Fenicia da Tiglat-Pileser III ad Assurbanipal." Pages 109–243 in *Studi storici sulla Fenicia: L'VIII e il VII secolo a.C.* Edited by Massimo Botto. Quaderni de orientalistica pisana I. Pisa: Università degli studi di Pisa, 1990.
Siddall, Luis Robert. "Tiglath-pileser III's Aid to Ahaz: A New Look at the Problems of the Biblical Accounts in Light of the Assyrian Sources." *ANES* 46 (2009): 93–106.
Tadmor, Hayim, and Mordechai Cogan. "Ahaz and Tiglath-Pileser in the Book of Kings: Historiographic Considerations." *Bib* 60 (1979): 491–508.
Walton, J. T. "Assyrian Interest in the West: Philistia and Judah." *ErIs* 33 (2018): 175*–82*.

Chapter 10

Brinkman, John A. "Elamite Aid to Merodach-Baladan." *JNES* 24 (1965): 161–66.
———. *A Political History of Post-Kassite Babylonia 1158–722 B.C. AnOr* 43. Rome: Biblical Institute Press, 1968.
Eph'al, Israel. "'Arabs' in Babylonia in the Eighth Century B.C." *JAOS* 94 (1974): 108–15.
Fales, Frederick Mario. "Moving around Babylon: On the Aramean and Chaldean Presence in Southern Mesopotamia." Pages 91–111 in *Bab-*

ylon, *Wissenskultur in Orient und Okzident*. Edited by Eva Cancik-Kirschbaum et al. Berlin: de Gruyter, 2008.

Luukko, Mikko. "How Could the Assyrian King Enter Babylon Conciliatory?" *NABU* (2007): 85–86.

Chapter 11

Grayson, Albert Kirk. *Assyrian and Babylonian Chronicles*. Winona Lake, IN: Eisenbrauns, 2000.

Kessler, Karlheinz. *Untersuchungen zur historischen Topographie Nordmesopotamiens*. Wiesbaden: Reichert, 1980.

Radner, Karen. "Salmanassar V. in den Nimrud Letters." *AfO* 50 (2003–2004): 95–105.

Yamada, Keiko, and Shigeo Yamada. "Shalmaneser V and His Era, Revisited." Pages 387–442 in *'Now It Happened in Those Days': Studies in Biblical, Assyrian, and Other Ancient Near Eastern Historiography Presented to Mordechai Cogan on His Seventy-Fifth Birthday*. Edited by Amitai Baruchi-Unna et al. Vol. 2. Winona Lake, IN: Eisenbrauns, 2017.

Chapter 12

Barnett, Richard D., and Margarete Falkner. *The Sculptures of Aššur-naṣir-apli II (883–859 B.C.), Tiglath-pileser III (745–727 B.C.), Esarhaddon (681–669 B.C.) from the Central and South-West Palaces at Nimrud*. London: British Museum, 1962.

Cogan, Mordechai. *Imperialism and Religion: Assyria, Judah and Israel in the Eighth and Seventh Centuries B.C.E.* Missoula, MT: Scholars Press, 1974.

Gross, Melanie, and David Kertai. "Becoming Empire: Neo-Assyrian Palaces and the Creation of Courtly Culture." *Journal of Ancient History* 7 (2019): 1–31.

Holloway, Steven W. *Aššur Is King! Aššur Is King! Religion in the Exercise of Power in the Neo-Assyrian Empire*. Leiden: Brill, 2002.

Kertai, David. "Embellishing the Interior Spaces of Assyria's Royal Palaces: The Bēt Ḫīlani Reconsidered." *Iraq* 79 (2017): 85–104.

Mallowan, Max E. L. *Nimrud and Its Remains*. Vol. 1. London: Collins, 1966.

Pedde, Friedhelm, and Steven Lundström. *Der Alte Palast in Assur: Architektur und Baugeschichte.* WVDOG 120. Wiesbaden: Harrassowitz, 2008.

Reade, Julian E. "The Palace of Tiglath-pileser III." *Iraq* 30 (1968): 69–73.

Yamada, Shigeo. "Names of Walls, Gates, and Palatial Structures of Assyrian Royal Cities: Contents, Styles, and Ideology." *Orient* 55 (2020): 87–104.

Index of Ancient Sources

Hebrew Bible/Old Testament

Genesis
25:12	151 n. 120
25:13	151 n. 122
25:15	151 n. 120

2 Samuel
9–10	109 n. 67

1 Kings
14:15–31	142 n. 72
14:19	142 n. 72
14:29	142 n. 72
15:7	142 n. 72
15:31	142 n. 72
20	18 n. 26

2 Kings
8:28–9	146
10:32–33	18 n. 24
14:28	109 n. 67
15:8–13	139 n. 61
15:19	139
15:25	139
15:29	25 n. 4, 144 n. 81
15:29–31	129 n. 3, 144 n. 81
15:30	145
15:32–16:20	129 n. 4
16:5–9	141 n. 66
16:6	145
16:7	25 n. 4, 143 n. 74
16:9	148
16:10	149
17:3	145 n. 90
19:13	87 n. 92
23:14–25	18 n. 26

1 Chronicles
5:6	25 n. 4, 144
5:26	144
18:9–10	109 n. 67

2 Chronicles
25:6	63
26:7–8	137 n. 45
27:1–28:27	129 n. 4
28:5–21	141 n. 66
28:16	143 n. 74
28:17	145
28:20	1, 25 n. 4

Isaiah
7:1–2	141 n. 66
7:1–25	129 n. 4
7:6	140
7:10–12	143
10:5	138 n. 55
10:8	52 n. 22
37:13	87 n. 92

Amos
1:10	52 n. 22
1:9–10	134 n. 32

Hosea
10:14	145 n. 92

Greco-Roman Literature

Herodotus, *Hist.* 1.95–106   83 n. 13

Index of Modern Authors

Abel, Félix-Marie 144 n. 83
Abou-Assaf, Ali 52 n. 20
Ackerman, Susan 1 n. 3
Ackroyd, Peter M. 142 n. 70
Alcock, Susan E. 23 n. 50
Alibaigi, Sajjad 6, 6 n. 26, 119 n. 16, 119 n. 18, 119 n. 20, 194
Al-Maqdissi, Michel 111, 111 n. 82
Al-Rawi, Farouk N. H. 29 n. 24
Alt, Albrecht 6, 6 n. 27
Alvarez-Mon, Javier 82 n. 70
Andrae, Walter 55 n. 38
André-Salvini, Béatrice 126 n. 56
Anspacher, Abraham S. 5
Archer, Robin 66 n. 26
Aruz, Joan 76 n. 39, 193
Aster, Shawn Zelig 90 n. 110, 138 n. 52, 194
Astour, Michael 6, 6 n. 26, 97 n. 3, 102, 102 n. 22, 102 n 25, 193
Avanzini, Alessandra 149 n. 111
Bachelot, Luc 42 n. 88, 174 n. 9
Badre, Leila 113 n. 92, 113 n 96
Bagg, Ariel M. 61 n. 1, 68 nn. 35–36, 69 n. 38, 102 n. 23, 131 n. 13, 178 n. 29, 188 n. 11, 191, 193
Baker, Heather D. xi, 4 n. 16, 44 n. 6, 54 n. 30, 63 n. 13, 169 n. 26
Balcıoğlu, B. 59 n. 63
Barnett, Richard D. 5 nn. 23–24, 6, 6 n. 28, 29 nn. 26–27, 30 n. 28, 30 n. 31, 93 n. 129, 171 n. 40, 172 n. 41, 174 n. 6, 175 n. 10, 189, 196
Bartlett, J. R. 141 n. 67
Bartoloni, Gilda 132 n. 18, 138 n. 55

Baruchi-Unna, Amitai 27 n. 14, 196
Begrich, Joachim 139 n. 57, 140 n. 64
Belli, Oktay 126 n. 56
Biga, Maria Giovanna 138 n. 55
Binandeh, Ali 82 n. 70
Black, Jeremy 40 n. 80, 127 n. 62
Blenkinsopp, Joseph 140 n. 64
Blocher, Félix 49 n. 2
Bordreuil, Pierre 52 n. 20, 110 n. 78
Botto, Massimo 130 n. 7, 195
Bounni, Adnan 111, 111 n. 82
Brandl, Baruch 152 n. 125
Bright, John 140 n. 64
Brinkman, John A. 25 n. 2, 26 n. 7, 28 n. 20, 56, 56 n. 47, 76 n. 39, 76 n. 41, 77 n. 44–45, 78 nn. 48–49, 154 nn. 5–6, 155 n. 9, 155 n. 12, 166 n. 7, 167 n. 9, 192, 195
Briquel-Chatonnet, Françoise 76 n. 40
Brown, Stuart C. 83 n. 73
Bryce, Trevor 2 n. 4, 97, 97 n. 2, 99 n. 11, 101 n. 16, 101 n. 18, 103 nn. 31–32, 104 n. 36, 105 n. 38, 107 n. 51, 108 n. 59, 109 nn. 66–67, 146 n. 93, 148 n. 102, 193
Budge, E. A. Wallis 30 n. 29
Bunnens, Guy 12 n. 5, 51 n. 15, 111 n. 80, 113 n. 92, 191, 193
Burstein, Stanley Meyer 2 n. 9
Byrne, Ryan 149 nn. 109–110
Cancik-Kirschbaum, Eva 72 n. 4, 196
Canning, Sir Stratford 5
Capet, Emma 113 n. 92
Carayon, Nicolas 131 n. 17
Chaaya, Anis 111 n. 83, 193

-201-

Charpin, Dominique   42 n. 88, 47 n. 20, 169 n. 29
Cifola, Barbara   32 n. 34, 34 n. 40, 190
Cingano, E.   147 n. 98
Cogan, Mordechai   6, 6 nn. 26–27, 27 nn. 14–15, 116 n. 113, 122 n. 42, 140 n. 64, 141 n. 67, 144 n. 80, 176 n. 19, 178 n. 29, 190, 192, 194–96
Cohen, Ada   1 n. 3, 36 n. 57, 68 n. 35
Cohen, Raymond   37 n. 57, 190
Cole, Steven W.   74 n. 24, 77 n. 45, 155 n. 9, 192
Crouch, Carly L.   138 n. 55, 139 n. 59
Curtis, John E.   29 nn. 23–25, 40 n. 80, 84 n. 75
Dalley, Stephanie   5 n. 20, 6, 6 n. 26, 29 n. 25, 51 n. 15, 52, 52 n. 21, 54, 54 n. 32, 66 nn. 24–25, 67 nn. 31–32, 84 n. 79, 190–91
Dalongeville, Rémi   75 n. 38
Damerji, Muayyad Said   29 n. 23
DeGrado, Jessie   32 n. 34
De Martino, Stefano   62 n. 10, 192
Dever, William G.   60 n. 72
Dezsö, Tamás   65 n. 21, 67 nn. 29–30
Diakonoff, Igor Mikhailovich   94 n. 135
Dietrich, Manfred   28 n. 21, 190
Donner, Herbert   x
Drews, R.   12 n. 5
Dubovský, Peter   66 n. 23, 67 n. 34, 129 n. 2, 132 n. 22, 134 n. 27, 137 n. 48, 139 n. 57, 141 n. 65, 148 n. 104, 152 nn. 123–124, 192, 194
Dupont-Sommer, André   52 n. 19, 66 n. 26
Durand, Jean-Marie   19 n. 31, 52 n. 19, 53 n. 24, 58 n. 57, 169 n. 29, 189
Dussaud, René   132 n. 20
Ebeling, Erich   115 n. 104
Ehrlich, Carl S.   137 n. 48
Elayi, Alain G.   14 n. 12, 112 n. 87, 194
Elayi, Josette   7 nn. 29–30, 14 n. 12, 39 n. 72, 40 n. 78, 62 n. 12, 111 n. 80, 112 n. 87, 176 n. 19, 190, 192–94
Engel, B. J.   179 n. 32

Eph'al, Israel   6 n. 26, 27 n. 15, 33 n. 38, 65 n. 21, 73 n. 15, 82 n. 70, 154 n. 6, 190, 192
Fagan, Garrett G.   66 n. 26
Fales, Frederick Mario   xi, 4 n. 17, 26 n. 9, 28 n. 22, 34 n. 43, 44 n. 6, 53 n. 24, 54 n. 34, 62 n. 10, 72 n. 4, 72 n. 10, 76 n. 39, 77 n. 46, 78 n. 47, 94 n. 135, 155 n. 11, 187 n. 8, 192, 195
Falkner, Margarete   5 nn. 23–24, 6 n. 28, 29 nn. 26–27, 30 nn. 28 and 31, 93 n. 129, 171 n. 40, 172 n. 41, 174 n. 6, 175 n. 10, 189, 196
Fantalkin, Alexander   136 n. 42
Faust, Avraham   90 n. 110
Fink, A. S.   109 n. 66
Forrer, Emil O.   27 n. 12, 43, 44 n. 5, 86, 86 n. 85, 88 n. 95, 88 n. 99, 113 n. 94
Frahm, Eckart   2 n. 9, 5, 5 n. 25, 43 n. 4, 47 n. 16, 59 n. 63, 60 n. 72, 69, 149 n. 111, 171 n. 37, 187 n. 8, 190
Frangipane, Marcello   99 n. 12, 99 n. 14
Frayne, D. R.   187 n. 9
Friedrich, Johannes   51 n. 10
Fuchs, Andreas   xii, 19 n. 31, 44 n. 6, 45 n. 11, 49 n. 2, 50, 50 n. 8, 63 n. 16, 65 nn. 19–20, 66 n. 26, 67 n. 34, 81 n. 67, 82 n. 69, 119 n. 20, 151 n. 121, 175 n. 12, 191
Gadd, Cyril John   77 n. 45, 151 n. 121
Gal, Zvi   91 n. 118
Galil, Gershon   6, 6 n. 27, 99 n. 13, 195
Galter, Hannes   57 n. 54
Garelli, Paul   11 n. 4, 12 n. 6, 15 n. 17, 17 n. 21, 18 n. 25, 27 n. 15, 34 n. 43, 42 nn. 86 and 88, 44 nn. 8–9, 53, 53 n. 25, 59 nn. 64–65, 59 n. 68, 60 n. 73, 64, 64 nn. 17–18, 67 n. 30, 72 n. 11, 73 n. 14, 78 n. 50, 79 n. 53, 85 nn. 82–83, 163 n. 54, 188 n. 13, 190
Garrison, Mark B.   82 n. 70
Garstang, John   99 n. 11
Gaspa, Salvatore   147 n. 98
Gehler, Michael   22 n. 48
Gelb, I. J.   27 nn. 13–14, 45 n. 11

INDEX OF MODERN AUTHORS

Gelio, Roberto 62 n. 10
George, Andrew 127 n. 62
Ghersetti, A. 147 n. 98
Ghirshman, Roman 119, 119 n. 19
Gibson, John C. L. 109 n. 65
Gibson, MacGuire 76 n. 42, 85 n. 80
Gilmann, Nicolas 42 n. 88
Gitin, Seymour 12 n. 5, 60 n. 72
Grabbe, Lester L. 147 n. 100, 195
Graham, M. Patrick 41 n. 69, 142 n. 72
Grandpierre, Véronique 187 n. 8
Grayson, Albert Kirk xi, 2 nn. 6–8, 4 n. 19, 14 n. 15, 17 n. 20, 20 n. 35, 21 nn. 38, 21 n. 40, 26 n. 9, 27 nn. 14–15, 43 n. 3, 44 n. 9, 46 n. 12, 47 n. 17, 49 n. 2, 53 nn. 24–25, 53 n. 27, 54 n. 31, 55 n. 35, 56, 56 nn. 48–50, 72 nn. 5–6, 153 n. 1, 159 n. 37, 161 n. 42, 165 nn. 1–2, 167 n. 8, 171, 171 n. 38, 189, 191, 196
Gubel, Éric 113 n. 92, 113 n. 96, 131 n. 12, 131 n. 18
Guidotti, Maria Cristina 4 n. 17
Gurney, O. R. 99 n. 11
Haas, Volkert 126 n. 56
Haellquist, Karl Reinhold 85 n. 80
Hämen-Anttila, Jaakko 150 n. 116, 195
Hassanzadeh, Youssef 82 n. 70
Hawkins, John David 52 n. 19, 98 n. 4, 98 n. 6, 99 n. 11, 101 n. 15, 107 n. 51, 108 n. 58, 194
Heffron, Yağmur 89 n. 104, 193
Hejebri-Nobari, Alireza 126 n. 56
Herles, Michael 77 n. 43
Herrero, Pablo 119 n. 15
Hoglund, Kenneth G. 142 n. 72
Holloway, Steven W. 178 n. 29, 196
Hübner, U. 172 n. 42
Hulin, P. 145 n. 89
Hutter, Manfred 57 n. 54
Hutter-Braunsar, Sylvia 57 n. 54
Irvine, Stuart A. 139 n. 57, 140 n. 64, 141, 141 n. 68, 195
Jankowska, N. B. 94 n. 135
Joannès, Francis 25 n. 3, 42 n. 88, 67 n. 33, 74 n. 28, 75 n. 38, 76 n. 39, 78

Joannès, Francis (cont.) n. 52, 87 n. 90, 92 n. 124, 94 n. 135, 95 n. 139, 106 n. 43, 124 n. 48, 149 n. 111, 161 n. 45, 162 n. 49, 169 n. 29, 176 n. 15, 179 n. 32, 193
Joukowsky, M. S. 12 n. 5
Kahn, Dan'el 6 n. 26, 97, 97 n. 3, 101 n. 17, 103 n. 29, 104, 104 n. 35, 105 nn. 38–39, 116 n. 113, 122 n. 42, 192, 194
Kalaç, Mustafa 98 n. 6
Kalimi, Isaac 142 n. 70
Kangas, Steven E. 1 n. 3
Kanzaq, Rassoul Bashash 82 n. 70
Kaplan, Jacob 6, 6 n. 26, 65 n. 21, 66, 67 n. 28, 192
Kargar, Bahman 82 n. 70
Kassler, P. 75 n. 38
Kataja, Laura xii
Katzenstein, H. Jacob 132 n. 22
Kertai, David 171 n. 37, 174 n. 9, 175 n. 13, 196
Kessler, Karlheinz 88 n. 99, 113 n. 94, 124 n. 49, 125 n. 52, 131 n. 16, 168 n. 20, 196
Kirleis, Wiebke 77 n. 43
Klenger, Horst 12 n. 5
Knauf, Ernst Axel 150 n. 112, 172 n. 42
Knoppers, Gary N. 141, 141 n. 69
Kroll, Stefan 119 n. 12
Kuhrt, Amelie 83 n. 73
Kwasman, Theodore xi, 189
Landsberger, Benno 27 n. 14
Lanfranchi, Giovanni Battista xi, 28 n. 22, 30 n. 29, 34 n. 43, 35 n. 43, 62 n. 10, 80 n. 62, 81 n. 64, 82 n. 71, 84 nn. 75 and 78, 85 n. 81, 87 n. 95, 101 n. 15, 114 n. 99, 146 n. 93, 147 n. 98, 192–93
Larsen, Mogens Trolle 17 n. 21, 140 n. 64
Lauinger, Jacob 115 n. 103
Laxer, James 186, 186 n. 7
Layard, Austen Henry 3, 3 n. 11, 5, 174, 174 n. 7-8
Lemaire, André 11 n. 4, 12 n. 6, 15 n. 17, 18 nn. 25–26, 19 n. 31, 52 n. 19, 53 nn. 24–25, 58 n. 57, 59 nn. 64–65, 59

Lemaire, André (cont.)
  n. 68, 60 n. 73, 67 n. 30, 72 n. 11, 73 n.
  14, 78 n. 50, 79 n. 53, 82 n. 70, 85 nn.
  82–83, 136 n. 42, 146 n. 93, 163 n. 54,
  188 n. 13, 189
Levine, Louis D.   119 nn. 14, 119 n. 19
Lewis, Theodore J.   36 n. 57, 68 n. 35, 190
Lewy, Julius   47 n. 20
Lindsay, John   141 n. 67
Lion, Brigitte   47 n. 20, 191
Lipiński, Edward   19 n. 31, 52 n. 19, 53 n. 24, 72, 72 nn. 9–12, 73 nn. 13–19, 74 nn. 24–25, 74 nn. 27–31, 76 n. 39, 90 nn. 114–116, 101 n. 18, 105 n. 38, 109 n. 65, 109 n. 68, 110 nn. 77–78, 111, 111 n. 79, 111 n. 81, 111 n. 83, 112 n. 84, 112 n. 86, 113 n. 92, 115 n. 102, 115 n. 105, 130 n. 7, 131 n. 13, 131 n. 15, 139 n. 59, 139 n. 62, 144 nn. 82–84, 145 n. 92, 191–92
Liverani, Mario   11 n. 1, 23 n. 50, 42 n. 86, 77 n. 44, 80 n. 57, 84 n. 75, 89 n. 100, 98 n. 4, 99 nn. 12–14, 119 n. 13, 124 n. 49, 138 n. 55, 187 n. 8, 188 n. 15, 192, 194
Loftus, William Kennett   5
Loretz, Oswald   28 n. 21, 190
Luckenbill, Daniel David   ix
Lund, John   111 n. 80
Lundström, Steven   180 n. 42, 197
Luukko, Mikko   xii, 89 n. 104, 107 n. 50, 150 n. 116, 158 n. 29, 166–68, 189, 192, 195–96
MacGinnis, John   86 n. 88, 90 n. 117
Machinist, Peter   138 n. 55
Magen, Ursula   20 n. 34, 54 n. 34
Malamat, Abraham   52 n. 22
Malbran-Labat, Florence   110 n. 78
Mallowan, Max E. L.   93 n. 131, 174 n. 5, 196
Manitius, Walther   66 n. 26
Marzahn, Joachim   149 n. 111
Maraqten, Mohammed   149 n. 111
Marcus, D.   147 n. 98

Marriott, John   66 n. 26
Marti, Lionel   13 n. 10, 189
Matthiae, Paolo   111 n. 83, 132 n. 18, 193
Mattila, Raija   114 n. 99, 150 n. 116, 195
May, Natalie Naomi   28 n. 19, 58, 67 n. 29, 174 n. 9, 190
Mayer, Walter R.   59 n. 63, 147 nn. 99–100, 195
McCormick, Robert   76 n. 42
McKenzie, Steven L.   141 n. 69
McMahon, Gregory   123 n. 44
Medvedskaya, Ina N.   117 n. 2
Meissner, Burkhard   66 n. 26
Melchiorri, Valentina   111 n. 81
Melikišvili, G. A.   xii
Mellink, Machteld   98 n. 5
Meyer, G. Rudolf   51 n. 10
Michalowski, Kazimierz   5
Miglus Peter A.   22 n. 47, 190
Milano, Lucio   62 n. 10, 147 n. 98, 192
Millard, Alan R.   xii, 1 n. 2, 25 n. 4, 52, 52 n. 20, 53 n. 23, 103
Mollasalehi, H.   82 n. 70
Morandi Bonacossi, Daniele   35 nn. 48–49, 41 n. 85, 63 n. 13, 126 n. 59, 192
Mühl, Simone   22 n. 47, 190
Münkler, Herfried   187, 187 n. 10
Muscarella, Oscar   132 n. 19
Myers, Jacob M.   142 n. 73
Naʾaman, Nadav   6, 6 n. 27, 33 n. 38, 90 n. 117, 112 n. 84, 113 n. 94, 131 nn. 12–13, 136 n. 37, 137 n. 44, 140 n. 64, 194–95
Nadali, David   147 n. 100, 148 n. 102, 187 n. 8
Nehmé, Leila   2 n. 5
Neumann, Hans   149 n. 111
Neumann, Jehuda   77 n. 43
Nigro, Lorenzo   132 n. 18
Nissen, Hans-Jörg   76 n. 42, 131 n. 13
Norris, Edwin   3
Notley, R. Steven   142, 142 n. 71
Nougayrol, Jean   xi
Novák, Mirko   76 n. 39, 193

INDEX OF MODERN AUTHORS

N'Shea, Omar 60 n. 69, 191
Oates, David 5 n. 20
Oates, John 5 n. 20
Oded, Bustenay 92 nn. 122–123, 92 n. 125, 93 n. 128, 95 n. 138, 96 n. 141, 113 n. 94, 132 n. 22, 139 n. 57, 140 n. 64, 195
Oren, E. D. 136 n. 42
Otzen, Benedikt 140 n. 64
Owen, David I. 47 n. 20, 191
Parker, Barbara 67 n. 28
Parker, Bradley J. 95 n. 136
Parpola, Simo xi–xii, 28 n. 22, 34 n. 43, 60 n. 72, 77 n. 43, 99 n. 11, 124 n. 49, 150 n. 116, 167, 189, 195
Parrot, André 132 n. 19
Pecchioli Daddi, Franca 4 n. 17
Pedde, Friedhelm 180 n. 42, 197
Pitard, Wayne T. 18 n. 25, 146 n. 93
Ponchia, Simonetta 3 n. 13, 56 n. 48, 85 n. 80, 115 n. 103, 191
Porter, Barbara Nevling 13 n. 10, 189
Porter, Michael 99 n. 11, 124 n. 49
Portuese, Ludovico 32 n. 35
Postgate, John Nicholas xi, 5 nn. 20 and 23, 53 n. 27, 55 n. 36, 59 n. 67, 63 n. 14, 66 nn. 24, 66 nn. 26–27, 75 nn. 32–33, 79 n. 56, 89 n. 100, 89 n. 102, 89 n. 104, 115 n. 103, 121 n. 31, 127 n. 62, 175 n. 10, 191–93
Purser, Bruce H. 75 n. 38
Radner, Karen xi, 17 n. 22, 22 nn. 47–48, 34 n. 43, 43 n. 4, 44 n. 7, 47 n. 16, 59 n. 62, 60 n. 73, 63 nn. 15–16, 66 n. 26, 79 n. 56, 80 n. 62, 83 n. 74, 84 n. 77, 85 n. 80, 86, 86 nn. 86–88, 87 n. 92, 87 n. 94–95, 88 n. 96, 88 n. 100, 89 nn. 103–109, 90 nn. 110–117, 92 n. 127, 106 n. 48, 107 n. 50, 108 n. 60, 109 n. 64, 109 n. 69, 110 n. 71, 114 n. 99, 118 n. 9, 119 n. 12, 120 n. 26, 123 n. 44, 143 n. 78, 148 n. 106, 166 nn. 6–7, 167, 167 n. 9, 167 n. 11, 168 n. 19, 169 n. 26, 169 n. 28, 187 n. 8, 189, 193, 196

Rainey, Anson F. 136 n. 42, 142, 142 nn. 71–72
Rassam, Hormuzd 5
Rawlinson, Henry Cresswicke 3, 148
Reade, Julian E. 5 nn. 22–23, 6, 6 n. 28, 54 n. 34, 75 n. 33, 80 n. 57, 120 n. 21, 171 n. 39, 175 n. 10, 177 n. 24, 194, 197
Reich, Ronny 136 n. 42, 152 n. 125
Rezael, Iraj 119 n. 18
Rezvani, Hassan 82 n. 70
Rigo, Monica 30 n. 29
Roaf, Michael 44 n. 6, 80 n. 62, 82 n. 71, 83 n. 75, 84 n. 75, 192–93
Robson, Eleanor 63 n. 16
Röllig, Wolfgang x, 101 n. 15
Rollinger, Robert 2 n. 9, 22 n. 48, 34 n. 43, 35 n. 43, 80 n. 62, 82 n. 71, 84 n. 75, 114 n. 99, 192–93
Romano, Licia 132 n. 18
Rost, Paul 3, 3 n. 12, 6, 130 n. 6, 154 n. 2, 189
Roustaei, Kourosh 82 n. 70
Sader, Hélène 109 nn. 65 and 67
Saggs, Henry William Frederick 5 n. 20, 130 n. 10, 149 n. 110, 152 n. 126, 155 n. 8, 166, 166 n. 5, 167 n. 9
Salvini, Mirjo x, 2 n. 5, 97, 97 n. 3, 119 n. 13, 126 n. 56, 194
Sancisi-Weerdenburg, Heleen 83 n. 73
Sanlaville, Paul 75 n. 38
Saporetti, Claudio 130 n. 7, 166 n. 6, 195
Sarlo, Daniel 92 n. 122, 92 n. 124, 93 n. 128
Sazonov, Vladimir 32 n. 34, 62 n. 11
Schäfer, Jérôme 75 n. 38, 193
Schloen, J. D. 109 n. 66
Schmidt, Oliver 66 n. 26
Schrader, Eberhard 3
Scurlock, Jo Ann 83 n. 73
Seux, Marie-Joseph 32 n. 34, 62 n. 11
Seymour, Michael 76 n. 39, 193
Shea, William H. 139 n. 60
Shavit, Alon 136 n. 42

Siddall, Luis Robert 6, 6 n. 27, 139 n. 56, 142, 142 n. 73, 195
Simon, W. 75 n. 38, 193
Smith, George 3
Sommer, Michael 66 n. 26
Spieckermann, H. 140 n. 63
Steadman, Sharon R. 123 n. 44
Stieglitz, Robert R. 131 n. 15
Stone, Adam 89 n. 104, 90 n. 117, 193
Svärd, Saana 150 n. 116, 195
Tadmor, Hayim xi, 3, 3 n. 10, 3 n. 13, 4 n. 15, 6 n. 27, 17 n. 22, 26 n. 9, 27 n. 15, 28 n. 18, 33 n. 38, 39 n. 73, 62 n. 10, 65 n. 21, 71 n. 3, 103–4, 104 n. 34, 104 n. 37, 108 n. 60, 111 n. 84, 119, 122 n. 42, 123 n. 43, 123 n. 45, 127 n. 61, 130 n. 8, 131 n. 14, 132 nn. 22–23, 135, 141 n. 67, 143 n. 75, 144, 145 n. 90, 154, 167 n. 9, 170, 170 n. 36, 171, 171 n. 40, 172 n. 42, 173, 174 n. 8, 189–190, 192, 194–95
Thalmann, Jean-Paul 111 n. 83
Thomas, Félix 28 n. 21, 190
Thureau-Dangin, François 57 n. 53, 179, 179 n. 32
Trundle, Matthew 66 n. 26
Uehlinger, Christoph 172 n. 42
Unger, Eckhard 54 n. 34
Ungnad, Arthur 43 n. 1, 51 n. 10
Valerio, Miguel 28 n. 19
Van De Mieroop, Marc 36 n. 57
Villard, Pierre 11 n. 2, 47 n. 20, 68 n. 34, 95 n. 137, 192
Virolleaud, Charles xi
Vogt, Ernst 6, 6 n. 27, 132 n. 22
Von Soden, Wolfram ix, 53 n. 23, 170
Waetzoldt, Hartmut 75 n. 38, 193
Wagner, Jörg 98 n. 5
Walker, Christopher 40 n. 80
Walton, J. T. 137 n. 47, 195
Ward, W. A. 12 n. 5
Watanabe, Kazuko xi, 19 n. 31, 26 n. 9, 191
Weeks, Noel K. 142 n. 72
Weidner, Ernst F. 51 n. 10
Weinfeld, Moshe 65 n. 21
Weippert, Manfred 131 n. 13, 143 n. 75, 172 n. 42
Westbrook, Raymond 36 n. 57, 68 n. 35, 190
Whiting, Robert xii
Wild, Stefan 132 n. 20, 144 n. 83
Wilhelm, Gernot 47 n. 20, 68 n. 34, 174 n. 9, 191
Winter, Irène J. 13 n. 10, 26 n. 8
Wiseman, Donald John
Worthington, Martin 89 n. 104, 193
Xella, Paolo 111 n. 81
Yamada, Keiko 27 n. 14, 167, 170, 196
Yamada, Shigeo xi, 3, 3 n. 13, 12 n. 6, 14 n. 13
Yener, K. Alishan 99 n. 12
Younger, K. Lawson 69 n. 42
Zawadski, Stefan 6, 6 n. 26, 147 n. 98
Zylberg, Peter 90 n. 110

INDEX OF PERSONAL NAMES

Adad-bêlu-ka"in, governor of Assur, eponym in 748 and 738   47, 49, 55, 91
Adad-idri. *See* Bar-Hadad II and Hadadezer
Adad-it'i. *See* Hadad-yis'i
Adad-nârârî I, king of Assyria (1307–1275)   61
Adad-nârârî II, king of Assyria (911–891)   12–13, 32
Adad-nârârî III, king of Assyria (810–783)   2, 14–15, 19, 20 n. 32, 21, 27–28, 32, 47, 49–50, 52–53, 53 n. 23, 56, 86, 97, 146–47, 174, 177, 180
Adbeel, Ishmael's son   151
Adia, queen of the Arabs   149
Ahab, king of Israel (ca. 874–853)   1
Ahaz, king of Judah (ca. 742–726)   xvi, 1, 6 n. 27, 134, 139 nn. 56–57, 140 n. 64, 140–43, 141 nn. 67–68, 142 n. 73, 143 n. 75, 145, 148–49, 185, 195
Ahuni, king of the Bît-Adini   14
Antiochus I, Seleucid king (281–261)   2
Argishti I, king of Urartu (787–766)   19, 51
Ashipâ, governor in northern part of the empire, possibly of Tushhan   158, 162
Ashurbanipal, king of Assyria (668–627)   40, 47, 62, 86, 149
Ashur-bêl-kala, king of Assyria (1073–1056)   2
Ashur-da"inanni, eunuch, governor of Zamua, eponym in 733   56, 91, 120
Ashur-da"in-aplu, son of Shalmaneser III   15

Ashur-Dân II, king of Assyria (934–912)   12, 43 n. 3
Ashur-Dân III, king of Assyria (772–755)   19-21, 27-28, 32, 43, 45, 47, 49, 54, 56, 174
Ashur-nârârî V, king of Assyria (754–745)   2, 19–23, 27–28, 43–47, 49, 53–54, 56–57, 98, 101, 105, 115, 174, 177
Ashurnasirpal II, king of Assyria (883–859)   1 n. 3, 2, 12–13, 13 n. 10, 22, 25, 30 nn. 29–30, 32, 36, 68, 92, 106, 174–75, 177–78, 184, 187, 189
Ashur-remanni, governor of Kullania   91
Ashur-shallimanni, governor of Arrapha, eponym in 735   55, 91, 157, 162
Assur-uballit I, king of Assyria (1365–1330)   11, 62
Atalia, wife of Sargon II   29
Attar-shumkî, king of Arpad   50, 99
Attarshumqa. *See* Attar-shumkî
Azriyau, king of Hatarikka   104 n. 34, 108–9
Bâba-ah-iddina, king of Babylon (813–812)   14
Balâssu, leader of the Bît-Dakkûri   116, 157, 159, 184
Banîtu, queen of Assyria, possibly the same as Iabâ   29
Bar-Ga'yah, king of *KTK*   19, 52–53, 115
Bar-Hadad II, king of Damascus (ca. 853–843)   14, 146
Bar-Rakib, king of Sam'al (Zincirli) (ca. 733–713/1)   1, 25, 109

Barsur, father of Panammû 109
Bâtânu, king of Bît-Kapsi 39, 80, 118
Bêl-Dân, governor of Nimrud, eponym in 744 and 734, eponym and chief cupbearer in 750 44–45, 47, 49, 54–56, 58, 91
Bêl-duri, possibly governor of Damascus 91
Bêl-êmuranni, governor of Rasappa, eponym in 737 91
Bêl-Harrân-bêlu-usur, palace herald 4, 20, 47, 49, 53–54, 58 n. 58
Bêl-lêshir, palace herald 53
Bêl-lû-dâri, governor of Tillê, eponym in 730 56, 91
Berossus, Babylonian priest (end of fourth century BCE) 2, 2 n. 9
Bisihadir, ruler of Kishesu 80
Dadîlu, king of Kaska 110
Daiân-Ashur, commander-in-chief of the army, eponym in 853 and 826 15, 17
Daltâ. See Taltâ
David, king of Israel and Judah (ca. 1010–970) 163
Deioces, founder of the Median Empire 83
Dur-Ashur, governor of Tushhan, eponym in 728 56, 91
Eni'ilu, king of Hamath 110
Esarhaddon, king of Assyria (680–669) xi, 5 n. 23, 40, 47, 81 n. 64, 138 n. 55, 174, 189, 196
Hadad-ezer. See Bar-Hadad II and Adad-idri
Hadad-yis'i, king of Gûzâna, governor of Gûzâna, Sikanu and Zaranu 52
Hadiânu II, king of Damascus 20, 50, 146
Hadyan. See Hadiânu II
Hamapi, possibly a tribal leader 116
Hanunu, king of Gaza xvi, 39, 69, 93, 136–37, 139, 152
Hazael, king of Damascus (mid-ninth century to 803?) 14, 17–18, 18 n. 25, 146, 146 n. 93

Hazael, king of Qedar 149–50
Herodotus, Greek historian (fifth century BCE) 14, 83, 83 n. 73, 136 n. 42
Hezekiah, king of Judah (ca. 719–699) 126, 147
Hosea, biblical prophet 138
Hoshea, king of Israel (ca. 731–722) 135, 145
Hiram II, king of Tyre (ca. 739–730) xvi, 110, 133–35, 139, 152
Hullî, king of Tabal 135
Iabâ, Assyrian queen, wife of Tiglath-pileser III 28–29
Iatie, queen of the Arabs 149
Idibi'ilu, Arab sheikh, gatekeeper at the border of Egypt 136–37, 137 n. 45, 151, 151 n. 119
Ipiq-Adad II, king of Eshnunna (early second millennium) 187
Iranzu, king of Mannea xv, 81, 117, 117 n. 2, 120, 184
Irhuleni, king of Hamath 14
Isaiah, biblical prophet 36 n. 57, 52, 138, 138 n. 55, 139 n. 57, 140 n. 64, 141, 141 n. 68, 190, 195
Ishmael, son of Abraham 151
Ishme-Dagan, king of Ekallâtum 11
Ittoba'al I, king of Tyre and Sidon (ca. 888–856) 163
Ittoba'al II, king of Tyre (ca. 701) 105, 110, 134
Jehoahaz, full name for Ahaz. See Ahaz
Jeroboam II, king of Israel (ca. 783–743) 139, 146
Joachaz, king of Judah (ca. 814–803) 18
Joas, king of Judah (ca. 803–790) 18, 18 n. 26
Jotham, king of Judah (ca. 749–743) 140
Kakî, possibly ruler of Bît-Zatti in western Iran 80
Karib-il, king of Saba 149, 149 n. 111
Kashtiliash IV, king of Babylon (ca.1232–1225) 11
Khilaruata, ruler of Melid in the first half of the eighth century 99

INDEX OF PERSONAL NAMES 209

Kushtashpi, king of Kummuhu 97–99, 103, 105
Liphur-ilu, governor of Habruri, eponym in 729 56, 91
Lulî, king of Tyre and Sidon (ca. 728–695) 163
Mannu-kî-mât-Ashur, governor of Gûzâna, eponym in 793 51 n. 10
Mannu-kî-sâbî, ruler of Bît-Abdadâni 81
Marduk-apla-iddina II. See Merodach-baladan II
Marduk-balâssu-iqbi, king of Babylonia (ca. 818–813) 14
Marduk-Shallimanni, palace herald in 751 and 741, eponym in 741; possibly governor of Gûzâna and eponym in 727 45, 53
Marduk-sharra-usur, possibly governor of Kurbail, eponym of 784 22
Marduk-zâkir-shumi I, king of Babylonia (854–819) 78
Mati'el. See Matî'-ilu
Matî'-ilu, king of Arpad 52, 98-99, 103, 115
Mattan II, king of Tyre (ca. 729) 135
Mattanba'al II, king of Arwad (ca. 738–732) xvi, 39, 113, 132–33
Menahem, king of Israel (ca. 750–738) 110, 139, 139 n. 60, 140
Merodach-baladan II, Chaldean chieftain of the Bît-Yakîn, king of Babylon (721–710, 704 or 703) 116, 155, 155 n. 12, 157–58, 195
Metenna. See Mattan II
Mikî, ruler of Halpi 81
Misharu-nasir, son of Bêl-Dân 55
Mitâki, ruler of Urshanika and Kianpal 80
Mitinti, king of Ashkelon xvi, 116, 135, 137, 137 n. 49, 139
Mukîn-zêri. See Nabû-Mukîn-zêri
Mushallim-Marduk, chief judge 51
Nabonassar. See Nabû-nâsir

Nabû-bêlu-usur, governor of Arrapha, eponym in 745; possibly then of Simme, eponym in 732 46, 55
Nabû-da'inanni, commander-in-chief, eponym in 742 49, 55, 71
Nabû-êtiranni, chief cupbearer, eponym in 740 49, 55
Nabû-mukîn-zêri, chief of the Chaldean tribe of the Bît-Amukkâni, king of Babylonia (731–729) 153, 156–58, 158 n. 28, 159–61
Nabû-nâdin-zêri, king of Babylon (734–732) 153
Nabû-nammir, official 48, 74 n. 23, 158, 162
Nabû-nâsir, king of Babylon (747–734)
Nabû-shuma-ukîn II, rebellious candidate to the throne of Babylon (732) 153, 159
Nabû-ushabshi, leader of the Chaldean tribe of the Bît-Shilâni 156, 159–60
Nâdinu, ruler of Larak 116, 157, 159
Narâm-Sîn, king of Eshnunna (early second millennium) 187
Nergal-nâsir, governor of Nasibîna, eponym in 746 43, 46
Nergal-uballit, governor of Ahi-zuhina, eponym in 731 56, 88, 91
Ninurta-bêlu-usur, a eunuch of Shamshî-ilu, governor of Arpad/Kâr-Shalmaneser 49, 55, 57–58, 91, 94
Ninurta-ilâya, possibly governor of Nisibîna, eponym in 736; possibly governor of Kâr-Shalmaneser from the late 730s or early 720s 49, 55, 58, 91, 106 n. 48, 107, 179
Ninus, mythic figure 2
Oded, biblical prophet 141
Osorkon IV, pharaoh, probably of the Twenty-Third Dynasty (ca. 730) 137
Panammû. See Panamuwa II
Panamuwa II, king of Sam'al (Zincirli) (ca. 740–733) 1, 109–10
Peqah, king of Israel (ca. 737–732) 134, 139, 140, 144–45

Peqahiah, king of Israel (ca. 738-737) 139
Phulos. *See* Pulû
Piankhy, pharaoh of the Twenty-Fifth Dynasty (ca. 747-716) 67
Pisîris, king of Carchemish (ca. 738-717) 105
Piye. *See* Piankhy
Poros. *See* Pulû
Pûl. *See* Pulû
Pulû, other name of Tiglath-pileser III xvi, 1-2, 162
Qaush-malaka, king of Edom 145
Qurdi-ashur-lâmur, Assyrian official, governor of Simirra, possibly settled at Ushu 91, 116, 116 n. 113, 138
Rahiânu, king of Damascus (ca. 750-732) 105, 134, 136-37, 137 n. 50, 138-40, 145-48, 151-59, 181
Ra/umateia, ruler of Araziash (or Kazuqinzani) 80-81, 117, 117 n. 2
Remaliah, father of Peqah, king of Israel 139
Rezin. *See* Rahiânu
Rûkibtu, king of Ashkelon 137
Rusâ I, king of Urartu (730-714) 728
Salâmânu, king of Moab 145
Sammuramat. *See* Semiramis
Samsi, queen of the Arabs xvi, 112, 116, 134 n. 31, 139, 148-52, 179, 184
Samsî-Addu. *See* Shamshî-Adad I
Sanîpu, king of Bît-Ammon 145
Sardanapalus, last Assyrian king according to the Greek authors 2
Sarduri II, king of Urartu (765-733) xv, 2, 6 n. 26, 21, 38, 41, 65, 97, 97 n. 1, 98, 98 n. 8, 99, 101-3, 105, 122-23, 123 n. 43, 125-126, 128, 193
Sargon of Akkad/ Agade, king of Assyria (ca. 2335-2279) 62, 187
Sargon II, king of Assyria (722-705) xi-xii, 6, 6 n. 26, 7, 7 n. 29, 11, 26, 26 n. 9, 27 n. 15, 28, 28 nn. 19-21, 31, 36, 37 n. 58, 39-40, 41 n. 85, 46-47, 47 n. 15, 54 n. 30, 58, 58 n. 57, 58 n. 60, 59

Sargon II (*cont.*)
n. 65, 60 n. 70, 65-66, 66 n. 22, 66 n. 27, 68-69, 69 n. 41, 77, 77 n. 45, 81, 81 n. 67, 82, 82 n. 69, 91 n. 120, 119, 119 n. 20, 128, 128 n. 63, 149 n. 109, 151, 151 n. 121, 167, 167 n. 12, 170, 171 nn. 37-38, 173, 173 n. 1, 175, 175 n. 12, 181, 181 n. 49, 188, 188 n. 12, 189-91
Sasinnu, *See* Zasinnu
Seduri. *See* Sarduri
Semiramis, legendary queen of Assyria and Babylonia 2, 14, 50
Sennacherib, king of Assyria (704-681) 1, 7, 7 n. 29, 26, 31, 37, 37 n. 58, 68, 72, 126, 126 n. 58, 147, 147 n. 100, 163, 163 n. 56, 165, 167, 171 n. 39, 173, 173 n. 2, 175, 181, 181 n. 49, 188, 188 n. 14, 194-95
Sha-Ashur-dubbu, governor of Tushhan 124 n. 49
Shallum, king of Israel (ca. 750) 139
Shalmaneser I, king of Assyria (1273-1244) 115
Shalmaneser III, king of Assyria (858-824) 1-2, 12-15, 17, 32-33, 33 n. 38, 50, 62, 64, 68, 78, 83, 92, 120, 122, 125, 146-47, 174, 178, 185-86
Shalmaneser IV, king of Assyria (782-773) 19-20, 27-28, 32, 47, 49-51, 53-54, 56, 146, 174
Shalmaneser V, king of Assyria (726-722) xi, xvi, 3 n. 13, 5 n. 20, 8, 27, 27 n. 14, 28, 28 n. 20, 29, 40, 54 n. 30, 138, 165-67, 167 n. 15, 169 n. 24, 169 n. 26, 166, 166 nn. 30-31, 166 n. 35, 171, 171 n. 40, 172, 188-89, 193
Shamash-ahu-iddina, possibly governor of Subutu 91
Shamash-ahu-iddina, chief eunuch active in the west 110
Shamash-bunaya, prefect and possibly governor of northern Babylonia 48, 74 n. 23, 91, 158-59, 161-63
Shamash-kenu-dugul, high dignitary 45

INDEX OF PERSONAL NAMES 211

Shamshî-Adad I, king of Ekallâtum (ca. 1807-1776)   11, 11 n. 2, 187
Shamshî-Adad V, king of Assyria (823-811)   12, 14-15, 31-32, 92
Shamshî-ilu, commander-in-chief, governor of the land of Hatti, of the land of the Guti and all the land of Namri   8, 19, 19 n. 31, 20-22, 44-45, 49-51, 51 n. 10, 51 n. 15, 52, 52 nn. 21-22, 53, 53 nn. 23-24, 54 n. 32, 55-57, 58 n. 57, 59, 71, 74, 146, 189, 191
Shipitba'al II, king of Byblos (ca. 737-732)   110, 133
Sibitti-bi'il. *See* Shipitba'al II
Sîn-taklâk, treasurer, eponym in 739   49, 55
Siruatti, Arab Me'unite   137, 137 nn. 44-45
Solomon, king of Israel and Judah (ca. 970-931)   163
Sulaya, possibly governor of Tu'imme   91
Sulumal, king of Melid   99, 103, 110, 181
Tabeel, an unnamed person whom Peqah and Rezin conspired to make king of Judah   140
Tabua, queen of the Arabs   149
Taltâ, king of Ellipi (737-713)   81, 117, 117 n. 2, 120
Tanus. *See* Tunî
Tarhulara, king of Gurgum (ca. 742-711)   99, 103, 105
Tarqularu. *See* Tarhulara
Te'elhunu, queen of the Arabs   149-50
Tefnakht, pharaoh (ca. 736-729)   137
Tiglath-pileser I, king of Assyria (1114-1076)   12, 76
Tuba'il. *See* Ittoba'al II
Tuhamme, king of Ishtunda   110
Tukultî-apil-Esharra, Akkadian name of Tiglath-pileser III   25, 27
Tukultî-Ninurta I, king of Assyria (1243-1207)   11, 31-32

Tukultî-Ninurta II, king of Assyria (890-884)   2, 12-13, 74
Tunaku, possibly king of Parsua   80
Tunî, ruler of Sumurzu in Namri   80, 88
Tutammû, king of Unqi   xv, 39, 107-8, 116
Uassurme, king of Tabal   110
Ubru-Nergal, Assyrian officer   168
Ulûlâyu. *See* Shalmaneser V
Upash, ruler of Bît-Kapsi   118
Urballâ, king of Tuhana   110
Urik. *See* Uriakki
Uriakki, king of Que (last part of the eighth century BCE)   105
Urikki. *See* Uriakki
Urimmi, king of Hubishna   110
Ushitti, king of Tuna   110
Uzakku, ruler of [...]   81
Uzziah, king of Judah (768/7-740/739)   137 n. 45
Yasmah-Addu, king of Mari (ca. 1782-1774)   11
Yautha', king of Qedar   149
Zabibe, queen of the Arabs   110, 149
Zakkur, king of Hamath   18 n. 26, 50, 108, 146
Zaqiru, leader of the Chaldean tribe of Bît-Sha'alli   116, 156-157, 159-60
Zasinnu, one of Mukîn-zêri's men   158
Zechariah, king of Israel (ca. 750)   139

www.ingramcontent.com/pod-product-compliance
Lightning Source LLC
Chambersburg PA
CBHW030826230426
43667CB00008B/1391